GENERAL SIR DUNCAN CAMERON

THE WAIKATO WAR

TOGETHER WITH
SOME ACCOUNT OF

TE KOOTI RIKIRANGI.

BY JOHN FEATON.

[New Edition, Revised by Captain Gilbert Mair.]

The Naval & Military Press Ltd
in association with
The National Army Museum, London

Published jointly by

The Naval & Military Press Ltd
Unit 10 Ridgewood Industrial Park,
Uckfield, East Sussex,
TN22 5QE England

Tel: +44 (0) 1825 749494
Fax: +44 (0) 1825 765701

www.naval-military-press.com
www.military-genealogy.com
www.militarymaproom.com

and

The National Army Museum, London
www.national-army-museum.ac.uk

In reprinting in facsimile from the original, any imperfections are inevitably reproduced and the quality may fall short of modern type and cartographic standards.

PREFACE

It was in 1879—more than thirty years ago—that I compiled an account of the Waikato war, in many of the stirring events of which I had taken a willing if inconspicuous part. Since then many of the men who participated in the wars and alarms of the sixties have been gathered to their fathers, and we who saw something of the stirring events of those early and strenuous days of colonisation have become a small and rapidly diminishing band. To a new generation some account of a campaign in which their fathers—perhaps in more instances their grandfathers—participated, should not be without interest.

One or two works on the subject, written by Imperial Officers, have been published in England, but they are very scarce and cannot now, without some difficulty, be obtained, and, although they are excellent from a military point of view, as detailing the operations of the Imperial Forces, they have almost entirely ignored the services rendered by the Colonial Militia and Volunteers. This important omission the author has endeavoured to rectify, and has given full prominence to the services of the Colonial Forces wherever found worthy of notice.

Since the war all has changed. Townships have sprung up where clustered the native whare, and cultivated fields have taken the place of barren wastes. The shrill scream of the railway engine startles the pukeko (swamp hen) as the train rushes across the morass, over creeks, and through deep cuttings, taking a few hours on its journey, when before the canoe took days. All has changed.

In placing the history of the Waikato war before the public, the author has not attempted to dive into the political history of the campaign. To do so would involve much time and trouble in gathering details from musty old Blue Books, and would not greatly interest the general reader. What the author has endeavoured to do is to give an authentic history or detailed account of the operations of both the Imperial and Colonial Forces that were engaged in the Waikato war of 1863 and 1864, obtained from the dispatches of General Cameron, the author's own personal observations, and various other authentic sources.

I have made no attempt to alter or amplify the earlier work, but present it as written in 1879, when, besides the greater availability of documents, memory was comparatively active and reliable, and not subject to the tricks of an advancing old age.

Auckland. July 1, 1911.   J.F.

PUBLISHERS' PREFACE.

So few people now survive of those who took an active part in the Maori war of half a century ago that no apology is required for presenting to the public in permanent form the narrative of an eye-witness of many of the stirring scenes of those trying times in the history of New Zealand. The "History of the Waikato War," by the late Mr. John Featon, was published serially in the "Auckland Star" in the years 1911 and 1912, and was so well received by thousands of readers that it has been deemed well to issue it in book form. Mr. Featon having been, in his own words, an inconspicuous but willing actor in the events of that campaign, his account of it is in no way deformed by personal bias or by partisanship of any kind. It is, in fact, a plain statement of facts as they presented themselves to him, and he is perfectly candid and impartial as between the combatants on either side. As regards the merits of matters that were in dispute between the Colonial and Imperial authorities, he completely ignores the political aspect of affairs, and thus escapes becoming involved in fruitless controversy. The publishers present this plain, unvarnished tale as a contribution towards the true history of the war in the Waikato and Bay of Plenty.

The present edition of the history gains additional value from the fact that it has been completely revised by Captain Gilbert Mair. Mr. Featon's history of the wars which followed the escape of Te Kooti from the Chatham Islands has been, to a considerable extent, re-written, in order to incorporate information supplied by Captains Gilbert Mair and G. A. Preece, who took an active part in the expeditions which were organised with the object of capturing Te Kooti and dispersing the armed band of rebel natives he had gathered around him.

(1923.)

SIR GEORGE GREY, K.C.B.,
Governor of New Zealand.

CHAPTER I.

In the early part of the year 1863 the storm clouds of war which had for so long hung like a funeral pall over and devastated the fair Province of Taranaki, banked up on the southern horizon of Auckland, and the daily increasing hostile attitude of the Waikato Tribes towards the settlers might have been likened to the thunder which, muttering at a distance, portends the coming storm.

The sugar and flour policy which the Government had adopted seemed to do no good, being looked upon as a sign of weakness on the part of the Pakeha, who would give anything to conciliate the proud Waikatos. A road that had been constructed over the Pokeno Ranges towards the Waikato gave great offence to the natives, and at several large meetings that were held it was decided that if the Pakehas moved one step further towards the Waikato the tribes should at once rise and sweep the hated white man off the face of the earth.

The temporary cessation of hostilities at Taranaki liberated large numbers of the Waikatos who had been actively assisting the Taranaki Tribes in their operations against the Troops, and these returning to their several districts helped in no small way to fan the glowing embers of rebellion into a flame. The few missionaries and Pakeha Maoris residing with the natives had sharp notice to quit. Their goods and chattels were appropriated, and in some instances the Maori wives and half-caste children of the Pakeha were taken from them. A printing establishment which the Government had erected at Te Awamutu was broken into by a mob of natives, who smashed the machinery to pieces, and ejected the superintendent, Mr Gorst, who shortly afterwards returned to England and gained a somewhat unenviable notoriety by his virulent attacks upon the New Zealand colonists.

One of the Waikato Natives who took a prominent part in destroying the printing press, Aporo by name, had the hardihood to make his appearance in Auckland, where he was promptly seized by the police, tried and sentenced to some two or three years' imprisonment. The arrest and incarceration of Aporo increased the wrath of the Waikatos, and especially the Nagtimaniapotos, to which tribe Aporo belonged. Meetings were held to consider what steps should be taken to recover their lost brother. The result was that an impudent letter was forwarded to the Governor demanding the release of Aporo, and in the event of non-compliance it threatened that the natives would at once march upon Auckland, destroy the town and liberate the prisoner. As the reader will imagine, no notice was taken of the natives' threat and Aporo remained in gaol.

The Kingites, as the Waikatos styled themselves, were so called on account of their having set up for themselves a King. Their reigning potentate was Tawhiao, son of their first king, old Potatau, who died a short time before this period. The idea of having a king, or the king movement, was started by

TAWHIAO, THE MAORI KING.

Wiremu Thompson, one of the leading Waikato chiefs, who was afterwards called "The King-maker." This great and good chief, always friendly disposed towards the Pakehas, tried in vain to stem the growing spirit of rebellion amongst his countrymen, and he predicted what he afterwards lived to see, viz., the confiscation of their lands, and before he died, which event took place some years after the war was ended, he exhorted his countrymen to live on friendly terms with the Pakeha.

The remains of Wiremu Thompson are buried on his ancestral ground at Matamata, and an inscription on a stone monument over his grave informs the traveller that it was erected to his memory by his friend, J. C. Firth, Esq., of Auckland.

The Maori king resided and held his court at Ngaruawahia, which is situated at the junction of the Waipa and Waikato rivers. Here important matters were discussed and decided by the king and leading chiefs, who, when occasion required, assembled from all parts of the Waikato. The following account of a state visit that the late King Potatau paid to Waiuku will give the reader an idea of the pomp which surrounded the dusky monarch upon his travels.

On Thursday morning, the 8th of March, 1860, a fleet of canoes from the settlements within the Manukau, manned by a considerable body of natives, arrived at Waiuku laden with dried shark, potatoes, and other eatables. Next day Potatau with a large party of Waikato natives arrived at Pura Pura, and on Saturday the old chief (king) came over to Waiuku in state.

The procession consisted first of from seventy to a hundred natives about four deep, then came a body-guard of from twenty to thirty carrying fowling pieces, next the standard-bearer with a green streamer having painted on it a red cross and the words "The Truth"; old Potatau came next seated on a pony with a tartan shawl thrown over it. The pony was led, and two women of the household walked alongside. Then came the general body of natives, women laden with kai kai and baggage bringing up the rear. On reaching the royal tent the standard was stuck into the earth, and the old chief seating himself on the ground received a general greeting.

The Maoris living in the vicinity of the out-settlers prepared for the coming struggle, which all could see was inevitable, by converting their live stock into cash, with which they bought powder, caps, and guns—from whom has long been an open question. No doubt a good deal of ammunition and many stands of arms found their way into the hands of the natives from Sydney traders who ran their schooners into Kawhia for that purpose; the natives have confessed as much to the writer, but we cannot disguise from ourselves the dreadful fact that traitors were in our midst, who trafficked with the natives secretly for the sale of munitions of war, one of the most dreadful of crimes, and for which death alone is the just punishment.

A strict Arms Act was in force, but there were few if any convictions, and to this day there are no doubt some who stalk proudly amongst us, with a bold front, in the full glare of the noonday sun, and who live on the fat of the land purchased with their blood money. Their face is fair, but the brand of Cain is upon their brow although invisible to human eyes.

When bullets and caps could not be obtained by the Natives, old lead, matches, and boxes of brass eyelets were eagerly sought after, and were used as munitions of war. The heads of the matches were placed in the brass eyelets, which fitted on the nipple of the gun, and made not a bad substitute for caps.

The firearms that the Maoris possessed were not such as to inspire their owners with confidence, being an assortment of old Tower and ship muskets and single and double fowling pieces. They had very few revolvers or bayonets, for which their tomahawk was supposed to be a substitute. Some of their old muskets were so very ancient that they might have done duty at Waterloo, and were quite as dangerous to the party who fired as to the enemy aimed at.

The Natives growing more insolent day by day, the settlers in outlying districts had an anxious time of it, and became alarmed at the attitude which the Maoris assumed towards them, with whom in most cases they had been on amicable terms for years. The hitherto friendly greeting and shake of the hands ceased, and each party viewed the other with suspicion.

It was no uncommon thing for armed Natives to stalk boldly into the settlers' houses, squat down in the rooms unbidden, walk into the kitchen, appropriate the contents of the pots on the fire, and demand tobacco, pipes, or matches, and if these were not given with a good grace, the unfortunate settler was treated with threats of a bloodthirsty character. To appeal to the law was useless; it was powerless, and the Queen's writ a myth. The settlers had to put up with the insolence of the Natives as best they could, to wait, hope, and pray that if the time for hostilities had nearly come it would come soon, in justice and mercy to both races alike.

CHAPTER II.

The out-districts of Auckland towards Waikato at the commencement of the war extended but little further south than Drury, and the country beyond was almost a *terra incognita*. From Drury to the Waikato, some sixteen miles, there existed but a short time before only a rough bridle track over the densely-wooded Pokeno Ranges, with here and there a few settlers' homesteads cleared out of the primeval forest, but in view of eventualities, the time had come when the solitude of the woods was dispelled, for several detachments of troops had just completed a cart road over the ranges and on towards the Waikato River, which ran gleaming like a silver thread through the King Country.

Dr. Hochstetter, in his work on New Zealand, speaking of this Prince of New Zealand rivers, says:—"The impression made by the sight of the majestic stream is truly grand. It is only with the Danube or Rhine that I can compare the mighty river which we have just entered. The Waikato is the principal river in the North Island. Both as to the length of its course and quantity of water, it surpasses all the others. The pieces of pumice stone which its waters are continually carrying along, piling them up on its banks and at its confluence with the sea, point to its origin in the vicinity of the extensive volcanic hearth in the centre of the island. Its sources spring from the very core of the land. Its waters roll through the most fertile and most beautiful fields, populated by numerous and most powerful tribes of the natives, who have taken their name from it. No second river of New Zealand has such an importance as the grand thoroughfare for the interior of the country. The Waikato is in truth the main artery of the North Island, and this grand stream wants but one thing, i.e., an open unobstructed entrance from the sea.

"While a great many other rivers of New Zealand, as for example the nearest neighbours of the Waikato, the Piako and Waihou, or the Wairoa in the North, are emptying into protected bays of the sea, widening near their mouths into broad estuaries by which the sea penetrates far into the interior of the land, and where the regular change of ebb and flow enables larger and smaller vessels to pass from the river into the sea, there are huge sandbanks piled in front of the mouth of the Waikato upon which the sea breaks in foaming surges. This is a matter of great importance, for those sandbanks which prevent the passing in and out of larger vessels are a natural bulwark for the natives. They look upon the Waikato more than upon any other river of New Zealand as being the river exclusively their own. Never up to the time of my journey (1859) had a boat of European construction been known to float upon the proud native stream, the Mississippi of the Maoris.

"Two mission stations, the one at its mouth (Putataka), the other at Taupiri, were at that time the only European settlements on the banks of the river where the Maori King had taken up his abode. From his residence at Ngaruawahia, where the Waipa mingles its waters with those of the Waikato, the national flag of Niu Tireni was floating proudly in the breeze, and from among the bushes of the flax plant, the toetoe-grass, and the ti-trees, the Maori huts were everywhere peeping forth, now single, now in clusters of miniature villages, and surrounded by thriving plantations. Flats are alternate along the course of the river, with fern hills, or with dusky wood-clad mountain ridges, and the picturesque landscape sceneries are developing themselves there where the river in a narrow gorge of rocks is breaking through the mountain chains. The Waikato, at the junction of the Mangatawhiri, has a breadth of about half a mile. It encompasses several wood-clad islands, and after having passed in an almost precise south then north direction through extensive low lands, the lower Waikato basin, it makes here a sudden bend to the west. It breaks through a low coast range, and empties twenty miles further below on the West Coast into the sea."

"Never," says Dr. Hochstetter, "never up to the time of my journey had a boat of European construction been known to float upon the proud native stream—the Mississippi of the Maoris," and if the natives had retained possession of the river, no boat of European construction would have floated on it to the present day, for the canoe is far better adapted to make headway against the rapid river than a boat, be it ever so well manned. Again, running into the main stream, there are numerous small creeks obstructed with logs and snags. Though these retard the passage of a boat, the canoe, on account of its light draught, floats over them easily.

The quantities of maize, potatoes, flax, and pigs that the Waikato natives used to ship away and pour annually into the Auckland market would scarcely be credited. For transit to Auckland the route was down the Waikato River, then up the Awaroa tidal creek not far from the Waikato Heads to Pura Pura, the landing place close to Waiuku. The freight was then carted across the portage some two miles, and shipped in cutters or small schooners to Onehunga. At Pura Pura there was a bacon-curing establishment that was able to forward bacon to Auckland by the ton, equal in quality to the best Canterbury bacon of the present day.

Sometimes cargoes of maize, wheat, potatoes, and flax were shipped direct from the Waikato to Sydney or other ports in schooners that used to cross the bar for that purpose.

Those were halcyon days for the Waikatos. Money they were never short of. The Waikato Heads provided them with an abundance of fish, from the schnapper to the dainty "guard," whilst in the fresh water, higher up the river, shoals of whitebait and the esculent eel were to be had for the trouble of getting. Their plantations were luxuriant with maize, wheat, potatoes, pumpkins and kumaras, and their gullies swarmed with the wild pig and not a few cattle. For clothing, if they did not care to purchase that of European make, the flax plant rustled in the swamps and on the side of every river bank.

Perhaps no savage tribes that ever existed in any part of the globe had such an abundance of the good things of this world. But a few years had passed since they were cannibals. Many of them still in the prime of life could remember and had partaken of a cannibal feast.

The Rev. B. Y. Ashwell, to whom and his brother missionaries the Waikatos are said to owe so much, mentions in his interesting brochure, entitled "Recollections of a Waikato Missionary," a cannibal feast at which he was a spectator. He says: "On my arrival at Otawhao, I found the Ngatiruru, with their chiefs Puata and Mokoro, had just returned from Rotorua. They had been victorious, and were carrying baskets of human flesh to cook. Not less than sixty backloads were brought into the pa at Otawhao. The next day, July 30, 1839, was a great feast of human flesh. I quitted the pa in disgust, and I said to the Whare Kura, i.e., those natives disposed to Christianity, 'Come, let us leave this pa, and build a pa for Christ.' This they assented to readily and more than two hundred left. A site was chosen on the Awamutu (where the barrack and large bridge now stand), and a pa was built; and, at the request of the Whare Kura, I drew up laws and regulations for them."

With the commencement of hostilities, the prosperity of the Waikatos was destroyed, and has not since been restored. They are like a changed people.

What the political cause of the war was it is not my province to enter into here. Some say one thing, some say another. For my own part, I do not know, but I do know that apart from all politics the settlers as a body did not want war. To them it meant in many cases ruin and a cruel wasting of the best and strongest years of their lives. I also do know that the Waikatos, some time before hostilities commenced, openly despised the Queen's authority, and assumed such a front and bearing towards their European neighbours that if the Governor had not taken upon himself to have declared war, the settlers would have been compelled to have done so, whatever might have been the consequences, their very existence as a body being menaced.

The Waikatos hated the settlers with an exceeding great hate, and how a native can hate the reader will be able to judge from the fact of its having been known that whilst vehemently declaiming against the pakeha at a meeting the declaimer has worked himself up into such a frightful state of excitement as to fall down dead. Pride and jealousy perhaps, more than anything else, more, perhaps, than land, were the root of the evil, especially as far as the Waikatos were concerned. The wise Wiremu Thompson, son of the great Te Waharoa, knew of the pride and jealousy that raged in his people's hearts. He cautioned them against it and foretold their doom. They heeded him not. They cared more for the crafty and ferocious Ngatimaniapoto chief Rewi. The doom that he prophesied was the doom of the pakeha. When he wrote to the Taranakis urging them to attack the soldiers, he said, "Red plumes! Plumes of the Kaka! The doom has been fixed at Kawhia! Once the fighting! twice! three! four times! Seize your weapons! Twist the fastenings tightly! Bind them fast! Now unbind! Strike! Fell! Let it fall!!"

Shortly after the completion of the military road, Colonel Leslie, with a detachment of the 40th Regiment, took up a position at Pokeno, on the Waikato side of the ranges, and commenced throwing up a large redoubt, which was called the "Queen's." This post commanded the approach to Auckland by an enemy from the Waikato River, and afforded a base from which operations could be directed against the Kingites.

Numbers of natives from the neighbouring settlements came each day, watching the soldiers at work, and holding great arguments amongst themselves concerning it as they squatted on the ground. At times they would mingle with soldiers, beg tobacco, matches, etc. At last the day arrived when the redoubt was finished, and over which, from the top of a flagstaff,

REWI, CHIEF OF THE NGATIMANIAPOTOS.

the British ensign flapped in the breeze, at which the natives stared, and pointed up to it with their dirty pipes, and traced on the ground with a stick a rough outline of the redoubt—flagstaff, flag, and all.

The frontier townships consisted of the Wairoa, Drury, the Mauku, and Waiuku, and at each of these settlements meetings were held by the settlers to discuss the advisability of taking immediate steps to defend themselves against any sudden attack from the natives, who, on the other hand, were afraid that the settlers would suddenly rise and shoot them down. The following incident will illustrate the state of the out-districts at the time, and the mutual distrust that existed between the natives and the settlers.

A few miles from the Mauku, towards the Waikato River, a hill called "The Bald Hill" rises up to a great height, and can be seen a long way off. To celebrate a marriage that took place a bonfire was foolishly lighted on the top of the hill by some of the settlers. When night set in the illumination was mistaken as a signal for the natives to rise and attack the settlers, and the natives firmly believed on the other hand that it signified a general rising of the settlers against them. The terrified settlers congregated for mutual protection, and the men stood under arms, some with fowling pieces, old muskets, axes, or any weapon they could lay their hands on, the whole night long, and how long such nights are can only be known to those who have undergone similar heavy hours of suspense. The sigh of the night wind in the woods, the falling crash of a tree's decayed limb or the distant bark of a watch-dog, denoted the approach of the enemy, and excitement was wrought up to the highest pitch. The natives, alarmed, deserted their whares, and with gun in one hand and tomahawk in the other, hid themselves in the forest. The next morning the affair was explained, and the settlers, re-assured, returned to their usual avocations, but some of the natives did not return to their settlements for two or three days.

And so the early part of the year had slowly passed away, and June dawned on the Auckland district with its cold winds, its rain, and long dark nights. "See the stars," said the natives, "how red they are. It is a sign of war."

CHAPTER III.

Active preparations were now made for an invasion of the Waikato. A camp had been formed at Otahuhu, and huts erected for the accommodation of a large number of troops. Colonel Leslie at the Queen's Redoubt had been reinforced, and an advanced post taken up at the Mangatawhiri Creek. In the meanwhile the Waikatos had not been idle. A large number of them had assembled at Rangiriri, and were busy throwing up extensive earthworks, and a fleet of canoes was collected for the purpose of conveying a force that was to march on and burn Auckland.

On the 23rd of June, a day memorable to the citizens of Auckland, a circular was issued from Government House by the Governor, Sir George Grey, calling out for active service four hundred militiamen from the first division of the Auckland district. These comprised all unmarried men capable of bearing arms, from sixteen up to forty years of age. The names of the militiamen liable to be drawn were written on separate pieces of paper or card of uniform size, and then placed in a bag. The officer appointed to command the militia, Colonel Thomas Rawlings Mould, of the Royal Engineers, in the presence of a Justice of the Peace, drew from the bag one by one as many pieces of paper or card as there were men required. The men whose names were drawn had to serve. The pay of the militia was 2s 6d per diem and rations such as supplied to Her Majesty's Regular Forces. The clothing consisted of one muffin cap, the same as worn by the troops, one blue shirt or jumper, one pair of trousers with a red stripe down, two pairs of boots, one pair of gaiters and one great-coat provided at the expense of the Government. When on service outside the Auckland militia district, one shilling a day extra pay was given.

The Governor's circular, as may be imagined, caused great excitement amongst the bachelors, who, however, did not respond to the call of duty so readily as the authorities desired. Numbers of them, to escape service, delayed no longer, but popped the question, and got married right away, to the great delight of the young ladies concerned; and others, hoping to be tied up in holy bonds some day, objected on principle to run the chance of being cut off in the flower of their youth and beauty. The martial flame of the Auckland citizens had evidently not been yet kindled, and they were not particularly eager to close with the wily savage in his native woods and swamps. The fact of a great many not coming forward for enrolment called forth shortly afterwards from the Deputy Adjutant General of Militia and Volunteers the following unique notice, which will doubtless be interesting to the readers of the present day:—

"Many Militiamen of the first-class (unmarried from sixteen to forty) not having enrolled their names as required by law, I request Militiamen and Volunteers now doing duty, or any other person who may know such individuals *who shirk their fair share of duty*, to enclose the *shirker's* name and place of residence in an envelope, and place it in the Post Office. addressed thus:

"*On Public Service Only.*
Deputy Adjutant-General of Militia and Volunteers,
Auckland."

"Legal proceedings will be taken against them. No postage stamps are required on the letter.

H. C. BALNEAVIS,
Deputy Adjutant General of Militia and Volunteers."

On July 3rd the headquarters of the 2nd battalion 18th regiment, consisting of 28 officers and 290 rank and file, arrived in Auckland harbour, from England, in the transport Elizabeth Ann Bright. The next morning they disembarked and marched through Queen-street, headed by the band of the 65th regiment, en route to the camp at Otahuhu, where the 14th and detachments of the 12th and 70th regiments had been quartered for some time previously. A few days afterwards, this force, including the newly-arrived 18th, numbering in all about 1,200 men, marched to Pokeno, forming on the way a camp at Drury where 170 of the 18th regiment were left behind.

The 65th regiment, then stationed in the Albert Barracks, Auckland, left their quarters at 4 a.m. on the 9th en route for the front, and were followed next day by Captain Mercer's Battery Royal Artillery, consisting of 170 men, 50 of whom were mounted, with 4 six-pounder Armstrong guns, 4 twenty-four pounder howitzers, and 1 nine-pounder. The Volunteers and Militia mounted guard in the Albert Barracks in place of the troops that had left. Immediately after the Artillery, General Cameron left Auckland for the front. Six large boats and thirty seamen from H.M.S. Harrier went up the Manukau harbour to Drury. The boats were then carted on to the Maungatawhiri Creek, for river service on the Waikato.

A strong force of some 2000 men being now assembled at the Queen's Redoubt, General Cameron upon his arrival immediately advanced, or, as military historians would say, threw the 14th regiment across the Maungatawhiri Creek, and occupied a strong position on the Koheroa Hills.

The Colonial Defence force, under the command of Colonel Nixon, and which did such good and hard service for the country, was now raised. Placards were posted about the town and suburbs inviting good horsemen to join the corps, the headquarters of which were to be at Otahuhu. Horses, arms, and appointments were furnished to non-commissioned officers and privates. The pay was, for sergeants, 7s 6d; corporals, 6s 6d; and troopers 5s per day finding their own rations, but when required forage for horses was supplied by the Government. A large number of settlers responded to the call, and in a few days one hundred saddles were filled ready for the field.

Simultaneously with the forward movement of the troops the natives living in the southern districts of Auckland received notice to take the oath of allegiance, and give up their arms, or failing which, they would be ejected. The following is a translation of the notice which the natives received:—

NOTICE.

All persons of the native race living in the Manukau district and the Waikato frontier are hereby required immediately to take the oath of allegiance to Her Majesty the Queen, and to give up their arms to an officer appointed by Government for that purpose. Natives who comply with this order will be protected. Natives refusing to do so are hereby warned forthwith to leave the district aforesaid, and retire to Waikato beyond the Maungatawhiri. In case of their not complying with this order they will be ejected.

By His Excellency's order.

Auckland, July 9th, 1863.

The Governor's notice to take the oath of allegiance or quit fell like a bombshell amongst the natives, and at almost every settlement they elected to leave, and join their comrades in the Waikato. Unfortunately most of them got away with their arms and ammunition, which they had been storing up for some time. The Princess Te Paea came down from Waikato to Mangere for the avowed purpose of unearthing the bones of her ancestors, and conveying them to a place of security in the Waikato. The ancestral bones were taken away in boxes, the oblong shape of which and heavy weight savoured more of arms and ammunition than of bones. A large escort of natives accompanied the Princess and the mysterious boxes in several large canoes across the Manukau at night, to Waiuku. The boxes were then taken overland to the Awaroa Creek, where a numerous party of armed Waikatos was awaiting their arrival. The whole party then proceeded in a number of canoes up the Waikato. The writer and several others who were in a cutter lying anchored waiting for the ebb tide in the Manukau Harbour, about sixteen miles below Waiuku, had a narrow escape of being murdered by the escort of the Princess as they passed, and were only prevented by the Princess Sophia herself, she probably thinking that they might be stopped at Waiuku, if, by any means, the crime should be discovered, and an alarm raised. At most of the settlements the night before the natives departed from their homes for ever was spent in speechifying, tangi-ing, going through the war dance, firing off guns, and rum drinking. A large fire was kept burning in the open, into which was cast nearly everything that they did not intend to take away on the morrow.

The settlers, now that the Governor had taken a decisive step and brought affairs with the natives to a crisis, were alarmed at their exposed and unprotected position. At Waiuku a stockade was commenced on rising ground in the centre of the township, and armed parties went each day into the bush for slabs. At the Mauku. it was decided, if attacked, to make a stand in the church, where to this day can be seen the apertures cut for the rifles to be pointed through. The majority of the settlers living with their families isolated in bush clearings hastily left their homes and crowded into Auckland homeless, and in not a few cases nearly penniless, their cattle wandering untended through the bush, their pigs and poultry running wild, and the severe work of many years left to go to wreck and ruin. Not a few homesteads were pillaged and burnt, and the live stock killed by the natives. In all cases it took years to repair the damage done.

And these were the colonists who were basely charged by certain high parties and religious fanatics in England of desiring a war with the Natives. God forgive them, for the New Zealand settlers find it difficult to do so, the calumny being so untruthful and wicked.

The Militia shirkers not having been unearthed in sufficient numbers, although a great many old scores were paid off by informing, had to be drawn out, for we find that at this time Colonel Mould, R.E., was instructed by the Governor to draw out with all convenient speed the whole of the first-class Militia. There was no escape this time. The badgers were drawn and had to serve.

Quite a crowd collected each day round the Militia office to give in their names. Auckland was getting intensely military. The young men who served behind the counters in the shops were full privates, and the baker's man who brought the bread was perchance a lance-corporal or a sergeant. The drill instructors had a busy and harassing time of it. Day after day the recruits endeavoured to form into line, to right-about face and to form fours, but they got hopelessly mixed up together in their frantic efforts to form fours, and when it came to right-about face nose was often pointed to nose amidst the laughs and jeers of the spectators, whose time had not yet come, but did shortly afterwards, when the second-class Militia were called upon, and respectable middle-aged parties who, after their cash, above all things believed in their personal dignity, had in their turn to succumb to the inevitable and become a prey to the drill sergeant. What dignity could possibly stand the goose step and the withering sarcasm of the drill instructor? And then of a night, instead of the cheerful bright fire and warm slippers in a comfortable room, to be ordered to go prowling about the outskirts of the town with a loaded gun, looking earnestly for the savage foe that was coming to fire and sack the city, and praying to goodness that he might never see him. No dignity that ever existed could stand such work as this. The constant trickling of water will in time even wear away a stone, and so steady drill wore away the awkwardness of the Militia so observable at first.

All sorts of dodges were tried to evade the Governor's edict. The quick-sighted suddenly became ophthalmic, and lost their vision beyond twenty yards, and the slightly rheumatic, helplessly lame, limped painfully before the inspecting doctor. It was in the bones, sir, where even the skilful eye of Esculapius could not penetrate, and many got struck off the roll in this way, real shirkers in every sense of the word.

The value of the Auckland Rifle Volunteers was now again demonstrated, as it had been before when the war first broke out at Taranaki, for here was a force that was already drilled and capable of taking up their duties at once, mustering some 400 bayonets. The battalion was under the command of Major Campbell, and comprised five companies. No. 1, under Captain Howell; No. 2, Captain (afterwards Colonel) Lyon; No. 3, Captain Heaphy; No. 5, Captain Derrom; and No. 6, Captain J. M. Clarke. There was for some reason or other, no No. 4 company. The Volunteer Naval Brigade, under Captain Daldy and Lieutenant Guilding, also did good service in relieving the Rifles and Militia of their duties. Shortly afterwards the strength of this Brigade was augmented by a No. 2 company, under the command of Captain John Copeland.

Those of the Militia who had volunteered for active service outside of the Militia district were under the command of Captain St. John (afterwards Colonel St. John), whose brilliant services in the field will long be remembered by New Zealand colonists. The Militia Volunteers were camped at Otahuhu.

To reinforce the Waiuku stockade and the Manukau district, a small number of about twenty-five men were enrolled and sworn in as special constables, their pay being 3s 6d a day and rations. These men seem to have been distinct altogether from the Militia, for they had to apply to Mr Joseph May at Epsom, who, being a J.P., no doubt swore them in, and had the corps all to himself.

Several fires taking place at this time in Auckland caused great excitement amongst the inhabitants, who made sure that it was the work of the Maori foe, who were sacking the town. The ringing of bells, bugles sounding the alarm, the hurried tramp of crowds of Militiamen and Rifles with their arms through the streets, women screaming, and the red glare of the fire overhead rendered more glaring by the blackness of night, threw the whole town into the greatest disorder, so much so that it became necessary for a notice to be issued requesting inhabitants in case of fire to remain in their houses, the Militia to assemble in the barracks, and the Rifles at posts selected in case of alarm.

CHAPTER IV.

The following notification forwarded to the Waikato chiefs by His Excellency Sir George Grey is specially interesting, showing, as it does, upon what grounds the Governor decided upon taking possession of the Waikato district.

CHIEFS OF WAIKATO.

Europeans quietly living on their own lands in Waikato have been driven away, their property has been plundered, their wives and children have been taken from them. By the instigation of some of you, officers and soldiers were murdered at Taranaki. Others of you have since expressed approval of these murders. Crimes have been committed in other parts of the island, and the criminals have been rescued or sheltered under the order of your authority. You are now assembled in armed bands. You are constantly threatening to ravage the settlement of Auckland, and to murder peaceable settlers. Some of you offered a safe passage through your territories to armed parties contemplating such outrages.

The well-disposed among you are either unable or unwilling to prevent these evil acts. I am therefore compelled for the protection of all to establish posts at several points on the Waikato river, and to take necessary measures for the future security of persons inhabiting that district.

The lives and property of all well-disposed persons living on the river will be protected, and armed and evil-disposed people will be stopped from passing down the river to rob and murder Europeans.

I now call upon all well-disposed Natives to aid the Lieutenant-General to establish these posts and to preserve peace and order.

Those who remain peaceably at their own village or move into such districts as may be pointed out by the Government, will be protected in their person, property, and land.

Those who wage war against Her Majesty, or remain in arms, threatening the lives of her peaceable subjects, must take the consequences of their acts, and they must understand that they will forfeit the right to the possession of their lands, guaranteed to them by the Treaty of Waitangi, which lands will be occupied by a population capable of protecting for the future the quiet and unoffending from the violence with which they are now so constantly threatened.

Auckland. July 11th, 1863.

The above notification was no clever stringing of words together by the Governor to cover an aggressive act, it being true in every particular, and it was none too soon when he decided to take steps for protecting for the

BISHOP SELWYN.

future the quiet and inoffensive from the violence with which they were so constantly threatened.

This then was the cause of the Waikato War. It was a struggle for supremacy of law and order against no law and no order except that of outrage. Such a state of things could not last—impossible—it being against the natural order of things. Law Courts had been formed and native assessors appointed in the Waikato, but when the Taranaki war commenced all semblance of law and order disappeared. The few well-disposed were unable or unwilling to stay the spirit of rebellion, so the Governor, Sir George Grey, was compelled to take steps for the future safety of the settlers. The time had to come, and may have to come again, and always will have to come, no matter when, whenever law and order comes into juxtaposition with no law and no order.

Sir George Arney, the then Chief Justice of New Zealand, ruled that every man, woman, and child domiciled within these shores are subjects of Her Majesty, and must obey the laws. He stated that it was his duty to say so.

A writer, treating of this subject at the time, says, "The Maoris, who have hitherto had the advantage of living in a sort of political ferry boat always available to convey them to the side most remote from danger or responsibility, must now be considered by all as bound down to one position. They are British subjects, and must obey British law." It is not, perhaps, very difficult to perceive how an opinion frequently contradicting this first sprung into popularity with a class of persons in this country.

A generous mind will always be ready to make allowance for many shortcomings in a people situated as the Maori people have been. This indulgence towards individuals naturally extended itself to the race, and the law was in practice allowed to be different in its operation towards the native and the European. Such a practice admitted, the step was an easy one which founded that distinction upon some undefined but radical difference in the sovereignty of Her Majesty over the native and European inhabitants of New Zealand.

As we have said, the root of this error was a generous one, but the error was great, and has proved very fatal, notwithstanding. The Maori felt that he was not under the subjection of law as his European neighbour was, and this led him to assert that the Queen and the law belonged to the white man, and another law belonged to the Maori. The European felt that the law did not protect him in his dealings with his native neighbour, while it was always ready to give the very greatest protection to his native neighbour in all transactions with him.

The doctrine that no natives or tribes of natives in this country have a right to wage war against one another or against the Queen's authority has only thus lately been placed plainly before the Maoris.

A large number (about 160) of refugee natives having congregated with the chief Ihaka's (Isaac's) Papakura Maoris, at Keri Keri, near Papakura, a party of the 65th regiment and Colonel Nixon's Defence Force were ordered to eject them. Bishop Selwyn and another clergyman also went to persuade the natives to leave. Whether it was politic of the Bishop to go and interfere at this crisis, and also on several other occasions, has been much questioned. Certain it is that he was at the time severely censured by a great many, however good may have been his intentions. Upon the arrival of the troops, the natives

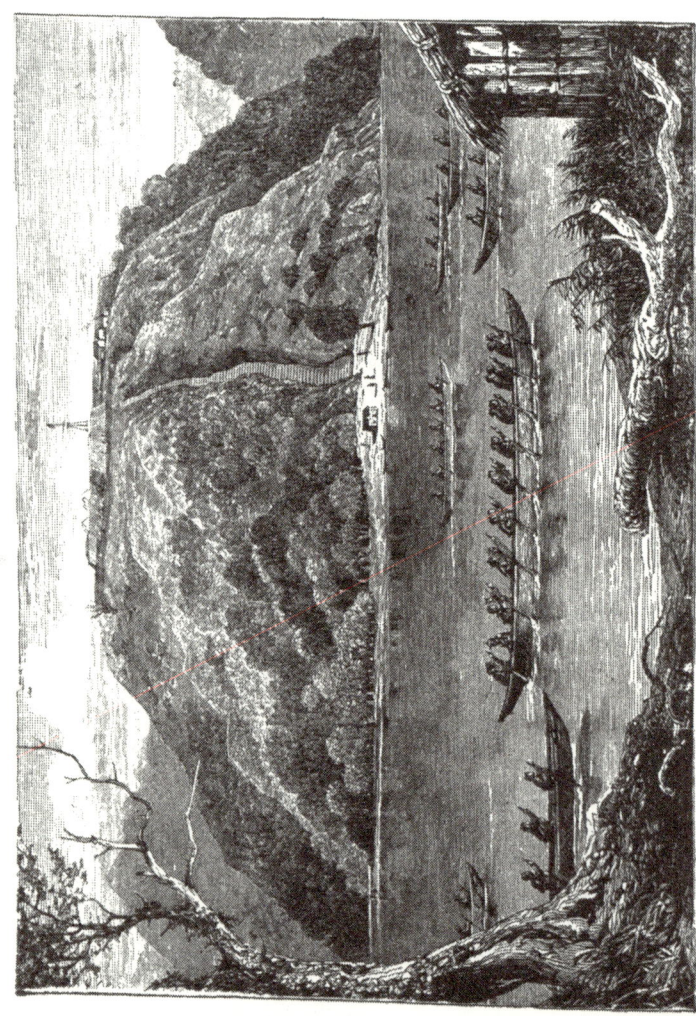

ALEXANDRA REDOUBT, AT TUAKAU.
(Constructed by the 65th Regiment.)

asked to be allowed to remain over Sunday, that day being Saturday, and the chief Isaac, who was not to be seen, was stated to be laid up in his whare with rheumatism. This was false, for the wily old rascal was as well as ever, but was lying on top of his gun and ammunition and would not move. The other natives had also hidden their arms and ammunition and would not move. After much parleying the time for them to leave was extended until the following Monday evening and the troops returned to camp.

On the next day, Sunday, a strong detachment of the 65th Regiment, under Colonel Wyatt, C.B., marched from the Queen's Redoubt to the native settlement at Tuakau, for the purpose of expelling the Maoris who had not left or given in their allegiance according to the Governor's order. The village was situated on the edge of the river, and justly considered one of the prettiest and most flourishing in the lower Waikato. The land was good; potatoes, kumaras, and corn grew luxuriantly, and each year filled the storehouses of the natives to overflowing. A water mill close by ground their wheat into flour, and their fruit trees were loaded with apples and peaches, whilst the branches of the vine bending under their juicy weight trailed in the swift running stream. No wonder the natives were loth to leave their beloved home. The 65th debouched suddenly from the bush in the rear of the settlement, and surprised the natives, who hastily collected their lares and penates, moved mournfully down to their canoes, and with many tears and deep sighs paddled away.

The object of the expedition having been completed, it returned to the Queen's Redoubt, with the exception of a company who were left behind to throw up and occupy a redoubt on a high cliff overlooking the river.

Early on the Tuesday morning most of the natives left Keri Keri, the rheumatic old chief, no doubt, as nimble as the youngest. They dispersed, and prowled, with tomahawk and loaded gun, through the Hunua ranges, and some towards Shepherd's Bush. The mounted orderly, as he galloped along the road hard by with dispatches from the General to His Excellency the Governor, passed safely through the bush, saw nothing, heard nothing but the piping of the tui, or the harsh scream of the kaka, and the day wore slowly on and on until the sun went down and the shades of evening mingled with the gloom of night, and the stars came out one by one, and with their bright twinkling eyes pierced even the deep gloom of the forest, and saw the evidence of a dark crime that had that day been committed.

Early the next afternoon a rumour reached Auckland which thrilled everyone with horror. It was to the effect that two settlers had been found murdered by the natives. Later on this rumour was confirmed. Extras were issued from the newspaper offices, which stated that Mr Meredith and his young son, a mere lad, had been found in Shepherd's Bush, tomahawked, evidently by the Maoris. They had been out the day before to work as usual, and, not coming home at night, a search party had gone out that morning, and discovered their bodies. The first victims had been sacrificed. Hostilities had commenced. The natives had now struck the first blow, a cowardly one, 'tis true, but they had drawn first blood, and that to the Maori was something. It remained to be seen where the next blow would be struck.

Although the natives opposed to us possessed but inferior arms, they had a great advantage over the troops in their intimate knowledge of the country, and could number altogether nearly 3000 fighting men, that is counting the tribes outside of the Waikato, who in various ways assisted the Kingites. These dispersed into bands of from 200 to 400 men, roving through and having the advantage of the deep cover afforded by the extensive bush, over thirty miles in length by twelve in breadth, which fringed our frontier settlements from the Wairoa to Waiuku, rendering them a formidable foe, as they could, if so minded, strike suddenly for outlying districts, and retreat back into the bush. To guard all the frontier settlements, and at the same time push forward a strong force into the heart of the Waikato, would require all and more than all the men and means at the disposal of the General. Most of our townships at this period were almost defenceless, and each expecting to be attacked. No one could tell when or where a party of natives would emerge from the long fringe of bush.

The troops were, except those at Drury, all at the front at the Queen's Redoubt and Maungatawhiri, and the Rifles and Militia were still in Auckland. Each hour was an anxious one.

CHAPTER V.

Heavy rains now set in, and made the roads almost impassable. Fortunately the road to the Queen's Redoubt, or the Great South Road, was metalled, otherwise it would have been a most difficult task to have conveyed stores to the troops already at the front. As it was, the teams were sorely tried, and the escorts, composed on the first stage from Auckland of Militia and Volunteers, and thence on to the front of Regulars, were, day after day, soaked to the skin. The little township of Otahuhu at this time was a scene of bustle and excitement; all day long the main street was thronged with Regulars, Militia, and Volunteers, whilst convoys, on their way to the front, halting, blocked up the road, and from the reveille to tattoo bugles were sounding.

On the morning of the 17th July, some hours before the break of day, 60 Volunteer Cavalry, under Colonel Nixon and Captain Walmsley, were in saddle and galloping along the road to Papakura, where they joined about 400 Regulars, under Colonel Murray, of the 65th Regiment. At 6 a.m. they were on the march for Keri Keri, where a large number of natives had occupied a pa, the same no doubt who were concerned in the murder of Mr. Meredith and his son. The natives surprised, made no opposition, and the troops took the chief, Ihaka (Isaac), and eighteen men, women, and children prisoners, together with a flag, a keg of powder, on which a native was sitting, and twelve stands of arms. A large number of natives who were camped in the pa, which was erected in the bush, fled with their arms and ammunition.

The prisoners were escorted to Drury, and the Hon. Dillon Bell, the Native Minister, for some reason best known to himself, but which has never been found out by anyone else, forwarded to his Maori pets several bags of sugar and a quantity of tobacco. It will be, however, a satisfaction for the reader to know that after passing through the hands of the troops very little of it reached those for whom it was intended.

Four horses that had been taken at the same time as Isaac's party were sold for £20 each, and the money, to the astonishment of everyone, was handed over to the prisoners. They also were allowed far better rations than the troops, who not unnaturally grumbled considerably. It appeared that by some great stretch of imagination on the part of the authorities, Isaac's party were considered to have voluntarily given themselves up, although they had refused to take the oath of allegiance, and were captured with arms and ammunition in their possession.

Numerous similar gross acts of favouritism shown towards the rebel natives during the progress of the war by the colonial authorities, who were said to be influenced in no small way by the clergy, and afterwards by certain religious fanatics, who held their meetings in Exeter Hall, London, caused the war to be very unpopular with the troops, both Imperial and Colonial.

The prisoners were conveyed under a guard and accompanied by Bishop Selwyn to Otahuhu, and were there received by a crowd of settlers, who hissed and hooted both at the Bishop and the prisoners. The tumult increasing, Ihaka and his party were removed into the Military Stockade.

The chief Ihaka, on account of his good behaviour in having given himself up, did not have his land in the Papakura Valley confiscated, and at the present time it is in the hands of his family, and of very considerable value.

The roads beyond Drury were now declared not safe, and warning of their insecurity was given to the out settlers who had not already come in. The church at Drury was converted into a depot for the reception of the refugees until they could be forwarded under escort to Auckland.

It has been stated by one writer, a missionary, that the reason why the Maoris were incited to commit murder was because directly the natives left their settlements the settlers came with carts and carried away their goods and chattels, the Maoris watching this operation from the bush. Such may have been the case in one solitary instance, but, as a general rule, the goods and chattels left behind by the natives were not worth mentioning, and they were astute enough to know that directly they left their settlements to take up arms against the Queen and her subjects they were outlawed, were in open rebellion, and their lands and effects from that moment were confiscated, as stated in the notice which they had received from the Governor.

At most of the settlements deserted by the natives, greater or less quantities of potatoes and kumaras were left, for the reason that the Maoris did not care to be hampered with their carriage. These were, as might be expected, appropriated either by the settlers or the troops.

The writer passed through several deserted settlements shortly after the natives had left, but never saw anything that would tempt anyone to take the trouble of even picking up. There was, however, one notable exception to the usual heap of old rags, for, of all things in the world, there stood a piano, an article of furniture that could not be conveniently carried away. The popular supposition that music soothes the savage breast did not seem to hold good in this instance, or it may have been that the owner was unable to produce from his instrument other than discordant sounds, which perhaps rather tended to irritate than soothe. The Maori chief to whom the piano belonged was, I believe, shot dead at Rangiriri.

Whether the settlers had taken anything from the native whares or not, murder, no doubt, would have been committed all the same, it being the Maori method of declaring war.

Some of the soldiers at the Queen's Redoubt, thinking that the natives had left their settlement at Pokeno, went to seek for potatoes, but the Maoris, not having departed, opened fire upon them, but without effect. The marauders beat a hasty retreat. A detachment of troops marched out the next morning from the Redoubt, but found the settlement deserted.

For service in the field the troops, who were armed with the Enfield rifle, were provided with a serviceable blue serge tunic in place of the regulation red

THE WAIKATO WAR.

coat, which was left at the headquarters in Auckland, and their shakos were discarded for the time being. The regimental colours were also left behind, as well as the mess plate of the officers, and the bandsmen put on one side their instruments, and joined the ranks of their several corps at the front.

No pomp or splendour of war could attend the "fight" that was about to ensue. The struggle would be carried on in an almost wild, uncultivated country in the deep tangled forest, amid swamps or barren fern hills.

The Kingites opposed to our forces could not be considered as organised. They had no one leader or chief, for their King, Tawhiao, was a mere puppet, taking no active personal part in the affairs. His council of chiefs arranged and decided everything of moment. Of the chiefs who took the most prominent part in the war, Rewi, perhaps, stands first. Before hostilities commenced he it was who incited his tribe, the Ngatimaniapotos, to break into and destroy the printing establishment at Te Awamutu, and when Apora was incarcerated, Rewi strongly advocated a raid upon Auckland. During the struggle Rewi, no doubt, had more than any other chief to do with directing the native operations.

In the matter of commissariat the natives were not badly provided. Large supplies of flour, potatoes, and kumaras could be sent down the river from the Upper Waikato, where were situated several flour mills and their most extensive cultivations. Supposing that this resource should fail or be cut off, nature gave them an almost inexhaustible supply of food, for when in the bush the nikau was at their side, and when on the open ranges the fern root was at their feet.

CHAPTER VI.

At daybreak on the 17th of July, the same day that Ihaka and his party were captured at Keri Keri, the outposts of the 14th Regt. on the Koheroa reported the Natives in considerable force about two miles off, entrenching themselves in rifle pits, evidently with the intention of arresting the further advance of the troops. The Koheroa range extends in a horse-shoe shape some three or four miles from the Maungatawhiri Creek to the Waikato River and the Whangamarino Creek, which skirts the base of the range in the south, in the same manner as the Maungatawhiri in the north. The elevation of the range is greatest where it rises up from the Maungatawhiri Creek; at this point the 14th Regt. was posted. The range then slopes away to its extremities at the Waikato River. Colonel Austen, the officer commanding the advanced post at the Koheroa, at once made his disposition for dislodging the Natives; but having to wait for reinforcements from the Queen's Redoubt, consisting of detachments from the 12th and 70th Regts., which were followed by General Cameron, it was 11 o'clock before he was able to advance. The 14th Regt. led the way, supported by the 12th and 70th Regts., in all about 500 men. After marching some two miles, the advance guard came into collision with the Maori skirmishers, who had been thrown forward some distance in front of their rifle pits. As the 14th advanced, the Natives retreated, firing, to their intrenchments, which the Maoris occupied in force. When the 14th were within 200 yards of the rifle pits, the Natives opened on the attacking column such a heavy fire that the advance was checked, and here and there some men of the 14th staggered and fell. This regiment being a newly-formed 2nd Battalion, was composed in a great part of young soldiers, many of them growing lads, new to war, and who had never been under fire. From the veterans of the 65th, 12th, and 40th Regts. they had heard of the savage character of the foe they now confronted; and the destruction of the grenadier company of the 40th Regt. in the Taranaki swamps was still fresh in their memory. General Cameron—the same Cameron who led the Black Watch up the blood-stained heights of Alma nine years before—was close up with the attacking column, and, seeing them waver, ran forward some yards in front of the 14th, and, waving his cap in the air, called upon his young soldiers—not in vain. Captains Strange and Phelps, with Lieuts. Glancy and Armstrong, rushed forward sword in hand in front of their companies, who with loud cheers charged the Maori intrenchments, which they carried at the point of the bayonet. The main body of the Natives, who had not time to re-load, hastily retreated; those who remained were bayonetted.

The routed Natives, pressed by the 14th, 12th and 70th supports, fled over the range and down into a swamp, which they had to cross before they could get cover in a belt of bush that edged the river-side. In crossing the swamp the Natives suffered severely from the heavy fire which the troops poured into them from the range above.

The remnant of the Natives who had crossed the creek were allowed to retreat without further pursuit, the troops having no means of crossing.

In this engagement the troops lost only one killed and twelve wounded. amongst whom was Colonel Austen slightly wounded in the arm. The casualties were confined to the 14th Regt. The Natives opposed to the troops numbered about 300, of whom 150 were killed and wounded. One native, a boy, was taken prisoner, he having been found lying on his face in the fern, shamming dead.

The reason that the troops lost so few men, was, no doubt, due to the fact that the Natives rarely take deliberate aim. They get too excited, and fire very often without even raising their piece to the shoulder.

The Natives left on the field a number of spades, some double-barrelled fowling-pieces and flint muskets, two or three tomahawks, and a quantity of ammunition.

General Cameron sent word by some friendly natives to the enemy that he would allow one of his surgeons to attend their wounded, whom the Maoris had managed to carry away. This very generous offer was, however, refused, the Natives conveying their wounded up the river in several canoes. It so happened that they were passed on their way up by two Europeans who had been detained at Ngaruawahia by the Kingites. One of them, Mr. England, a shoemaker, had been kept behind by the natives for the purpose of making leather covers for cartridge boxes, which were of wood with a number of small auger-holes bored for the reception of the cartridges. The natives did not molest Mr. England's party, who paddled swiftly down the stream and reached Waiuku, where they resided, in safety. The Maori treatment of their wounded is very simple; for a gun-shot wound they plug up the orifice made by the ball with clay, to exclude the air, and the patient has to take his chance. Some remarkable and speedy cures have been effected in this way. The dock-root is also used extensively for wounds and sores. The following is the official account of the engagement:—

Headquarters, Queen's Redoubt,

July 18, 1863.

Sir,—I have to inform your Excellency that, at eleven o'clock yesterday morning, Lieutenant-Colonel Austen, 2nd Battalion, 14th Regiment, commanding the camp at the Koheroa, having observed a large body of natives collecting on the hills in his front, instantly ordered his battalion to get under arms, and moved with praiseworthy promptitude against them, followed by detachments of the 12th and 70th Regiments, which had just arrived at the camp as a reinforcement, the whole force amounting to about 500 men. A report of the circumstances reached me as I was on my way to the Koheroa, and I hastened towards the column, which I overtook on its march. After we had proceeded in skirmishing order about two miles, the rebels opened fire upon us, and as we advanced upon them they retired along the narrow crest of the hills towards the Maramarua, making a stand on every favourable position which the ground presented. Some of their positions which had been recently fortified by lines of rifle pits, and which, from the nature of the ground, could not be turned—they defended with great obstinacy; and, as we had no artillery in the field, they could only be dislodged from them by successive attacks with the bayonet, which were executed by the 2nd Battalion, 14th Regiment, with great gallantry and success. We pursued them from one position to another, a distance of about five miles, until we drove them in great confusion across the mouth of the Maramarua, some escaping up the Waikato in canoes, and others along its right bank, after crossing the Maramarua. A considerable portion of them, however, before reaching the Maramarua, escaped down a gully to the left, seeking shelter in a swamp, and suffered severely from the fire of our men on the heights. As we had no means of crossing the Maramarua, I ordered the troops to return to camp. All the troops behaved remarkably well. I am greatly indebted to Lieutenant Colonel Austen, 2nd Battalion, 14th Regiment (who was wounded in the arm), to Major Ryan, commanding detachment 70th Regiment, and Brevet-Major Miller, commanding 12th Regiment, for the manner in which they led and directed the movements of the men under their respective commands. Among the officers conspicuous for their forwardness in the attack were Captain Strange, 14th Regiment, who commanded the leading company of the column; Captain Phelps, who greatly distinguished himself at the head of his company when charging a line of rifle pits, and Lieutenants Glancy and Armstrong, also of the 2nd Battalion, 14th Regiment; Colonel Mould, C.B., Royal Engineers, was with the column during the engagement, and ready to give his valuable services if required. I enclose a list of casualties, which are small, considering the time the engagement lasted, and the nature of the ground, which was exceedingly favourable for defence. The enemy must have had fully 300 men in the field, almost the whole of them belonging to tribes of the Waikato. There can be no doubt their loss was considerable, upwards of twenty dead having been counted by us on the ground, several of whom were chiefs of consequence, and among them an uncle of the King.

D. A. CAMERON,
Lieutenant-General.

His Excellency,
Sir George Grey, K.C.B., Etc., Etc.

CHAPTER VII.

Standing on the highest point of the Pokeno range, where the bush is cut away for the road, leaving a blank in the sky-line that can be seen miles away, a beautiful scene presents itself to the wandering eye of the traveller. To the north is stretched, like a panorama, a large expanse of seeming level country, dotted here and there with patches of bright green, and white specks that you know are houses; and here and there dense clumps of bush; whilst on the horizon, like dark clouds, rise up the cones of extinct volcanoes, looking dim and blue in the distance. The largest of the cones is the Mount of Eden, and under its shadow, by the waters of the Waitemata, rests Auckland City. To the west the broad bosom of the Manukau glitters in the sun like an immense sheet of glass; and the hills that girt its western shore are the ranges that ward off the stormy seas of the wild Pacific. If the wind should chance to be light and westerly, at times even the distant boom of the ocean as it bursts upon the Manukau bar can be heard. On this bar it was that on the 7th of February, 1863, was totally lost H.M.S. Orpheus, 21 guns, together with Commodore Burnett, 22 officers, and 167 seamen and marines. This ill-fated ship left Sydney for the Manukau, on her first voyage to New Zealand, with a crew of some 250; and had on board a large quantity of stores for the different ships of war stationed in New Zealand. On the morning of the 7th February the New Zealand coast was sighted, and before noon the vessel had come up with the land. Earlier than usual the hands had been piped down to dinner, which, being finished, the vessel headed straight for the bar, coming in from seaward through the north (or main) channel. This passage runs between two long sandbanks that stretch some four or five miles out to sea, which, excepting in very calm weather, breaks heavily on the banks, especially with the flood. The wind was fair, blowing a stiff breeze from the west; the sun was shining brightly, and, under steam and press of canvas, the Orpheus entered the north channel. She had scarcely done so when she struck heavily several times, and then, swinging round, settled firmly on the bank. Several boats were lowered, but were immediately smashed against the side of the ship, and the crews drowned—the first lieutenant being in charge of the first boat that was lowered. One boat and crew, however, got away clear in charge of the paymaster, Mr. Amphlett, who made for the Pilot Station to get assistance. At the Pilot Station there was, beside the usual pilot boats, a lifeboat (but it was scarcely, if ever, used), and the hands at the station, unable to launch it, had to proceed to the wreck with the boats they had in use. The steamer Wonga Wonga, bound south, on her way through the south channel, observed the Orpheus on the bank and went to her assistance. When she arrived, the crew of the Orpheus were on the yards and rigging, with a heavy sea bursting over the decks. Having no rocket apparatus, the Wonga Wonga could only lay by in the channel as close as possible to the bowsprit of the Orpheus. Some of the Orpheus' men, sliding down the foretopmast-stay, jumped into the sea, and were picked up by the people of the Wonga Wonga; others, in the attempt, were drowned. At this time the masts of the Orpheus suddenly went over the side, carrying with them the unfortunate seamen and marines who were clinging to the yards. With a loud cry they disappeared in the heavy surf that was breaking over the doomed ship. Whilst this dreadful tragedy was being enacted on the bar, another ship of war, the Harrier, was lying calmly at anchor at Onehunga—only some 22 miles from the scene of the wreck—but it was night before the sad news of the wreck reached that ship, and it was then, of course, too late to render assistance. In those days there was no telegraph. Out of the whole of the ship's company only about 70 or 80 were saved. One seaman—a coloured man—was picked up inside the heads, floating in with the flood-tide. He was completely doubled up like a ball, and had floated in that strange position. Although in a dreadful state of exhaustion when picked up he afterwards recovered. Parties of settlers went on the coast the morning after the wreck, but no bodies had been washed ashore, and the only indications of any disaster having taken place were some spars pounded to pieces with the action of the surf. It was nearly a week after the wreck before any bodies came ashore. The loss of the Orpheus is said to have been caused through the sandbank (a shifting one) on which she struck not being marked on the Admiralty chart. Owing to the recent hostilities at Taranaki, men-of-war were continually crossing and recrossing the bar in nearly all weathers; in fact, when H.M.S. Harrier first crossed the Manukau bar it was blowing a hard gale with a tremendous sea running, yet she came safely through the same channel taken by the Orpheus. Official information that should have been in the hands of the commodore was evidently not there, or if there was not used.

On the southern side of the Pokeno range the view is altogether different—here the range falls abruptly to the flat, in the centre of which was situated the Queen's Redoubt; further on rise up the fern hills of Koheroa, with the Mangatawhiri stream at its base, running through a swamp tract until it joins the Waikato, which glides like a silver thread through the King Country. At the back of the river broken wood and fern-clad ridges obstruct the further view. The road over the Pokeno ranges, cut through a dense bush, is rough and uneven, up hill and down dale, with here and there sharp pinches difficult for the transport of stores. Several streams crossing the road were roughly bridged over. Whilst the fight was taking place in the Koheroa hills, the distant rattle of musketry being plainly heard on the Pokeno ranges, a convoy of six carts, escorted by 50 soldiers of the 2nd Battalion, 18th Regiment, under command of Major Turner and Captain Ring, wound its way slowly along the road over the Pokeno range en route from the Queen's Redoubt to Drury. Arriving at a part of the road called the "Stone Depot," so-called on account of the metal for the road being stored there, the convoy halted to water and feed the horses. Whilst so engaged, a detachment of the 18th passed by on its way to the Queen's Redoubt; they reported the road all clear of natives. Thus assured, Major Turner rode on by himself, leaving the escort to follow in charge of Captain

THE WAIKATO WAR. 37

ATTACK ON ESCORT, NEAR SHEPHERD'S BUSH, GREAT SOUTH ROAD, JULY 17th, 1863.

Ring. The horses having been fed and watered, the convoy resumed its march, the rear guard, consisting of fourteen men, being some little distance behind the last cart. The escort, not dreaming of danger, were marching at ease, when suddenly, near Martin's farm, a heavy fire was opened on the convoy from the bush on both sides of the road. Major Turner, who by this time was some distance on in front, must have ridden unknowingly through the ambuscade. The suddenness of the attack threw the convoy momentarily into confusion; the horses plunged and reared, and some being hit, fell on the road in their traces. Quickly recovering from the surprise, the escort, with great coolness, returned the fire of the natives, who kept under cover of the bush. The natives seeing the rear guard some distance behind the main body, attempted to cut them off; a mob of about forty rushed across the road. Four of the rear guard were already hors de combat, when the remaining ten brought their bayonets to the charge and rushed at the Maoris, who, although four to one, declined the contest, and scrambled back hastily under cover of the bush, thus enabling the rear guard to double up to the main body. Gallantly fighting as it went, the convoy continued its march until they were reinforced by the detachment of the 18th, which had passed them at the "Stone Depot"; but hearing the firing, had doubled back to assist their comrades. Upon their arrival the natives retreated. Shortly afterwards more reinforcements arrived from Drury. In this affair the escort lost five men killed and eleven wounded. Some of the bodies were dreadfully mutilated; one soldier was found with his tongue cut out. Where the convoy was attacked, the road was strewed with pieces of harness, broken boxes, pools of blood, and the bodies of the killed and wounded soldiers; these being lifted on to the carts, the troops returned with the convoy to Drury. How many men the natives lost is not known, as they managed to carry their dead and wounded away with them. The camp at Drury was that evening reinforced by the arrival of the Naval Brigade, some 200 strong, under Captain Sullivan, of H.M.S. Harrier. The Naval Brigade was composed of seamen and marines belonging to the different ships of war on the station; they had several boats with them for service on the Waikato River. The Brigade arrived in the Harrier, which crossed the Manukau and steamed up the Papakura channel, landing the men in boats up the Drury creek.

CHAPTER VIII.

The attack on the escort proved that the natives intended not to retreat to the Waikato, but to hover in the long belt of bush which covers the Hunua and Pokeno ranges, and so threaten the General's communication between the Queen's Redoubt and Auckland.

It therefore became necessary to establish posts at intervals along the road passing over the Pokeno ranges. This duty absorbed about 400 men, composed of drafts from the 40th and 2nd Battalions, 18th Regiments, and 60 of the Volunteer Militia, under Ensign Jones, who held one post at Baird's farm. Whilst the redoubts were being thrown up, the troops were in tents, and had to keep continual watch day and night, each picket taking turn and turn about every four hours, during which time the picket lay concealed behind logs and stumps waiting for the enemy to make his appearance. He, however, did not do so, being evidently well posted up in the strength and tactics of the troops. During this time the soldiers suffered severely, the weather being wet and cold.

The regiments in the field with General Cameron at the commencement of hostilities consisted of the 65th, 40th, 12th (except one company, which was at Hobart Town, but arrived shortly afterwards), the 70th, 2nd Battalion, 14th (less three companies stationed at Wellington), and one wing headquarters of the 2nd Battalion 18th Royal Irish; Captain Mercer's Field Battery Royal Artillery, and a company of Royal Engineers—in all, about 4000 Imperial troops. The 57th Regiment was in New Zealand, but stationed at Taranaki and Wanganui, and did not take an active part in the subjugation of the Waikato tribes. To supplement the above forces, considerably over 1000 Militia and Volunteers were placed in the field. (At a later period of the campaign the General received further large reinforcements in the shape of the remaining wing of the 2nd Battalion, 18th Regiment, the 50th, 43rd, and 68th Regiments of Foot, together with another Field Battery of Artillery, the Military Train, Detachments of Royal Engineers and Army Hospital Corps.) To these Imperial troops were added four Regiments of Colonial Militia recruited in the Australasian colonies, each regiment being 1000 strong. These were destined for the permanent military occupation of the Waikato. The above army was materially assisted by the Naval Brigade, formed of seamen and marines landed from the different ships of war on the station, under the direction of Commodore Wiseman, H.M.S. Curacoa.

Immediately after the engagement at Koheroa and the attack on the escort, the citizens of Auckland were called upon to take the field and share with Her Majesty's forces the honours and fatigues of war. Accordingly, on Saturday, July 18, the Albert Barracks, Auckland, presented an unusual scene of bustle and excitement. The Militia and Volunteers were ordered to Otahuhu for active service. Crowds of citizens assembled to give "God speed" to their relations and friends. There were many aching hearts in Auckland city that day. Fathers pressed the hands of their sons; mothers embraced their boys—many of them but 16, and not strong enough to bear the fatigues of a march hampered with the heavy rifle and accoutrements served out. Some of these lads, it is said, fell down on the march exhausted. Sweethearts came to cry, and wave their handkerchiefs to their beloved; and numbers came out of curiosity to see them off, as they would have come to have seen a regiment of regulars, or a spectacle of any sort. The detachments would not be away long, only a week, it was said—delusive hope to the fond mothers who tried to console themselves with the idea that their boys would be with them again in a few days. The days passed and they did not come; weeks went; and it was over a month before they returned. Many of them, never; and many came back only to pine away, and die—for they had been smitten by a foe more terrible than the Maori, a foe called Fever and Ague, wrestled with in wet tents and the malarious camp at Drury. But the bugles are sounding the fall-in, the detachments form into line, and the command is given, "Fours right; quick march!" the Volunteer Band in front strikes up a lively air, the sentry at the gate presents arms, and the companies march out, followed by a cheering, surging crowd.

CHAPTER IX.

Captain Mackintosh, of the 1st Class Militia, and Captain Derrom, of the Rifle Volunteers, were in command of the detachments that marched out to Otahuhu. This advance force numbered about 200 bayonets, drafted from the different companies of Militia and Volunteers. Other detachments followed shortly afterwards. All classes of society were represented by these citizen soldiers, as may be seen by the roll of one company of the 1st Class Militia, which consisted of 1 Custom-house officer, 29 clerks, 3 surveyors, 1 seedsman, 4 farmers, 3 builders, 1 cabinetmaker, 14 carpenters, 2 shipwrights, 1 boat builder, 1 painter, 1 grainer, 1 mason, 2 bricklayers, 5 blacksmiths, 1 tinsmith, 2 bootmakers, 2 printers, 1 storeman, 1 storekeeper, 1 grocer, 1 chemist, 2 carters, 4 labourers, 2 teachers, 1 photographer, 1 keeper lunatic asylum, 3 gentlemen, 8 servants, 1 ostler, and 2 without either trade or calling.

The sudden withdrawal of so many artisans from their business occasioned great loss and inconvenience to the tradespeople. Some trades were completely paralysed for a time, and one newspaper had to suspend its issue, having no compositors to set up the type—they had gone to the front.

Fifty of the Auckland Naval Brigade, under Lieutenant Guilding and Sub-Lieutenant Stevenson, marched to Onehunga on the same day as the Militia and Volunteers left the barracks, with the object of cruising round the Manukau in boats to pick up and destroy any canoes they might find. They were to have been accompanied by 50 friendly Natives who had arrived from Rotorua and were armed with rifles supplied by the Government, but the Navals refused to march in company with armed Natives. The townspeople took the matter up and a deputation waited on the Governor and Native Minister, the Hon. Dillon Bell, and the result was that the natives were disarmed.

Five hundred of the 1st Class Militia were required for service outside of Auckland, and the departure of so many able men from the capital caused great uneasiness to the inhabitants, who were afraid that they might be attacked. Auckland in 1863 was very different from the Auckland of the present day, and although the capital of the colony and seat of Government, did not contain more than about 10,000 inhabitants, including men, women, and children. Where the densest part of Newton now stands there were fern ridges and gullies. Ponsonby did not exist, and Parnell was but a mere straggling suburb. Those who were not on the Militia roll offered to do night patrol duty, and amongst others at Parnell, Bishop Selwyn himself came forward to act as a night watchman unarmed, although what use an unarmed watchman, if attacked, would be against an armed Maori it is difficult to see. One night the sentry on duty in Freeman's Bay fired his piece at what he supposed to be a Maori, and caused such an alarm that the excited inhabitants in that quarter turned out en masse. But it was nothing; no natives made their appearance. The sentry had fired at a stump or something of the sort, and the trembling denizens returned again to their troubled couches, most of them to pass the remainder of the night in anxious suspense.

The following letter written at the time by one of the Militia forcibly illustrates the gross incompetence and neglect of the Militia authorities in caring for the welfare of the men, many of whom they had literally dragged from their homes. In the midst of abundance of supplies there was no excuse for the wretched ignorance and want of forethought displayed by the Colonial authorities. The writer says:—"The men marched out in good spirits, and, though somewhat disheartened with the prospects of the incumbrance which sixty rounds presented to their progress, they marched cheerily. Tired and weary, they arrived at Otahuhu only to find that they were not to return, and that no preparations had been made for their reception at the camp. After a long delay, the men standing all the time in the wet and mud, numbers of them actually shivering with cold, these men were packed into huts which were dirty, cold and miserable. The camp authorities had only received notice that 200 men were coming, and no stores were sent. Six officers and 223 men were sent on Saturday night. On Sunday two officers and 100 men came in from Onehunga, and one officer and 50 men from Panmure and Otahuhu, being nine officers and 373 men sent to camp without stores and without other preparations. Those who have felt the piercing cold (with continual wet boots and stockings) of the last few days will now be able to appreciate the delights of damp, cold, miserable and cheerless huts; with wind whistling through the crevices; no fire; and huddled together like sheep, with one candle to each hut, and nothing to eat. This was our situation; nor is it yet much improved. On Saturday night, short commons; on Sunday, no bread served out till 10 p.m. Raining fast, we could not stir from the huts without being up to ankles in mud. After dark, no stirring out at all without the chance of falling into ditches which intersect one another like cobwebs, varying from ten inches to five feet in depth; mud on the floor of the huts from four to six inches thick; my hand, from cold, is almost numbed, and I can scarcely feel the pen with which I scrawl these lines. We receive rations—but what are they? Bread that smells like vinegar, and sugar more black than brown. The men were drawn from their homes without warning; they were not supplied with anything, but just as they stood in Albert Barracks, were marched through the mud of the Otahuhu road and the still heavier slush of the Otahuhu camp; wet and cold feet were the consequences, and leave has been refused to go to Auckland for an outfit. My boots were wet on Saturday night; they were wet when I put them on on Sunday morning, and they have not been dry since, and so wet are they that they will not be dry for two days. Yet I am one of the lucky ones, having put on a pair of strong boots. Others, thinking they would be home on Saturday night, came away in the boots they were wearing in dry and comfortable workshops. What is the consequence? Their paper boots are gone, and they have nothing to replace them with. I do not want a feather bed, but, with the rest of my comrades, expect to have necessaries as far as practicable."

THE WAIKATO WAR.

CHAPTER X.

Before the Auckland Militia were fully formed, Colonel Moule had resigned his command, and was with the General at the front. The Militia, however, were fortunate in having, as Colonel Moule's successor, Major-General Galloway, who had lately been gazetted from the colonelcy of the 70th Regiment, and who, instead of returning to England, at the request of General Cameron accepted the command of the Militia and Volunteer forces in the Auckland district. Two days after the arrival of the Auckland Rifle Volunteers at Otahuhu, they, together with the Onehunga Volunteers—in all, about 400 men—were moved on towards Drury, under command of Major Lyons. The column that night encamped at Papakura, and the next day General Galloway arrived, and forwarded Major Lyons with a strong detachment of Rifles and Militia Volunteers over to the Wairoa for the purpose of taking up a position there and throwing up a redoubt. Building redoubts was now the order of the day. An officer of the Royal Engineers marked out the position of the earthworks to be thrown up, and the citizens of Auckland had no help for it but to set to with pick and shovel. The majority of the men, unused to laborious work, made but slow progress in building redoubts; their hands blistered, and their backs ached not a little, and many glances of envy were cast at their more fortunate comrades with corporal's or sergeant's stripes, who had nothing to do but look on, and give, now and again, the back-aching, hand-blistered diggers and delvers a gentle hint that they were awfully slow, and if they did not look out they would have the natives upon them before they were finished; and this was not altogether a jest, for numbers of the enemy were prowling about in the dense fern and bush with which the country was covered. At night time the sentinels could see the fires of the enemy all along the ranges, and the wonder is that the natives did not make a dash at the Rifles whilst throwing up the earthworks. Major Campbell, at this time, was in charge of the camp at Papakura, and pushed the works forward as fast as he could; but it was impossible for him to transform, even on an emergency, men and lads who had never done two days' work in their lives with pick and shovel, into navvies.

Colonel Wyatt, of the 65th, having arrived to inspect the redoubt, severely lectured the men for the slow progress they had made, and they duly felt the enormity of their crime in not being able to handle such ancient and well-known instruments as the pick and the shovel. After a great deal of grumbling and growling, the redoubt was at length finished, to the satisfaction of all parties, and the natives had then lost the opportunity of making a dash.

Not accustomed to anything approaching strict discipline, and used to the great freedom and independence of colonial life, it was some time before the Militia and Volunteers could be made to understand their true position, which event only took place when many of them got into serious trouble for disobedience of orders, and found themselves in the military cells minus their thick crop of curly black or brown hair, as one well-known citizen soldier sadly remarked, looking more like convicts than gentlemen Volunteers.

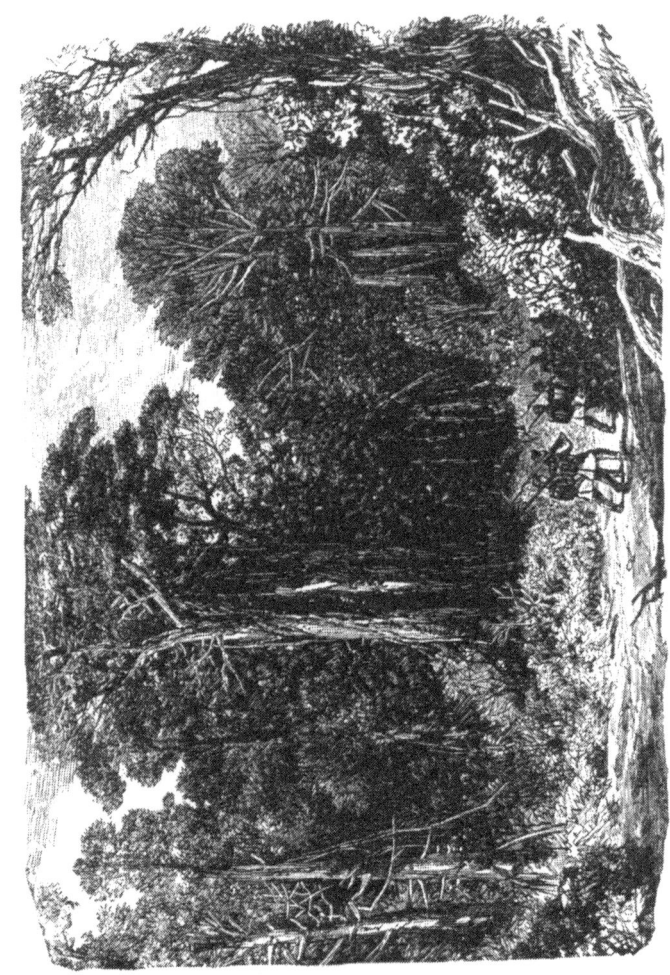

THE DEVIL'S NEST, ROAD THROUGH THE BUSH, DRURY, 1863.

CHAPTER XI.

After the murder of Mr Meredith and his son, it might have been expected that the settlers would have been careful not to have ventured in the bush—especially in the vicinity of where the natives were known to be. The Government had given those settlers who had not come in, warning of their insecurity, but notwithstanding this, and the fact that the natives had already, on two occasions, been engaged with the troops, at Koheroa, with severe loss to themselves, many families still persisted in clinging to their homesteads, at the imminent peril of their lives.

On July 22, a Mr Greenacre and three men went into the bush, not far from Mr Hay's house, between Papakura and Drury, for the purpose of cutting wood. Whilst so engaged they were suddenly attacked by about 50 Maoris, who fired a volley at them. Mr Greenacre and party dropped their axes and ran off as fast as they could out of the bush and back to Mr Hay's house, followed by the natives, who kept on firing. Not very far from Mr Hay's house, in the open ground, one of the men, named James Hunt, received a ball in the back and fell mortally wounded; the natives ceasing further pursuit, Mr Greenacre and the other two men escaped, and gave the alarm to the troops stationed at Drury and Papakura. A party of the 65th and some Marines from Drury were soon on the spot; they skirmished through the bush, but the natives had gone. The body of James Hunt was found where he had been shot, and was not tomahawked. The troops returned to Drury with the body. They had no sooner arrived than news was brought by Mr Anderson, veterinary surgeon, R.A., that a detachment of the 18th was surrounded in the bush at Keri Keri by a large force of Maoris. Colonel Wyatt, with the 65th, immediately marched towards Keri Keri, where heavy firing was going on, accompanied by Mr Anderson and Ensign Hay, of the Militia, as guide. When the alarm was given at Papakura that the natives were in the bush near Mr Hay's house, and had killed a settler, Captain Clare, of the Militia, at once started with a detachment of his men, and sent an orderly to Captain Ring, who had charge of the 18th camp on the Wairoa road. Captain Ring, with his detachment of the 18th, soon joined the Militia, and they advanced towards the bush at Keri Keri. Lieutenant Rait, with some Mounted Artillery, scoured the open ground. The 18th and Militia entered the bush in skirmishing order, some distance to the left of where the 65th had been, and came immediately into collision with the natives, who at once opened fire and fell back, followed by the troops. The Militia now, for the first time in the Waikato War, exchanged shots with the enemy. The detachment was composed principally of men used to the bush, and eager spirits who had volunteered for active service outside of the Militia district. Whilst advancing, the men kept well up with the 18th, and brought one native to the ground, shot by Private Jackson. Continuing to follow the retreating Maoris into the heart of the bush, Captain Ring's party were suddenly outflanked by a superior force of the enemy. At this time the troops were in a clearing surrounded by dense bush, and whilst endeavouring to charge the natives one of the 18th was killed and one severely wounded. The natives having splendid cover in the bush, kept up a heavy fire on Captain Ring's party. Fortunately, in the clearing was an earthwork that had been thrown up a few days before by the 18th, but afterwards abandoned. Captain Ring at once availed himself of this position, and under cover of the earthworks kept the natives from emerging into the open. Several desperate attempts were made by the enemy to get possession of the body of the 18th man who had been shot, but the fire of the troops was too severe for them to effect their object, although, after losing several men, they succeeded in obtaining the soldier's rifle and bayonet. Clouds of powder smoke hovered amongst the dense foliage surrounding the combatants, and the rattle of the firing was incessant, the bullets pinging and pattering against the trees like hailstones. Captain Ring's party had evidently fallen into a trap, and if no relief should soon arrive, their case was desperate. The afternoon was fast passing away, and already the shades of evening were beginning to fall upon the bush. The sharp rattle of rifles was now heard rolling through the forest and approaching nearer every minute, and the fire of the natives somewhat slackened. A bugle call sounded clear above the din—it was the regimental call of the 65th, which, with a loud cheer, charged through the bush, driving the enemy off. The 18th had one man killed and three wounded, and the 65th had one man killed. It being nearly dark, the troops hastily returned with their dead and wounded to the camp at Drury. The loss of the natives was not known. Appended is Captain Ring's official account of the affair:—

Camp near Keri Keri,
Wairoa road, July 23rd, 1863.

Sir,—I have the honour to state for your information, that at noon, the 22nd instant, I received information that two settlers had been fired upon by a body of natives, and that one of the settlers was killed, and hearing firing in the vicinity of Pukikiwereke, about two miles from my camp, I immediately proceeded with 100 men of the detachment under my command, and close to the abovenamed place I fell in with natives who were engaged with a party of Militia Volunteers. I opened fire, and the natives retreated to my former entrenchment above the whare at Keri Keri. The fire of the skirmishers drove them down the hill into the brushwood, the leading skirmishers on the right, under Lieutenant Wray, took possession of the hill and kept up fire on them. I, with another body of skirmishers, proceeded to take them on the right flank, but found that the natives, who mustered a strong force, nearly surrounded me. Here I lost one man killed, whose rifle and bayonet were taken possession of by the natives, though not without serious loss to them. I then concentrated my men in the entrenchment, and having heard from an Artillery officer who rode up to my position, that the 65th Regiment was in my immediate vicinity, I requested that he would inform the officer commanding the 5th that there was a track on the enemy's rear, and if an attack were made in that direction it would be of great service, as it was quite impossible for me to follow so

THE WAIKATO WAR.

strong a force of the enemy into the bush with my small force. I remained in the entrenched position until close on sunset, keeping a steady fire on the enemy, who were endeavouring to obtain possession of the body and ammunition of the private who was killed, and whom I would not leave. I repeatedly tried to obtain possession of the body by sending out volunteers of the man's company, but desisted, finding it would entail greater loss. I was about retiring, leaving a rear guard in the entrenchment, when the Mounted Artillery arrived; immediately after I saw the 65th appear. The natives then drew off their right flanking movement, and retreating into the bush, enabled me to obtain the body of the man of my detachment; this accomplished, the whole force withdrew. Casualties: 1 private killed and 3 wounded. The officers engaged on this occasion were Lieutenant Wray, Ensign Jackson, and Ensign Butts, whose assistance, coupled with the steadiness of my men, merits unqualified approbation.—I have, etc.,

JAMES RING,
Captain Royal Irish Commanding.

CHAPTER XII.

Discovering that it was much easier and safer to obtain a victory over one or more surprised settlers than the troops, the natives accordingly, on July 24, started on the war path to hunt for victims. Early in the morning one party of braves surrounded the house of Captain Calvert, which was situated on the Wairoa-road, near Papakura, and not very far distant from the 18th camp. Fortunately at the time the only occupants of the house were Captain Calvert and his son. Several natives having effected an entrance into the kitchen alarmed the inmates, who no sooner appeared than they were fired at. Young Mr Calvert fell mortally wounded, and Captain Calvert, discharging his revolver amongst the natives, rushed at them with his sword, when the intruders beat a hasty retreat. Help being obtained, young Mr Calvert was carried to the camp and shortly afterwards expired. On the same morning a Mr Cooper, living at the Wairoa, was out in his paddocks looking after his cows when suddenly a volley was fired upon him by a party of Maoris. The unfortunate man fell dead, a ball passing through his head. The savages afterwards set fire to his clothing, his body when found being partially burnt. The Maori braves, when they returned to camp that night, no doubt round the whare fire recounted to their admiring brethren the glorious deeds they had done that day and were prepared to do again if an opportunity occurred. These murders caused great excitement and consternation in Auckland, but it was impossible to protect every settler who persisted in remaining upon his isolated and exposed homestead. Many settlers no doubt preferred to run the risk of the natives to leaving their homes and having their houses ransacked, which in almost all cases invariably took place directly they were left; and it must be said that the natives were not always the guilty parties, for there is good reason for supposing that more than one deserted farm house was looted and the furniture destroyed by some of the rough and lawless characters that are always to be found amongst a body of troops, who, in war time, consider they have a right to take and destroy everything they can lay their hands upon, notwithstanding regimental orders to the contrary. The natives, reinforced on the Hunua and Pokeno ranges, had now evidently command of the long belt of bush, and threatened General Cameron's positions on all sides. The General, until he could organise a force to sweep the natives out of these ranges, was compelled to remain on the defensive. To advance further up the Waikato could not well be done until a steamer could be placed at his disposal on the river. To supply this want a small light-draught paddle steamer, named the Avon, had been purchased by the Government and fitted out for the purpose at Onehunga. The Avon was supplied with bullet-proof iron plating, and pipes were fixed in connection with the boiler, so that a stream or jets of scalding water could be thrown upon any party of natives attempting to board. For armament she had one 12lb. Armstrong gun at the bows. Captain Hunt, of Onehunga, was in charge of the vessel, under the command of Commander Mayne, H.M.S. Eclipse, upon whom devolved the onerous duty of taking the Avon up to the General's position on the Waikato river—a difficult and dangerous task on account of the many (then unknown) shallows with which the river abounds, and in the face of an enemy who could easily obstruct the passage of the steamer. It had been blowing a hard westerly gale for several days, but on the morning of the 25th of July, 1863—a momentous day for the Waikato, as it hailed the advent of steam and the march of civilisation—the weather was fine and clear on the Waikato bar. The sea broke white as Alpine snow, bright and sparkling, on the sandbanks on either side, but the bar itself was clear of break. About mid-day the natives at the settlement of Putataka, overlooking the bar, discerned the smoke of two steamers making for the entrance. Approaching closer, the vessels stopped for some little time, then the smaller of the two made straight and swift for the bar, the larger one turned round and steamed back from whence she came and ere long was lost to sight under the land. The small steamer approached the bar, a long heaving swell catches her up and carries her safely on its crest; another long heaving swell runs up behind and sends her riding swiftly along. The sea now breaks in curling waves on each side, but the channel ahead is clear, and the natives looking on know that the eye of the Waikato is put out, that a Pakeha steamer for the first time floats on the Waikato river. The natives intended to greet her with a volley, but were dissuaded from doing so by Mr W. Spargo, an old settler who resided near the heads. The Avon steamed up the river, but got ashore on the flats before reaching Kohanga, where she took on board Mr Strand, who had a knowledge of the channel and acted as pilot. After taking the ground several more times on her passage, the Avon reached the Bluff on the afternoon of the 27th, without having been molested by the enemy in any way, although they were doubtless aware of her arrival in the river. The following official letter gives an interesting and detailed account of the passage of the p.s. Avon from the Manukau to the Waikato river:—

Avon, off the Bluff,
Waikato, 27th July, 1863.

Sir,—I have the honour to inform you that I left Onehunga in Her Majesty's ship under my command, with the steamer Avon in tow, on the morning of the 16th, and steamed to the Manukau Heads. The signal "Bar unsafe" being made from the station, we anchored on the Huia bank, and remained there till Monday, the 20th. The ship dragging into shoal water, we then shifted berth round Puponga, and remained there till Saturday, the 25th. On the morning of the 25th, proceeded over the bar, with the Avon in tow, and reached the Waikato Heads at 1 o'clock. Took 30 of our men on board the Avon and sent Eclipse back to Manukau, and crossed the Waikato bar in the Avon at 2 o'clock.

After grounding several times on the flat which crosses the river inside the entrance, we ran on the bank about two miles below Kohanga, and had to remain there until 4 o'clock next morning.

We then hauled off, and steamed on till nearly daylight, when we again grounded. During the day we lightened the vessel by putting coal and some other heavy things into a large canoe which we towed up, and at high water (4.30 p.m.) the vessel again floated. Steamed on till 6, and anchored eight miles below Tuakau; started at daylight next morning, and reached the Bluff at 4 p.m.

The only natives we saw were a few at the Heads, who hoisted a white flag as we passed; 20 or 30 at Kohanga, and as many at Cameron. No one appeared the least disposed to dispute our passage.

Captain Greaves, Deputy-Assistant Quarter-Master-General, accompanied the vessel, and it is owing to his knowledge of the river and unflagging energy that the service was accomplished so successfully. He preceded the vessel the whole way, sounding and showing the channel. I request that you will bring to the notice of the Colonial Government the services of Mr Strand, of Kohanga. He accompanied the vessel from that place to Cameron, and materially assisted Captain Greaves in conducting her over one or two difficult places in which the channel had lately shifted.—I have, etc.,

J. C. MAYNE,
Commander H.M.S. Eclipse.

To Commander F. W. Sullivan,
Senior Officer in New Zealand, Naval Brigade, Camp, Maungatawhiri.

The ship Norwood arrived in Auckland harbour from Portsmouth, Aug. 2nd, with left wing of the 2nd Batt. 18th Royal Irish, under Colonel Carey; also 132 officers and men of the Royal Engineers, under command of Captain Brooke.

On Sunday night, August 2, it being moonlight, General Cameron made a reconnaissance of a position at Paparata, which the natives had formed and occupied in force. From this place, situated about 10 miles from the Koheroa Redoubts towards the East or Hauraki Gulf, the natives could direct their operations against the troops over the ranges, and could also receive reinforcements and supplies from the interior by way of the Piako. Colonel Mould, of the Royal Engineers, was in command of the reconnoitring force, which consisted of 300 officers and men. The object of the expedition having been fulfilled, the troops, after a weary march, returned to camp. A few shots were exchanged with the enemy, one soldier being dangerously wounded. It was in connection with Paparata that the gallant Von Tempsky first came into special notice in New Zealand. General Cameron desiring a plan or sketch of the enemy's works, Von Tempsky undertook the dangerous task, which he successfully carried out. Lying concealed amongst the dense scrub and flax in the very midst of the natives and their prowling dogs, he sketched the enemy's position and returned safely to camp. For this service Von Tempsky received his first commission in the Colonial Forces; for less than what he did at Paparata many a soldier has received the Victoria Cross. Several years afterwards this gallant officer lost his life in attempting to storm a rebel stockade on the West Coast, between Wanganui and Taranaki. His loss was deeply regretted by his comrades in arms and all who knew him. Captain, afterwards Colonel, Thos. Macdonnell was with Von Tempsky, and was eventually awarded the N.Z. Cross for this service.

CHAPTER XIII.

A force was now organised by General Cameron for the purpose of scouring the bush and contesting the possession of the same with the enemy. This force consisted of a flying column composed of volunteers from the Regulars, about 200 strong, and a corps of Forest Rangers under Lieutenant Jackson, consisting of volunteers from the Militia, numbering 50. These men were armed with revolvers and a breech-loading carbine, a much handier weapon in the bush than the long Enfield rifle. Another corps of Forest Rangers was shortly afterwards raised under the command of Von Tempsky. The pay of the forest rangers was 8s. per diem, without rations, the men finding their own. Lieutenant Jackson had almost a roving commission, and his corps, in a great measure, were free from the strict discipline of the troops; the work they had to do was the most harassing and exciting that the soldier is called upon to perform. From day to day their lives hung upon a chance; for on each expedition they were liable to be surrounded in the heart of a dense bush and cut off to a man; assistance could not be, and was not, relied upon.

A correspondent who accompanied Lieutenant Jackson on one of his expeditions gives the following interesting account of his journey. The writer says:—"On my way to the Wairoa I received an invitation from Lieutenant Jackson, commanding the Forest Rangers, to accompany him on an expedition through the ranges. I gladly complied, and we started the following day (Thursday) at 9 a.m.; a delay in forwarding biscuit from Papakura prevented an earlier start. Smith's Inn being the headquarters of the corps, we proceeded thence in a south-easterly direction towards the Hunua. Passing the spot where Mr Cooper was shot, close to his house on the first slope of the range, we ascended through some clearings on to the first ridge. A narrow bush track led us after that down the other side, a luxuriant vegetation obscuring any chance of a fair view of the country. Towards 12 o'clock a sudden turn of the track brought the bright light of an open country across our forest-roof, and the Hunua opening, the old lair of the enemy, came in sight. Carefully we approached this neighbourhood, but, after a little scouting, were satisfied that the field was still unoccupied, and we had our dinner in the neighbourhood of Williams's hut. While the men were resting, Lieutenant Jackson, Ensign Hay, Sergeant Cole (the corps guide), and myself, went to scan the surrounding district with our glasses. A magnificent view of valleys, ridges, fern and forest land lay before us—the heights of Paparata to the far south-east, and the thin line of our track towards the junction of the Tiara Keenu Block serpentining through the fern. No signs of anything new or unusual denoting an enemy's presence could be discovered, and the order for the march was given. We passed the blackened site of Williams's hut, burnt to the ground by the retiring enemy; and after turning a flanking height of the high forest ground, the abodes of the Hunua war party came in sight. They are still in good repair, as the attempt of Lieutenant Steele's party to fire them failed through the wetness of the thatch. Two hours' march through high fern brought us to the remains of Warner's hut, close on the forest; that was after having hit upon the enemy's track on his retreat, pointing evidently towards Paparata. This was an important discovery, and Lieutenant Jackson would have followed it up had his force been stronger, our whole complement consisting only of two officers, forty privates, eight non-commissioned officers, one volunteer: in all fifty. We next entered the forest, intending to hit by a cross-cut through the bush a piece of unfinished road in the neighbourhood of the Mangawheau, a tributary of the upper course of the Wairoa. Up to this we had been guided by men thoroughly acquainted with the neighbourhood, their knowledge being correct, and proving the inestimable importance of having such guides. Later in the afternoon the labyrinth of gullies and hills, interwoven by a most provoking network of supplejack, proved even too much for the most experienced, and we had to consult the never erring guide, the compass. During the struggle with supplejacks the judicious equipment of our party became apparent, the short carbines and the general light style of accoutrements making it alone possible to wind our way through the interminable mazes. The capabilities of the men, too, as bushmen, were displayed in a most satisfactory manner. They carried a swag composed of one blanket, one great coat, twenty rounds of ammunition, all enveloped in a so-called waterproof, and a haversack containing three days' rations of meat and biscuit, half a bottle of rum, a revolver, cartridge-box, carbine, some with sword-bayonets, others with tomahawks, and all these little items hanging from their bodies made it a work of considerable difficulty to get along through the New Zealand forest without being thrown off one's equilibrium. Darkness soon added to our difficulties, and after one hour's scramble down precipitous hillsides closely set with supplejack traps, a little stream invited us to encamp. No fires were lit; each groped his way to some lair, spread out the components of his swag, and a violent attack on meat and biscuit ensued. Sentinels for night-watch were told off, posted and appointed, and those not thus engaged threw themselves with hearty good will into the arms of the forest Morpheus, a rough but kindly deity, seldom disappointing his votary. Lieutenant Jackson, Ensign Hay, and myself had, with the eye of connoisseurs, taken instant possession of the shelter of a most comfortable lair, tenanted probably the night previous by some knowing old boar. The rain that fell that night did not wet us much, as the slanting position of the old trunk and its forest parasites proved a perfect roof, at least for two of us. Before daylight the sentinels were doubled, that time being the hour for Maori surprises. At daylight we bolted biscuit and meat to our contentment, and, with belted swag and haversack, away we glided through the dripping forest with the rain rattling through the foliage. After a couple of hours our guides were nonplussed, confessed their helpless condition, and Mr Hay, compass in hand, took the lead—to some purpose, as it became apparent shortly after. By his guidance we hit upon the point we intended to make, proving thus the superiority of a general knowledge of country to that of a minute, though circumscribed, acquaintance with one locality. It rained heavily all day long. Of fern openings, we came upon two; the first is called Wharehinau nui, the second Wharehinau nuki—both old native plantations, and presenting the quintessence of rich volcanic soil.

"Towards four in the afternoon, after traversing a third opening of an old plantation overgrown with dense scrub, we encamped on a hill at an early hour, to be enabled to erect some shelter for the night. Soon a little forest township sprang into life, nikau and fern-palms being handy, and with eagerness we piled up shelter against the dropping rain. No fires were allowed till darkness had well set in, but all the wood was ready collected. At last the welcome word of 'fire' was heard, and here and there and everywhere through the forest gloom, carefully-tended sparks began to appear till the light of the fire, as it increased, shone upon men in all positions drying themselves with a grateful expression of countenance.

"The night-watch was once more told off: and let me tell you young men so eager for the eight shillings per day for bushranging, that unless you have a sound, well-seasoned constitution to boast of, you had better think twice before you venture on such work; for night-watching after a hard day's scramble, night-watching with rain filling your boots, will give you a trial too costly if unsuccessful. In a small corps such night duty comes round from man to man very often; in fact, almost too often. With daylight we were on the march again, Mr Hay once more taking the lead. After an hour's march we came at last upon the Mangawheau river—certainly in a roundabout way, but we hit it, anyhow, thanks to our intelligent Ensign. The river contains a considerable quantity of water; we crossed it over some rocks above a little fall, and came thus, at last, into the mysterious precincts of one of our enemy's natural strongholds. Up to this we had seen no tracks; no traces of Maoris except at the Hunua, and some scattered cattle tracks. Now, however, the scene changed. Here and there nikau was found freshly cut, and soon a distinct track was come upon. Sergeant Henry Southee was placed at the head, and the track was followed up. Mr Hay had repeatedly told me that we would have to cross the track from Paparata to Maketu if we carried out our original intention of scouring all the openings down to Pokeno. He now believed that the track we did hit was the one referred to, and after a little it was deemed advisable to follow it up in preference to crossing it, as the signs increased in freshness and number. Temporary whares for war parties of 60 to 100 men were come upon; and spots with pigeon snares for the summer season were passed. They consist of a hole—square or round—cut into some broad surface root of a large tree, filled with water and surrounded by snares attached to an adjoining little upright frame, and they are used in the summer season when water gets scarce. We were traversing a magnificent forest, topping long and sharp-backed spurs, sloping to the south-east coast. Before descending a very marked one, however, we resorted to our usual mode of observation, viz., in climbing some large trees. Two of our most expert climbers, Henry Southee and little Rowland—both of marine extraction—were this time assisted by Mr Cole, and the following result was obtained:—A wide, open fern country stretched to the south-east; a broad distinct track led up a heavy fern hill; a large house or whare was also visible in a hollow; a ridge ran due south and another north-west. It was then decided, instead of proceeding to Pokeno, to follow this track at all hazard. Very silently and carefully our long blue-shirted Indian file wound through the green bushes, and considering the short time of enrolment, the men were careful enough in the all-important necessity of silence and stealthy step. Matters were becoming decidedly interesting now, and a little wholesome excitement tingling in one's blood gave spring and elasticity to the physical man. The signs became more and more pregnant with importance. We had seen soldiers' trousers—two pairs—in one hut; remains of stretchers for the wounded, in another place; but now we came upon the most significant of all—a double track, one leading open to the right, and another hidden by artfully-laid branches to the left. Here was evidence of this path leading to something worth finding, and we slipped into it with eager curiosity and bated breath. Traces of pigs abounded; and the track of a dog riveted our attention. Something like a distinct bark had been heard previously, and the certainty of something being close at hand took possession of everyone. The forest was dense in every direction around us—we could seldom see above 20 yards ahead—when suddenly, 'Poaka, poak, poak,' was heard ahead of us. Riveted with the excitement of coming events we halted. A distant voice began speaking to some audience—Henry Southee acting as interpreter for me. I heard one say, 'Ah! if we had the Pakehas before us now we would give it them.' Then followed a war dance. 'Come on! Come on!' was the last sentence we heard, which was shouted close at hand, and then we threw ourselves in ambush; when alas! a cap went off on the piece of some eager man struggling among supplejacks. A long silence ensued on the part of the hidden enemy, and Lieutenant Jackson thought it advisable to take up a position further back on the high ground. The talking could again be heard as we retreated silently as we had come, halting once more on some eminence. Here it was decided that as the exact locality was not positively known by our leaders, and as we knew that we were in the heart of the enemy's country, and were totally in the dark as to the number we might rouse by any engagement; and as the explosion of the cap without igniting the charge showed that, in spite of all possible precautions, perhaps many pieces were in a similar condition, it was deemed necessary to retreat. By the same track we reascended the spur about half past two in the afternoon, and pushed on through the forest till long after dark, when, losing the track, we retraced our steps to a clearing that we had passed, and camped for the night. The next morning we made an early start, and found that the track we had travelled was the one from Paparata to Maketu, as Mr Hay had expected. Three hours' march brought us in sight of the old pa at Maketu. A woodland scenery of undulating ground appeared to the south; to the north were hilly gullies, where another pa and now abandoned huts were situated. To the west, right in front, Maketu village and plantations appeared, and in the same direction, marking the distant South Road, rose the white peaks over the redoubt of Lieutenant Rixon, at the entrance to Shepherd's Bush—the whole, with a bright gleam of the distant Manukau, forming a most beautiful landscape. A hearty tramp of a few hours brought us to the camp at Drury."

CHAPTER XIV.

On the 7th of August the steamer Avon left her moorings and steamed past the Koheroa for some miles up the Waikato river. Owing to the heavy rains during the winter, the lead indicated a good depth of water. On her way she was fired into by a party of natives lying in ambuscade on the river bank; the Avon returned the fire with her 12-pounder Armstrong, and the shells bursting amongst the brushwood close to where the natives were concealed quickly dispersed them. A few days afterwards a large number of natives commenced to entrench themselves on the Mere Mere—a slightly elevated ridge that runs up from the Waikato river some little distance beyond the Whangamarino creek. From the British outposts, with the aid of a glass, the Maoris could be plainly discerned throwing up rifle-pits in all directions; and from the numbers of them that swarmed the hill side it was evident that they intended to make a determined stand at this point against the further advance of the troops. The natives who had taken up the position at Mere Mere consisted mainly of the Ngatimaniapotos, who, with their chief Rewi, had come down the river to assist the Lower Waikatos after their disastrous defeat on the Koheroa. The Ngatimaniapotos considered themselves the fighting men par excellence of the Waikato. A great many of them had been in several skirmishes with the troops at Taranaki, and on one or two occasions with partial success, and they doubted not but that in their own country or district they would be able to give a good account of themselves and the soldiers. With the Ngatimaniapotos appeared the King's standard, which was set up on a ridge on the extreme left of the position. For a long time it was generally believed that, man for man and armed with the same weapons, the Maori was quite, if not more than, a match for the British soldier; but Dr. Thompson, one of the surgeons of the 58th Regiment, while stationed in New Zealand, upset this idea by the following experiment: The doctor had 147 Maoris measured, their average height being 5ft. 6¾in.; whilst 617 men of the 58th Regiment averaged 5ft. 7¾in. The average weight of the Maoris was 141lbs.; that of the men of the 58th Regiment, 143lbs. The average weight the Maoris raised was 367lbs.; the average weight raised by the soldiers was 422lbs. —being 55lbs. more than the Maoris. In circumference of chest the Maoris averaged from 35 to 36 inches, and the 58th, from 35 to 71 inches. By the above it will thus be seen that in sheer weight and strength alone the Maori is inferior and would have to give way, whatever some writers may say to the contrary.

Unmolested by General Cameron, the natives were enabled, in a short space of time, to complete their extensive works of defence on the Mere Mere range. On the west side the position was protected by the Waikato river, and on the east by the extensive swamps that stretch away towards Paparata. Close to the river side the natives had placed in position two old ship guns which they had picked up from some wreck on the coast, and dragged or carried some 200 miles to their present position. For shot, the Maoris used sash weights and pieces of old iron—any shape did so long as it would go into the muzzle. Weeks now passed and the General made no sign. Some guns were brought forward and placed in position in the redoubts on the Koheroa, overlooking the Whangamarino creek and Mere Mere. Now and again a shell was sent whizzing towards the enemy's works, and the natives, in reply, at times skirmished through the belt of bush that lay between Mere Mere and the redoubts, and took long shots at the sentries. Once or twice they crept up in the early dawn and surprised an unwary sentinel, but they made no attempt to storm the redoubts—that feat had been tried at Taranaki, and the success that they achieved was not calculated to inspire them with the idea of performing the same operation again. The Flying Column and Jackson's Forest Rangers scoured the bush from the Wairoa on one side to Waiuku on the other, but the natives had disappeared. They were evidently concentrated at Mere Mere, waiting to push back the troops whom they expected daily to advance, but they were disappointed, for the General made no forward march.

CHAPTER XV.

The city and suburbs of Auckland and Otahuhu district were at this time placed under the command of Colonel Carey, of the 18th. The majority of the men under his command in Auckland were composed of the Militia and Volunteers, who were not in the field, and, except when on parade, were pursuing their several and peaceable avocations in all parts of the town. In case of emergency it was most desirable that Col. Carey should be enabled to collect his scattered forces together at the shortest possible notice at any hour of the day or night. To accustom the men to assemble in case of attack, Colonel Carey issued a notice to the effect that he intended, within a few days, to sound the alarm by the firing of a certain number of guns, when the Militia and Volunteers were immediately to hasten to the Albert Barracks with their arms and accoutrements. Accordingly, in the daytime on the 20th August, the sound of guns was suddenly heard booming over the town. It was the alarm! The scene that then followed baffles description. The whole town was instantly in an uproar. Figures, in an excited state, came rushing out of doors and passages, clutching in their hands a rifle, and their belts, pouch, and bayonet slung round their necks. The clerk threw his pen down; the draper's young man suddenly disappeared from his astonished lady customer, vaulted over the counter, and made off; the baker left his dough, the tailor his goose, the tinsmith his soldering iron; the bricklayer his bricks; and the carpenter his chips—all were off to the Barracks, through the streets like mad, followed by cheering boys and yelping curs; whilst the natives in the town squatted on the ground and stared, open-mouthed, at the strange spectacle. When the guns had ceased booming the buglers took up the alarm, and in an incredibly short space of time there was in the Albert Barracks a very large muster of Militia and Volunteers, although, through not having time to put on their uniform, they presented a somewhat motley appearance. But the men were there, and could have shown a good front to a large force of Maoris. The moral effect of this turn-out was very great. Henceforth Auckland was considered comparatively safe from being surprised; and each citizen knew and felt that in case of any sudden attack they could rely upon one another. That both General Cameron and Colonel Carey were pleased at the alacrity shown by the citizens in assembling so smartly when suddenly called upon, may be seen by the following correspondence:—

Head Quarters Colonial Forces,
Auckland, August 24, 1863.

Sir,—I have the honour to forward for the information of Government the accompanying letter from the Lieut.-General commanding the forces, giving cover to a letter from the officer commanding at Auckland and Otahuhu.

It is a source of much pleasure to me that the conduct and soldier-like bearing of the force under my command should have merited and called forth such a gratifying mark of approval from the Lieut.-General commanding in New Zealand.—I have, etc.,

T. J. GALLOWAY,
Major-General Commanding Colonial Forces.

To the Hon. the Minister of Colonial Defence.

Headquarters, Queen's Redoubt,
23rd August, 1863.

Sir,—I am directed by the Lieut.-General commanding to forward for your information the enclosed copy of a letter, which he has received from Colonel Carey, commanding at Auckland and Otahuhu; and he feels sure that you will feel equally gratified with himself by that officer's account of the alertness and promptitude displayed by the Volunteers and Militia in repairing to their several posts on the occasion of the alarm being sounded in Auckland on the 20th inst. The Lieut.-Colonel avails himself of this opportunity to express, through you, his approbation of the conduct and services of all the corps of Volunteers and Militia since the outbreak of hostilities in this province. Having been called out suddenly for service in the field at the most inclement season of the year, encamped at great distances from their homes, and required to perform duties most trying and harassing even to regular troops, they have been subject to many hardships and privations, which they have endured with a constancy and cheerfulness reflecting the highest credit upon them.

The Lieut.-General is fully aware how much your personal influence and example have contributed to call forth and encourage this soldier-like spirit on the part of the Militia and Volunteers, and begs you will accept his warm thanks for the timely assistance given by you in accepting your present command at a very critical period, and for the cordial manner in which you have co-operated with him in all his arrangements for the defence of this province.— I have, etc.,

W. F. HUTCHINS,
Lieut.-Colonel, Assistant Military Secretary.

Major-General Galloway,
Commanding Colonial Forces, Auckland.

The following sketch will give the reader an idea of the kind of hardship endured by the Militia and Volunteers referred to by General Cameron in his complimentary letter:—Imagine a force of some 200 men, composed of Militia and Volunteers, marching along the road between Otahuhu and Drury. The route is ankle deep in mud, and with great difficulty the baggage carts keep up with the column. The men, marching four abreast, have no choice but to take the road as it comes; sometimes the mud reaches half-way up their leather gaiters. The baggage carts covered with tarpaulins are behind the main body, and are followed by a rearguard. Two brown blankets rolled horse-shoe fashion over the shoulder, in which was stowed their lares and penates, consisting mainly of one shirt, a comb, one towel, a piece of soap, and one pair of socks; some had great-coats served out to them, others had none, a rifle, bayonet, belts, and an enormous pouch containing fifty rounds of ammunition, completed the costume of the Militia, when in full marching order. No martial strains of music enlivened the march, but in lieu thereof the men break out singing popular airs. Those in demand at the time were "Maryland," "Marching through Georgia," "We'll hang John Brown on a sour apple tree," and other American ballads handed down from the Civil War. A smart driving shower of rain now chills the musical ardour of the men, and the damp rises from their heated bodies like steam. It is afternoon before the force, wet and weary, reaches their camping ground at Drury. The bugles sound the welcome halt: the arms are piled, waggons unloaded, tents into which is thrown wet fern for beds, are pitched, fragments of damp wood are somehow seduced into a blaze, and the kettles are under way for tea. Each man is then served with a tot of rum, and then! turn in? No! for the bugles are sounding, and some of the unfortunates are told off for outlying and inlying pickets, for they are now in front of the enemy. Some hot tea and biscuit is bolted, and they are marched out to do sentry go, till relieved, in the fern, where they are soon lost to sight in the gloom of a winter's afternoon. But the camp is not attacked by the enemy, for through the long hours of the night occasionally is heard a cry from No. 1 sentry that "all's well," then No. 2 repeats the signal "all's well," No. 3 "all's well," and so on along the line of sentries. At daybreak the bugles sound the reveille, the camp is roused up, and the men, stiff, aching, and as tired as when they turned in the night before, tumble out to breakfast and fatigue duty, cutting wood, throwing up trenches, etc., until picket time comes round again. And all along the Militia and Volunteers were villainously fed on the very worst of provisions. Many of those that had money used to buy extra provisions at the store, while others for a meal had to thank the generosity of the men of the 65th and 18th Regiments, who were quartered in the same camp, the regulars having far better rations than the Militia and Volunteers. Why this should have been the case is best known to officers at the head of the Colonial Commissariat, who must have had some motive for winking at the inferior quality of the rations served out to the unfortunate Militia and Volunteers.

One Sunday morning, the men at Drury were ordered out for fatigue duty to clean out the slaughter-house and assist to unload two cutters that had arrived with coals. The men refused duty, and were accordingly placed under arrest, tried, and sentenced to have their hair cut and seven days' cells. A detachment of the 18th unloaded the cutters, the coals being urgently required for the steamer on the Waikato river, whence it was conveyed by carts over the Pokeno ranges.

Occasionally an alarm was sounded by a sentry firing at what he imagined to be a Maori, and the whole camp turned out, standing shivering in the early frosty morning. Several fatal accidents occurred through an excited sentry firing at one of his comrades whom he had mistaken in the darkness for one of the enemy. At the Papatoitoi Redoubt, a sentry fired at what he supposed to be a native. The whole of the gallant defenders, at the sound of the bugle, quickly lined the banquette of the Redoubt, and poured for some time a smart fusillade into the supposed enemy, who, strange to say, did not return the fire. The next morning it was discovered that the gallant defenders had been firing into an unfortunate grindstone that had lain hors de combat on the ground. This affair was spoken of as the "Battle of the Grindstone." At Waiuku, one dark, windy night, the brave garrison of the stockade rushed out, headed by their lieutenant, sword in hand, and charged a band-box, which, being blown by the wind through the fern, caused a noise that might be mistaken for a moving body of natives. Dr. Topp, the medical man of the district, happened to be outside the stockade at the time; fortunately he tripped and fell. A storm of bullets instantly swept over him, cutting away the fern just above his prostrate form. Many of the men to this day believe that they charged a body of natives, who were crawling up through the fern to attack the stockade.

CHAPTER XVI.

Shortly after the Military posts had been established at different points over the Pokeno ranges, contracts were let for clearing away the bush for some distance on each side of the road. This work accomplished, the natives would not have the advantage of such good cover as heretofore in the event of their again attacking our escorts. The bushmen engaged on the contract received, on account of the danger attending their work, a high rate of pay; and whilst felling the trees were escorted each day by a party of soldiers, who also assisted in the chopping. At about 11 o'clock on the morning of the 25th August, some bushmen and a party of the 40th Regiment, 25 in number, were busy at work felling and clearing away the bush alongside the road, a short distance past Williamson's Clearing. The enemy were not supposed to be in the vicinity of the road, and the rifles of the 40th were piled in the usual manner, the men being busy with axes—suddenly, and without warning, a volley was fired from the bush, and two of the 40th fell dead. At the same instant a party of natives dashed out of the bush and seized the rifles that were stacked, 23 in number. A detachment of the 18th which was marching along the road arrived just then, and instantly opened fire on the Maoris retreating into the bush with their booty. Two of the enemy were shot by the fire of the 18th, and a third, before he could get away, was attacked and dragged down by a dog of the bloodhound breed belonging to one of the bushmen, and was shot on the ground. In the skirmish one of the 18th was wounded. The rest of the natives, with the 23 stand of arms, made good their retreat.

The enemy, evidently tired of waiting at Mere Mere for the advance of the General, had determined to take the initiative and send a force out to attack the troops. Three days after the attack on the 40th, a Mr Scott, an old settler, 70 years of age, who resided at Pukekohe, was shot at and severely wounded by the natives; the unfortunate old gentleman managed to crawl some distance to a house belonging to Mr Hawk, where he lay for 30 hours, when he was found in an exhausted state by a party of Militia from the Pukekohe stockade who were scouring the bush in the vicinity. Mr Scott was conveyed to Auckland, where he afterwards expired. On the morning of September 2nd a picket of the 18th at Pokeno, near the Queen's Redoubt, in charge of Ensign Dawson, was attacked by a party of natives. Ensign Dawson at once charged and drove the Maoris across the country for about half-a-mile to their village in the direction of Paparata. Here the natives, who were in force, made a stand. Ensign Dawson extending his men in skirmishing order held the enemy in check, until he was reinforced by Captain the Hon. F. Le Poer Trench, with a detachment of the 40th Regiment, when the enemy retreated. In this skirmish no casualties are reported as having occurred.

The barque Isabella arrived in Auckland Harbour Sept. 2nd from Hobart Town, with 109 rank and file of the 12th Regiment and the following officers, under command of Major Eager:—Captains Cole and Hinds, Lieutenants Featherstonhaugh, Ensign Cooper, and Staff-Surgeon Scott. The next day the first detachment of the Waikato military settlers arrived in the barque Kate, Sherlock, master, from Sydney. The detachment consisted of 80 men under Captain Drury, Lieutenant Abbott, Ensign R. J. Coulter, and Dr. Drake. On the 7th the s.s. Corio, Captain Turner, steamed into Auckland Harbour, from Dunedin, with 75 Waikato military settlers under Captain Horne.

General Cameron being desirous of utilising, as a highway, the Waikato River from the Heads to his advanced posts on the river side, made arrangements for the conveyance of stores by water as well as by land. The conduct of the water transport was placed in the hands of Mr Armitage, a gentleman who had been a Resident Magistrate for some time connected with the lower Waikato, and he engaged with Waata-Kukutai, and other friendly natives, to convey by means of canoes up the river a quantity of stores from the barque City of Melbourne, which had arrived at the Waikato Heads laden with commissariat stores. Kukutai was a chief very friendly disposed to Europeans; his settlement was near Kohango, not far from the Heads, where Dr. Maunsell had for many years his mission station. Mr Armitage made two trips up the river with stores, and the new route promised to be successful. On board the City of Melbourne, in case of attack, was stationed a guard of Militia, under Captain Lloyd from Waiuku. The captain of the vessel had discharged half of his cargo when information was received that the enemy intended to come down the river in force and capture the barque. The first favourable wind the captain sent the Militia ashore, tripped his anchor, and made sail for the Manukau, where he unloaded the remainder of his cargo which was taken by cutters up to Drury, and thence carted on to the Waikato. About half-way between the General's position on the Waikato and the Heads, a depot (called Cameron, after the General) was formed for the deposit of stores. On the 7th of September Mr Armitage started from the Bluff, a military post on the river, for the Heads. He was accompanied by two or three other canoes full of the chief Te Wheoro's tribe (friendly natives). On reaching Tuakau there was some delay on the part of the other canoes, and it so happened that Mr Armitage got ahead of them, and reached the depot at Cameron some half-an-hour before them, at about 8 o'clock a.m. On arriving, Mr Armitage got out of his canoe and went over to a house about 200 yards from the bank of the river, where there were two Europeans, Robert McKeown and William Strand—the former was a blacksmith who acted as clerk to Mr Armitage, the latter was a carpenter engaged in erecting a store at Cameron. A stockade had been erected at the depot for the protection of the stores, and was manned by a party of friendly natives under a chief named Toka. Accompanied by McKeown and Strand, Mr Armitage returned to the river bank, and they were about to get into the canoe for the purpose of proceeding to the Heads, when a volley was fired by some natives who were concealed in a bush close by. Mr. Armitage and his companions managed to scramble into the canoe and push off into the river. The natives, coming out of their ambush, kept on firing. One ball struck Mr Armitage, and although severely wounded in the abdomen, he jumped over the side of the canoe and directed his companions to do the same, so as to be under cover of the canoe and at the same time float down the stream. The so-called friendly natives in the stockade, as soon as the hostile natives opened fire, ran away into the bush. Some of the enemy getting into a canoe followed Mr Armitage and chopped off the hands of the unfortunate men that were clinging to the canoe; they then shot and tomahawked them in the water till they sank. Their bodies were not discovered for some time afterwards. The wretches tore from the body of Mr Armitage, before it sank, a portion of his clothes, together with his watch, chain, and ring. The victims having been despatched, the natives, who altogether were estimated at over 200 strong, disappeared in the dark recesses of the bush. They had no sooner done so than the natives who had fled when the firing commenced reappeared, and came down to the river side, fired a volley in the air, and rubbed noses with those natives who were suspiciously detained in their canoes, and who had just arrived too late to render any assistance, but in time to contemplate the clouds of smoke that rose up from about £600 worth of commissariat stores that the enemy had fired. Besides Mr Armitage, McKeown and Strand, a half-caste named Wade and a friendly native were killed.

The death of Mr. Armitage was keenly felt by the citizens of Auckland, by whom he was much liked and respected. The following notification of his death bears record to his great worth to both his fellow colonists and the natives:—

Colonial Secretary's Office,
Auckland, 11th September. 1863.

The Governor directs it to be notified that it is with great regret he has received a despatch acquainting him with the sad death of that useful and active public officer, Mr Armitage, the Resident Magistrate of the lower Waikato—who was a sincere and faithful friend to the native race, and whose loss is most especially to be deplored at this juncture of affairs.

ALFRED DOMETT.

At the time Mr Armitage and his companions were murdered, the Rev. Dr. Maunsell, his wife and family, together with Mrs Spargo, the wife of an old settler at the Waikato Heads, were at the Kohanga mission station, a few miles below Cameron, but were protected from the enemy by Wata Kukatai, who, however, lost a number of sheep, pigs, and cattle, killed by the murderers.

CHAPTER XVII.

The firing at Cameron was heard by the troops stationed at Tuakau, and the dense clouds of smoke rising up through the bush indicated that the depot was in flames. About noon, five friendly natives arrived in a canoe and reported the death of Mr. Armitage and the burning of the commissariat stores by the rebels. Captain Swift, of the 65th, the officer in charge of the Tuakau Redoubt, determined to at once proceed in the direction of the depot at Cameron, which he did, taking with him Lieutenant Butler and 50 men. After a march of two hours over a rough track, a distance of about seven miles, Captain Swift reached a clearing, which he passed through, and with his detachment ascended the top of a hill, from which he could discern some whares. At this time an advance guard was sent forward, but taking a different track, got separated from the main body, which they did not rejoin until the next morning. Captain Swift's party, moving on, passed along a track which led through some bush. After following this for about 200 yards, some Maoris were heard talking. Thinking that the natives were coming in his direction, Captain Swift prepared an ambuscade for them by extending his men on both sides of the track. Finding that the natives did not come on as expected, Captain Swift ordered his men to fix bayonets. The 65th then moved forward for about twenty yards, and when at a turn of the track, the natives, who were evidently aware of the approach of the troops, opened fire upon them, Captain Swift fell at the first volley, mortally wounded. Lieutenant Butler then charged the natives, and while so doing, being a few yards in advance of his men, was brought to the ground. Drawing his revolver he shot two natives, and requested Colour-Sergeant McKenna to take charge of the party. A smart skirmish then ensued for about half-an-hour; the fire of the 65th driving the natives back about 300 yards, with a loss of seven or eight men who were seen to fall. Darkness now put an end to the conflict, and the brave little band of the 65th, which had been holding its own against fearful odds, remained all night on the ground. At daybreak the next morning the detachment in charge of Colour-Sergeant McKenna with some difficulty got out of the bush, and reached the Tuakau Redoubt shortly before noon. Captain Swift died about 7 o'clock in the evening. He had been shot through one lung and the side. Corporal Ryan and Private Bulford remained with their respected Captain until he expired. They then secreted his body in the bush, and joined Lieutenant Butler, with whom were Privates Thomas and Cole. The night was bitterly cold, and Private Thomas taking off his coat wrapped it round his wounded lieutenant. At early dawn Corporal Ryan and the three privates conveyed their wounded officer back through the bush to the Tuakau Redoubt. On the road they were met by a strong detachment of the 65th, under Colonel Murray, who were pushing forward to support them, and with the view of searching for some men of the 65th who were missing. Corporal

THE WAIKATO WAR.

Ryan turned back with Colonel Murray to point out the spot where he had secreted the body of Captain Swift.

Colour-Sergeant McKenna, in his official report of the engagement, gives the following graphic account of the severe struggle that took place:—

Alexandra Redoubt,
Tuakau, 8th September, 1863.

Sir,—I beg to state for the information of the Lieutenant-General commanding, that at 10 o'clock p.m. on the 7th September, 1863, I proceeded under command of Captain Swift, with the force as per margin, to attack a party of natives who had set fire to the friendly native pa erected on the township of Cameron for the purpose of trying to rescue Mr Armitage and a party of friendly natives who were known to have been down there; also a quantity of commissariat supplies brought up from Waiuku. Proceeding in skirmishing order, we arrived at about 2.30 p.m. at the skirt of the bush leading to the ranges on which the pa was situated, and after an hour's struggle through the bush we came to a clearing. Halting, our captain ordered our half ration of rum to be distributed, sending on the advance guard immediately after. When, on having proceeded a few hundred yards, it became apparent that the advance guard had lost or struck off the track, but that we had gained it, I then proposed to Captain Swift to advance and act as scout to the party, to which he immediately assented, cautioning me not to proceed more than thirty yards in front of the main body. After advancing in this order for about three-quarters of a mile I observed tracks of natives, and in large numbers; this I pointed out to the captain, and a little further on I heard the natives in loud debate, on which (expecting that they were returning on the track that they were pursuing) I again informed Captain Swift, who ordered the men to lie down in the bush, at the same time ordering them not to fire until he gave them the word of command. However, on finding that the natives were not advancing, I crept up to within twelve yards of them, when, from their conversation, I judged they were under the influence of liquor. Captain Swift immediately called to advance, ordering the men to fix bayonets and charge; we advanced to within six yards of them, when they opened a most terrific fire; Captain Swift and Lieutenant Butler were at the time leading on the men, and after receiving the enemy's fire, the men gave a cheer and returned it in grand style; Lieutenant Butler shooting down a native on his right, turned his revolver to the left as quick as thought. I saw him come on his knee, at the same time discharging the remainder of the barrels of his revolver, bringing another native down at the same time that he fell himself. Seeing that he was wounded, I ordered Corporal Ryan and one of the men to take him to the rear, when he ordered me to lead the men to the front; on turning to my left I found Captain Smith mortally wounded, and after speaking a few words to him, he desired me to take his revolver and lead on the men, as at that time I was loading. With one loud hurrah, we charged, burning to avenge our officers. I now found myself in an open clearing of a few yards, the rebels flying to cover on our right and left, where they opened fire on my small party, who at this time numbered 2 sergeants, 1 bugler, and 35 men. Seeing that we were greatly outnumbered, I determined to hold on to our position if possible

E

till dark, trusting that the men in charge of Captain Swift and Lieutenant Butler had retired well to the rear, and been joined by our lost advance guard; if so, I knew they would be able to make well towards the redoubt before darkness set in, when probably I should be enabled to join them; but I found at about a quarter to 6 o'clock that the enemy had got round to our rear, thereby cutting off our retreat by the way we came. I immediately ordered a charge, but was met by a volley that killed 1 and wounded 3 men. On trying again, I found it hopeless to attempt it; I therefore determined to retreat down the hill which was covered with fern, and, sending on our wounded, I threw out a line of skirmishers, ordering the front rank to "fire and retire." In this order we retired down the hill in a steady and orderly manner, the natives coming out of the bush and raining down a complete shower of bullets on us, when, although we were not above 100 or 150 yards from them, not a man was hit. At this time it was near dark, but we managed to scramble through the bush, until at last we lost the track, when I ordered the men around me, and told them that I should stay there till morning, ordering not a word to be spoken, or a pipe to be lighted. I now found that four men were missing, and knowing that it would be completely useless to attempt at that time to find them, I determined to wait until morning, hoping in the meantime to hear them about in the bush. At 4.45 o'clock a.m. on the morning of the 8th, we commenced to try and gain a track out of the bush, and at about 8 o'clock a.m. we succeeded, and were met about half-way from the redoubt by Colonel Murray and his party, and then learned that our esteemed captain was dead. After detailing a man to return as guide to Colonel Murray, I continued my march to the camp, which we reached at about 11 o'clock a.m. completely exhausted. I am sorry to report our casualties were very great, but taking into consideration the number to which we were opposed—being near seven to one—we have every reason to be thankful that they were not greater. I hope it may not appear presumptuous on my part to bear testimony to the cool and gallant behaviour displayed by the late Captain Swift and Lieutenant Butler in this desperate affair; the Captain issuing his commands as if on parade, and even when wounded, refusing to take one man from the force to take him to the rear, until he was told that I would not be able to keep my position much longer; and Lieutenant Butler, even when brought on his knee, in the coolest manner possible deliberately fired the shots from his revolver into a crowd of Maoris. I need scarcely add that the men behaved most gallantly; in fact, it would be impossible to recapitulate the many acts of individual courage where each man emulated the other in acts of heroic bravery. I, however, beg to bring to your favourable consideration the valuable assistance I received from Sergeant Bracegirdle, who supported me throughout in a most intrepid manner; as also Lance-Corporal Ryan, Privates William Bulford, John Talbot, John Cole, and Benjamin Thomas, for the devotion they manifested to their officers, by staying with them until half-past seven p.m. on the night of the 7th inst. Captain Swift died at that time, after which they hid his body in the bush and waited until morning, and then, carrying Lieutenant Butler in their arms, they returned, meeting Colonel Murray and

THE WAIKATO WAR.

force. Corporal Ryan returned with Colonel Murray and pointed out the spot in which Captain Swift's body was hidden. I should estimate the loss of the enemy to be between 20 or 30 killed and wounded, 7 of whom I myself distinctly saw shot dead and dragged into the bush by the rebels.—I have, etc.,

E. McKENNA,
Colour-Sergeant 65th Regt.

W. Hutchinson, Lieut.-Colonel,
Assistant Military Secretary.

The 65th lost one officer and two privates killed and one officer and three privates wounded and one private named Bryan missing. It afterwards transpired that the unfortunate man, becoming separated from his comrades, wandered about the bush in a demented state for two days, when he was discovered by a party of natives and killed. Two other men who had lost their way afterwards returned to the redoubt at Tuakau. The enemy lost upwards of thirty men. The body of Captain Swift was conveyed to Auckland and buried with military honours in the Church of England cemetery. Lieutenant Talbot, although severely wounded, soon recovered and rejoined his company in the field.

For his services at Cameron, Colour-Sergeant McKenna afterwards received a commission and the Victoria Cross. Corporal Ryan, who remained with Private Bulford in charge of Captain Swift until he expired, also was awarded the Victoria Cross, but, unfortunately, never lived to wear it, being a short time after the engagement at Camerontown drowned whilst trying to save a drunken comrade who had fallen into the water. Private Bulford, and Privates Talbot, Cole, and Thomas, who attended to and remained with Lieutenant Butler, each received a medal for distinguished conduct in the field.

At Tuakau the 65th put up a memorial of their visit, formed of three blocks of sandstone raised on the stump of a tree by the river-side, which bore the following inscription:—

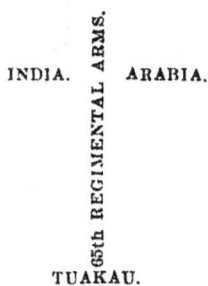

INDIA.   65th REGIMENTAL ARMS.   ARABIA.

TUAKAU.

At the top of the Bluff, near the redoubt, the body of Private Stephen Grace, 65th, killed in the action at Cameron, was buried. A wooden slab was erected over the grave in memoriam, and contained the following verse:—

No sound, no harmony, no joy,
Can art or music frame;
No thoughts can reach, no words can say
The sweet of thy blest name.

MAJOR LUSK.

CHAPTER XVIII.

Whilst Colour-Sergeant McKenna and his small band of heroes were yet struggling through the bush on their way to the redoubt at Tuakau on the morning of the 8th, a mixed force of Volunteers, consisting of 20 of the Mauku Rifle Volunteers, under Lieutenant Lusk, and the Forest Rangers, under Lieutenant Jackson, in all some sixty men, started from the Mauku stockade to reconnoitre the country in the direction of Patumahoe. After passing through some bush, the party came upon the deserted house of Mr Lusk, which was found to have been pillaged by the natives—thence some clearings were traversed and the bush once more entered. Signs of fresh Maori trails put the force on the alert, and in a short time a shot was heard some distance in their rear, then a volley. The order was given to right-about and return in the direction of the firing. After marching some distance, the halt was given, and the sound of Maori voices could be plainly heard. One party, under Lieutenant Jackson and Lieutenant Lusk, with the Mauku Rifles, proceeded towards the direction in which the shots were fired, and the Forest Rangers, under Ensign Hay, with Mr Hill as guide, went through the bush in an opposite direction, to cut off any natives between Lieutenant Jackson's party and the clearing where the firing was supposed to have been. The Mauku Rifles advanced through the bush, and came out into the clearing of Messrs Lusk and Hill. Here they found a bullock lying on its side that had evidently just been shot, the blood still oozing from a bullet-wound. No natives being visible, the party commenced skinning the beast. While thus engaged, a shot was suddenly fired from the bush, followed directly afterwards by another. The men were instantly on their feet, and made a dash towards the smoke which was still hanging about the trees. The bush was here very dense, and cumbered with fallen trees and supplejack vines, and the men with Lieutenants Jackson and Lusk had some difficulty in getting through. Forcing their way in, they suddenly confronted the enemy, who opened fire at a distance of a few yards, the white smoke from the fire covering Lieutenant Jackson's party like a cloud. The bush was so dense that the natives could not be seen, although only a short distance off. Directly after they had fired, the Maoris commenced shouting to the white skins to come on. Lieutenant Jackson's party answered this challenge by pouring a volley into the thicket. Some of the enemy were hit, for they directly commenced howling and opened fire again, which was replied to with vigour by the Mauku Rifles, who extended themselves in skirmishing order, remaining all the time well under cover. After keeping up the duel for half-an-hour, Lieut. Jackson gave the order to "Charge." which, with a loud cheer, was instantly done; but the natives finding at this juncture that Ensign Hay with the Forest Rangers was cutting off their retreat, fled precipitately. Lieutenant Jackson's party had no casualties, although several privates of the Mauku Rifles had narrow escapes. John Wheeler received a shot through his coat; Alfred Speedy one through his cap, and Worthington one through his trousers. After following the enemy through the bush for some distance, the party returned to the Mauku stockade.

On the same day as the above skirmish occurred a party of natives took up a position on some high ground overlooking the Razorback Redoubt on the Pokeno range. After exchanging shots with the defenders for about an hour, they retired. A few days afterwards the Maoris again put in an appearance in the vicinity of Cameron, and moving towards Tuakau under cover of a belt of bush adjoining the redoubt, opened a heavy fire on the position, which was returned by the 65th with interest. After wasting a good deal of ammunition the natives withdrew, not daring to make any attempt to storm the redoubt, but taking care to keep all the time well under cover.

The natives being again in force, roaming through the bush, the orderly duty between the Queen's Redoubt and Drury was attended with great risk. This duty was entrusted to troopers of the Mounted Artillery, who carried the despatches and mail. The orderlies, generally three in number—never less than two—used to start from the Queen's Redoubt in the evening after dark, and spurred their horses into a hard gallop the whole of the road over the Pokeno ranges to Drury. Strange to say, they were not molested by the enemy; probably on account of their travelling at night, the natives having a great antipathy to be abroad after sunset, being superstitious and afraid of the evil spirit Taipo. From Drury, if necessary, communication could be obtained with Auckland by telegraph, the wires at this time having been laid as far as Drury.

CHAPTER XIX.

Pukekohe Stockade, an isolated post, situated in the heart of the dense bush, some two miles from Martin's Farm, on the west side of the road, over the Pokeno Ranges, was attacked by a strong force of natives on Monday, September 14th. The stockade, in charge of Sergeant Perry, was held by a small party of Militia from Auckland, and Volunteers belonging to the district, who, in preference to deserting their homesteads, had decided to remain in the vicinity and guard their property. Although the garrison of the stockade did not number more than 30 men, Sergeant Perry, who arrived at Pukekohe some three or four weeks before the attack, decided to utilise the church, and having collected the few Volunteers in the district, took possession of the sacred edifice. The church was a small building, measuring only 30ft. by 20ft., situated in the centre of a 10-acre paddock, which had but a short time before been cleared, and the stumps of the trees were still standing. Heavy bush surrounded it on all sides. Finding that the walls of the church, composed of ¾-inch weather boards, and unlined, would not protect his men from the enemy's bullets if they were attacked, Sergeant Perry determined to build a bullet-proof wall, 7ft. high, all round the church, at about 10ft. from the building. The wall was pierced for rifles, and outside there was a ditch. To complete this the men went early and late vigorously to work. The wall was composed of young trees about a foot in diameter and 20ft. long, placed one on top of the other, and fastened with wooden treenails to stout posts on the inside. Whilst hauling the logs out of the bush, the men were more than once fired upon by the natives, who, for some reason, deferred their attack on the stockade until it was nearly completed. On the evening of the 13th (Sunday) Major-General Galloway and staff visited the post, and advised the men to be on the alert, as there was a large force of natives in the vicinity; and promising to send them a reinforcement, the General returned to Drury. Sergeant Perry and his little garrison passed the night in anxious suspense, the men lying down with their arms loaded and capped. The sentries, peering through the loop-holes in the stockade wall across the clearing, could scarcely tell whether the objects they saw in the gloom were Maoris or stumps, and each ear was strained to catch the faintest sound. Occasionally during the night a kaka would scream, or a decayed branch fall in the bush, and startle the garrison; and so the long night passed away, and when morning dawned there was no sign of the enemy, but the stumps in the clearing stood up sharp and distinct in the morning light. At about 9 a.m. on the Monday morning some of the men were at breakfast inside the church, and others were in the cook-house which was built outside the stockade. The sudden report of firearms caused the men who were in the cook-house to beat a hasty retreat inside the stockade and to close the gate.

Several bullets striking the shingle roof of the church dropped through. Quickly manning the stockade wall, the garrison returned the fire of the natives, who were seen issuing from the bush in large numbers, taking cover behind the stumps in the clearing, and gradually advancing nearer to the stockade. At the time of the attack a horse and cart was standing outside, as one of the men intended to start that morning to Drury, a distance of some seven miles, for provisions. The poor beast soon fell pierced with bullets, and the natives, making a dash, got good cover behind the cart, close up to the stockade. The enemy, who were estimated at considerably over 200, kept up a rapid fire—the bullets, however, striking harmlessly against the wooden wall of the stockade. Each stump in the clearing concealed one of the enemy, and a thick cloud of smoke hung over the stockade and 10-acre paddock. When the natives made a forward movement from one stump to another the garrison poured a volley into them, frequently sending some of them, with a loud yell, to the ground. At 11 o'clock the enemy had advanced to within 30 or 40 yards of the stockade, and although they were evidently aware of the small number of men defending the church, they had not the soul to storm the position, which the garrison expected every minute they would do. Instead of attempting to carry the position by assault, the natives fired for a few seconds as fast as they could, and then retreated into the bush, where they could be heard shouting to one another. The garrison still keeping to their posts—although some of the men desired to go out into the clearing and search for any dead or wounded that might have been left—waited to see what would be the next move on the part of the enemy. They had not long to wait, for in a short time the natives reappeared, again took cover behind the stumps, and poured volley after volley at the stockade—the thick wall, as before, stopping the bullets from doing any harm. One of the Maoris shouted out, in good English, for those inside the stockade to come outside and fight—an invitation declined by the garrison. Finding their fire had no effect, some of the natives commenced throwing stones over the stockade wall. At about 1 o'clock a detachment of 1 officer and 20 men arrived to reinforce the garrison. They came out of the bush on the opposite side to where the natives were, and making a dash across the clearing, managed to join the defenders of the stockade without losing a man. With 50 men inside the stockade the garrison felt themselves able to cope with the natives, and a flame of fire leapt out from each loop-hole of the stockade wall, sending a shower of bullets across the clearing, and keeping the natives well down in their cover. In about half an hour after the arrival of the first relief bugles were heard sounding in the bush, and the garrison knew that substantial aid was at hand; and very soon a number of soldiers issued from the forest into the clearing in skirmishing order. The force that had arrived consisted of 150 men belonging to the 65th and 18th Regiments, under Majors Saltmarsh and Inman, Having advanced into the clearing at the back of the stockade, they could not see the gateway, and called out to be shown the way. Sergt. Perry ran out to one end of the stockade, and pointed the road in, and as he was returning to the gate the natives crouching behind the stumps fired a volley after him, but without effect. At the same time a heavy fire was opened on the advancing soldiers, killing 3 and wounding 8, amongst whom was Major Saltmarsh. The troops at once charged the enemy, who fled precipitately into the bush; two, in their flight, stumbling over the logs that covered the ground, were bayonetted. Three wounded natives were found in the clearing, with supplejack tied to their heels for the purpose of dragging them away. These died from their wounds the same evening, and their bodies, with those of the other Maoris killed in the fight, were buried the next day. The natives lost on this occasion more than 14 men, killed and wounded. So late as a year and a-half ago, two skeletons of natives were discovered in the bush, not very far from the scene of the attack, who were supposed to have been killed in the fight, and after being dragged some distance no doubt were left by the enemy in their hasty retreat. The next day a force of Militia arrived, under Captain Moir, who relieved the garrison, which returned to Auckland, where Sergeant Perry, in consideration of the stubborn defence that he had made, received a commission as ensign in the 2nd Regiment Waikato Militia.

CHAPTER XX.

On Monday, September 14th, a large detachment of Military Settlers disembarked from the ship Star of India, which had arrived from Melbourne in Auckland harbour on the 12th. The force consisted of 407 officers and men under Captain Goldsmith, Lieutenants Lomax, Minnington, and Smith. The men raised in Victoria were called Pitt's Militia, on account of Colonel Pitt having superintended the enrolment of Volunteers in Melbourne for service and settlement in the Waikato. The Military Settlers as they arrived were clothed in the Militia uniform, drilled and drafted into Regiments—known as the 1st, 2nd, 3rd, and 4th Waikatos, the latter being mostly married men. As soon as possible, these regiments were moved forward to the posts held by the Auckland Militia and Volunteers, who, being relieved, returned to Auckland. Many of them, however, having acquired a taste for military service, to which was added the prospect of 50 acres of land, joined the Military Settlers or Waikato Militia. Several companies were raised in Auckland, and tempting advertisements, like the following, which appeared in the newspapers, soon filled their ranks with smart young men.

RICH WAIKATO LAND.

WANTED Twelve Men for the Company forming under Lieutenant Spencer. Fifty Acres of Land and a Town Allotment for all men who join this Company.
Apply at the "Daily Southern Cross" Office.

WAIKATO !   WAIKATO !

EPSOM COMPANY.

WANTED, a few young men of good character to complete Captain Hill's Company.
Apply at Exchange Hotel to Sergeant George Panter.

The conditions upon which the Military Settlers agreed to serve in the Waikato were published in the "New Zealand Gazette," as follows:—

MILITARY SETTLERS.

Conditions upon which land in the North Island will be granted to settlers willing to perform the after-mentioned military services:—

(1) No man above the age of 40 years will be accepted, and every applicant will be subject to an examination by an officer appointed by the Governor, and

must produce such certificates of good character, health, and general fitness for the service.

(2) Each accepted applicant, if not already in the Northern Island, will be provided with a free passage to a port to be designated by an agent of the Governor. Before embarkation he will be required to sign a declaration and agreement to the effect that he understands and will be bound by and fulfil these conditions.

(3) On arrival the men will be enrolled in the Militia for service in the Northern Island of the colony and formed into companies, constituted as nearly as may be as follows:—1 captain, 1 subaltern, 5 sergeants, 5 corporals, and 100 privates.

(4) Each man, according to his rank, will be entitled to pay, rations, and allowances until he is authorised by the Government to take possession of his land, when he will be relieved from actual service.

(5) Settlements will be surveyed and marked out at the expense of the Government in such localities in the Northern Island as the Government may select for that purpose.

(6) Each settlement will comprise not less than 100 town allotments and 100 farm sections.

(7) A stockade on the most eligible site in each settlement will be erected at the expense of the Government.

(8) A town will be laid out around or as near as conveniently may be to the stockade in one-acre allotments.

(9) Farms will be laid out around or as near as conveniently may be to the town. The size of the farm section allotted to each will be according to his rank in the Militia:—

    For a Field Officer .... 400 acres
    „ Captain .... 300 „
    „ Surgeon .... 250 „
    „ Subaltern .... 200 „
    „ Sergeant .... 80 „
    „ Corporal .... 60 „
    „ Private .... 50 „

(10) Every settler, under these conditions, who, upon being relieved from actual service, receives a certificate of good conduct, will be entitled to one town allotment and one farm section.

(11) Priority of choice for each rank will be determined by lot.

(12) After taking possession he will be entitled to receive rations free of cost for twelve months, upon the same scale as supplied to Her Majesty's troops. He will be allowed to retain possession, as a Militiaman, of his arms and accoutrements, and he will be supplied with ammunition for use, according to Militia regulations.

(13) No settler, after taking possession, will be permitted during the first three years after his enrolment in the Militia to absent himself from his settlement for more than one calendar month in any one year without the leave of the Governor being first obtained.

(14) During such three years he will be liable to be trained and exercised as other Militiamen; and whenever a portion only of the Militia shall be called out for actual service, each settler will be deemed a Volunteer Militiaman, and will be required to serve as such anywhere that may be required in the Northern Island of the colony. During such service he will be entitled to the same pay, rations, and allowances as other Militiamen.

(15) On the expiration of three years from his enrolment, each settler having fulfilled the conditions, but not otherwise, will be entitled to a Crown grant of the town allotment and farm section allotted to him, and will thenceforth be subject only to the same Militia service as other colonists.

(16) Any settler will be permitted to dispose of his land to any person approved of by the Government, and such person undertaking to be subject to the same liabilities will be entitled to the same privileges as the settler whose place he takes.

(17) In case of death of any settler before he shall have become entitled to his Crown grant, the land to which he is entitled will be granted to his wife or children, or to such other person as he shall by writing appoint—or it may be taken for the location of another settler under these conditions, or for any other purpose: but the value thereof, in such latter case, will be determined by valuation, and the amount paid by the Government to the settler's widow or children, or other person appointed as aforesaid. The pay of the Militia and Volunteers serving in New Zealand, with rations and other allowances, is as follows:—

Captains	11s 7d	per diem
Lieutenants	6s 6d	,,
Ensigns	5s 3d	,,
Sergeants	3s 6d	,,
Corporals	3s 0d	,,
Privates	2s 6d	,,

CHAPTER XXI.

The natives, on the 16th of September, appeared in the Wairoa district in force, and commenced ransacking the settlers' homesteads. The Wairoa (Lower) is on the river of the same name, which discharges its waters into the Auckland Harbour, some 28 miles south of the city. The river runs through the centre of a valley formed by rich alluvial flats, and surrounded by high wooded hills. Major Lyon commanded the district, the defence of which consisted of a redoubt (the Galloway) overlooking the river on the north, and a stockade on the south bank. Their position was about 8 miles from the mouth of the river, and in the heart of the valley settlement, and was defended mainly by a force composed of Wairoa Rifles, and of men from the different companies of the Auckland Rifle Volunteers, under the command of Captain J. McCosh Clark, No. 6 Company, with Lieutenant Tabuteau and Ensign D. A. Tole; this company, some time afterwards, had a uniform of green cloth, and were dubbed the "Grasshoppers." To strengthen their defences two detachments of the Volunteers, under Sergeants Gatland and Phillips, were detailed to cut slabs in the bush. Whilst so engaged they were suddenly fired upon by a party of natives, and returning the fire, fell back upon the redoubt, when the Maoris retired.

Major Lyon desiring to prevent the enemy, who were plundering the settlers' houses, from returning to their settlement at Otau, pushed forward with a small party to intercept them. This force consisted of a detachment of the Auckland Volunteers and 20 men of the Wairoa Rifles, with Lieutenant Steele. Coming upon the natives, the Volunteers at once, with the steadiness of regular troops, opened fire—killing two Maoris. The enemy returned the fire, and hastily retreating, made good their escape. From the body of one of the natives shot, Private Elley, of the Auckland Volunteers, obtained a gold watch, which was supposed to have been stolen from one of the settlers. Night at this time setting in, the force returned to camp; on the road they were met by a party under Captain Clark, A.R.V., and Lieutenant Russell, 18th Regiment, which was hastening to their support.

Lieutenant Russell declining to acknowledge Captain Clark as his superior officer, was the means of settling a moot point concerning the relative positions of the Regular and Volunteer Officers when on duty. Lieutenant Russell was placed under arrest, and his superior officers decided that he was in fault, a captain in the Volunteers taking precedence over a Lieutenant in the Regulars. The next morning at 4 a.m. Major Lyon marched from the Galloway Redoubt to attack the enemy in their settlement at Otau—where they were known to be in considerable numbers. The force detailed for this service consisted of 75 men under Lieutenant Jones and Ensign Johnstone; on the way the body of one of the natives, killed in the skirmish of the afternoon before, was found. The detachment arrived at daybreak on the bank of the river, on the opposite side of which stood the whares of the enemy, who were still wrapped in slumber. Placing his men under cover, Major Lyon ordered them to commence firing—instantly a stream of fire shot out along the river bank, and a shower of bullets whizzed across the stream and plunged into the whares, causing the occupants to rush out in all directions. As soon as the enemy had recovered from their surprise they returned the fire, but without effect. The range between the contending parties was about 300 yards. After keeping up a brisk fusillade for some time the Maoris retreated. Major Lyon, not being able to follow on account of the swollen state of the river, which prevented his force from crossing, returned to the redoubt without any casualties. The following is the official account of the affair:—

Galloway Redoubt, Wairoa,
17th September, 1863.

Sir,—I have the honour to report for the information of the Major-General Commanding Colonial Forces, that firing was heard in the bush on the other side of the river at different intervals in the course of the day.

About 4 p.m. a settler came to the Redoubt stating that two men were exchanging shots with some natives in the act of pillaging a house.

Lieutenant Steele, Wairoa Rifles, started immediately with 20 men, and I followed with 30. On arriving at the place, two bundles were found. I followed the track, passed through a chain and a-half of bush, and came out on rising ground. I could see the Maoris in a line with loads on their backs.

The men under my command were in skirmishing order, and fired into them. I then gave chase; many of them dropped their loads, making for Otau. Two Maoris were killed. I did not deem it advisable to advance further. From the number of shots proceeding from the bush and bank of the river, the natives must have been in strong force; it was also getting dark.

On my return I was met by Lieutenant Russell, 18th Royal Irish, with a party of 16 men, coming to our assistance, and Captain Clark, Auckland Rifle Volunteers, thinking we might require support.

This morning I started at 4 o'clock with 50 men from the redoubt, and 20 men from the Wairoa Rifles under the command of Mr Johnstone. We took the same direction and arrived within 300 yards of the Maori whares at daybreak.

The river was so swollen with the late rains that it was impossible to cross it. The Maoris were plainly visible, and many rounds were fired at them. They returned the fire, but without any effect, the men being well under cover. I sounded the cease firing, and proceeded to bury the body of one of the Maoris killed yesterday; he had been shot through the heart. The other we could not find.

It appears that the firing heard in the bush was for the purpose of diverting our attention while the natives were ransacking the houses. The men of the different detachments behaved, on both occasions, with great coolness.

I have the honour to bring under the notice of the Lieutenant-General commanding the names of Lieutenant Russell, 2nd Battalion, 18th Royal Irish; Lieutenant Jones, Militia Volunteers; Ensign Tole, Auckland Rifle Volunteers; and Mr McDonald, Native Interpreter. The exemplary conduct and soldier-like bearing of the non-commissioned officers and men of the different detachments who have been with me on these several occasions cannot be too highly commended; and more especially that of Quartermaster-Sergeant Davis, of the 3rd Battalion, Auckland Militia.—I have, etc.,

WILLIAM C. LYON,

Major-Commanding Galloway Redoubt, Wairoa.

After the force under Major Lyon had returned to the Redoubt, the same afternoon they crossed the river over a bridge opposite the Redoubt, and skirmished through the bush with the view of getting in rear of the native settlement. Upon arriving at the village they found the whares deserted, the enemy having retreated. The Maoris had evidently suffered severely from the concentrated fire poured into them in the morning. The whares were riddled with shot, and there were pools of blood both inside and out. Two Maori mats, one covered with gore and having a bullet-hole through it, were also picked up. Likewise two guns, a few tomahawks, and a variety of articles were taken. A quantity of plunder which had been looted from the settlers' houses in the district was also recovered. No signs of the natives being near, the force returned to camp, after destroying the settlement.

CHAPTER XXII.

When the natives retreated, after their attack on the stockade at Pukekohe, they did not leave the district, but dividing their force into small bands, ransacked the settlers' deserted homesteads lying between Drury and Waiuku. One party of natives leaving the bush the morning after the attack, surprised the occupants of a farm house belonging to Mr. Burt. A boy, the son of Mr. Watson, who occupied the farm, was shot—also one of the farm hands named McLean—the rest of the family managed to escape. At the time of the attack the boy Watson and Mr. McLean were working on the farm some distance from the house, in which were Mrs. Watson, who was bedridden, and her two daughters. James Hamilton, who resided on a neighbouring farm with a man called Sandy, hearing of the attack, prevailed upon Sandy to go with him to the rescue of Mrs. Watson and her two daughters. Upon arriving at the farmhouse, Hamilton found the Maoris firing into it and shouting out pakaru (kill) the pakehas. Hamilton and Sandy, armed with a rifle and revolver, at once opened fire on the natives, who decamped. The courageous conduct of Mr. Hamilton, on this occasion, was not overlooked by the Government, who awarded him a medal. Another party of natives plundered the houses in the vicinity of Waiuku; they broke into a deserted flax mill, owned by Messrs. Ninnis and Purchase, at the Waitangi, within gun-shot of the township, broke some of the machinery, and set the water-wheel going. At this time the cutter Undine arrived in the creek opposite the mill, loaded with stores, and several cases of arms and ammunition for the Waiuku Stockade. Strange to say, she was not fired upon by the natives. The cutter having been observed from the look-out on the top of the stockade, a boat with an armed party soon came alongside, and guarded her passage up the creek to the wharf.

On the 18th, Captain Lloyd, the officer in charge at Waiuku, whilst skirmishing through the paddocks with a party of his men, suddenly came across the natives, who had just been plundering one of the settlers' houses. The enemy, not observing Captain Lloyd's men, passed into the bush. One of them, however, a splendid specimen of the genus Maori, turned round; at the same instant the front men of Captain Lloyd's party fired, and a bullet struck the native dead, and his gun and ammunition were retained as a souvenir by one of the Waiuku Volunteers.

Having reason to believe that the enemy were in force in the bush, Captain Lloyd ordered his men back to camp.

Returning to the British advanced posts overlooking the enemy's position at Mere Mere, we still find that General Cameron did not appear to be making any preparations for an immediate advance. The natives, thinking that the troops had a difficulty in procuring stores, considerately sent a canoe load of provisions from Mere Mere, under cover of a white flag, as a present to the General. The General, however, was not idle; he was collecting a quantity of stores at the Queen's Redoubt, and was waiting for some large boats that were being built at Onehunga for the Waikato, and also for the arrival of the steamer Pioneer, a stern paddle-wheel vessel of large size and power, which had been constructed at Sydney from designs prepared especially for service on the Waikato River. On Saturday, October 3rd, the Pioneer arrived in the Manukau, after a stormy passage from Sydney, in charge of Captain Breton, Lieutenant O'Callaghan, Mr. Jeffrey, engineer, and 25 men—part of the passage she had been towed by H.M.S. Eclipse; but in a heavy gale the tow-line broke, and the vessels parted company. The Pioneer, although only drawing some two feet of water, made better weather than the man-of-war. The Pioneer was 140 feet in length, 20 feet beam, 8 feet 6 inches depth of hold, and drew only 2 feet 6 inches of water—built of ⅜ iron, bullet-proof, and fitted with four water-tight compartments. The propelling power consisted of an overhanging stern wheel with feathering floats driven by two engines of thirty horse-power each, supplied with steam from two boilers placed 54 feet forward of the engines, for the purpose of keeping the vessel of an even keel; on deck were placed two cupolas, each of 7 feet diameter. The cupolas, pierced for rifles, were placed one forward and the other aft, the communication being from below. To prevent her from being boarded, in the event of going aground, a three-inch pipe ran fore and aft, flush with the gunwale, and connected with one of the boilers; the pipe was pierced with a series of holes, so that a continuous jet of hot water could be thrown from her gunwale if an enemy came alongside. This fine vessel, some time after the war, broke from her moorings at the Waikato Heads, and drifted over the bar out to sea. Mr. Lodder, the officer then in charge of the vessel, started after her with several men in an open boat, and succeeded in boarding her. There being no coals in the bunkers, portions of the woodwork of the vessel were torn down, and the fires lighted—steam was got up, and an attempt made to fetch the Manukau. Unfortunately, when close to the bar, the Pioneer became unmanageable, and they were compelled to abandon the vessel, which broke to pieces, Mr. Lodder and his party miraculously escaping in their boat.

The natives on the Wairoa side of the ranges, after having been driven from their settlement at Otau, still continued to prowl about the district; and on the 13th of October murdered Mr. Job Hamlin, and tomahawked a boy named Wallace, at Henderson's farm, on the Wairoa-road. Mr. Hamlin, accompanied by the boy Wallace, was at the time engaged with a bullock-team in removing goods from the farm house, when they were surprised by the Maoris. The body of Mr. Hamlin, who had been shot through the head, was found lying in the road between Henderson's farm and Steele's. The boy Wallace was also found some distance from Mr. Hamlin, dreadfully tomahawked, the blow having fractured his skull, but he was still alive.

Wallace was carefully attended to, and his life saved by Dr. Thompson, of the 18th Regiment. A silver plate was placed over the fracture, inside the skin of his forehead, and he eventually recovered, being at this present time a strong

F

young man; the silver plate is not visible, the skin having grown over it. The next afternoon two men named Jackson and Sutherland, whilst engaged fencing behind Mr. Hay's house near Papakura, were fired upon by a party of the enemy. Jackson was shot and afterwards tomahawked, and Sutherland was found severely wounded. On October 15 Mr. and Mrs. Fahey, residing at Rama Rama, went out as usual to milk their cows, when the Maoris appeared, and fired upon them. When found, Mrs. Fahey was quite dead, and Mr. Fahey expired shortly afterwards.

THE WAIKATO WAR. 83

CHAPTER XXIII.

At about 10 o'clock on the morning of the 23rd of October, the force stationed at the Mauku were alarmed by the sound of heavy firing in the bush on Mr. Wheeler's farm at the Ti-Ti. On this farm a portion only of the bush had been cleared and burned, and in the centre of the clearing there remained several acres of felled timber that had not been burned off, but had been piled up in heaps ready for the brand. The fore-ground is open fern land, partially broken and intersected by a fresh-water stream and one or two shallow gullies. A detachment of 25 men of the Mauku Volunteers, under Lieutenant Lusk, advanced to the church from the Stockade, and the Maoris were then seen in considerable numbers about two miles off. Lieutenant Lusk immediately sent a request to Lieutenant Percival, of the 1st Waikato Regiment (a detachment of which was stationed in the stockade), to advance without delay and reinforce him at the church. Lieutenant Percival at once started from the stockade with twelve men, but instead of marching straight to the church, struck into the bush with the object of attacking the natives in the rear. Lieutenant Percival's small party soon came into collision with the natives, but after keeping up a steady fire for some time had to retire on account of the superior force of the enemy. Step by step the gallant little band were forced back out of the bush into the clearing, and in full view of Lieutenant Lusk's party at the church. Seeing the natives closing rapidly on Lieutenant Percival's small party, Lieutenant Lusk immediately advanced at the double to their support with the Mauku Volunteers. Upon observing Lieutenant Lusk's party advancing, the Maoris retreated and took up a position behind the logs and brushwood that had been piled up in the clearing. Lieutenant Lusk having joined Lieutenant Percival, the two detachments, numbering altogether some sixty men, moved forward in skirmishing order and opened fire on the natives, who replied vigorously, but without effect. Lieutenant Norman, who had just arrived at the Mauku from Drury, obtained a rifle and ammunition, and at about this time joined Lieutenant Percival's party, to which regiment he belonged. He had with him at the time the men's pay, amounting to about £50. The volunteers continuing to advance, firing all the while, the natives suddenly broke from their cover and retired hastily over the crest of a hill in the direction of the Bald Hill, followed by the volunteers, who were halted when they reached the crest over which the natives had retreated. On each side of the clearing through which the advance had been made, there was a strip of bush, and in order to prevent being lured into an ambush, the volunteers were ordered to retire. They had no sooner commenced to do so than fire was opened upon them from the bush on their right, the natives appearing immediately afterwards in force in front and on both flanks, opening a heavy fire on Lieutenant Lusk's force, which immediately took cover behind the stumps, logs, and brushwood, which lay about the clearing. The natives having developed their strength, which consisted of over 200 men, boldly advanced on the handful of volunteers opposed to them, swarming behind every stump and log all over the clearing. Here a desperate and unequal contest took place and lasted for some time. Every volunteer was fighting for dear life. A hasty retreat would have doomed the whole force to destruction. Each retiring step had therefore to be contested. Behind a log fell the gallant Percival, foremost among his men, but not before several of the enemy had dropped by his hand. Lieutenant Norman also was shot, after an heroic struggle in which five or six natives bit the dust from his rifle. The retreat of Lieutenant Lusk's party being cut off by the way they had advanced, they were compelled to retire through an angle of the bush which projected into the clearing. In effecting this, they had to dislodge some of the Maoris stationed there, which they succeeded in doing, but several of the men got cut off from the main body and had to run through a heavy cross-fire, in which one was shot, and Worthington, of the Mauku Rifles, running in another direction from the main body, was pursued through the bush by the natives and tomahawked. Lieutenant Lusk's party having got fairly under cover of the dense bush, the natives ceased following the retreating volunteers, who without further molestation returned to camp. They had, however, suffered severely, having lost two officers and six men killed, and one man wounded. The natives, owing to the desperate resistance made by the volunteers, must have lost at least 20 or 30 men killed and wounded, as a number of rough stretchers used by the Maoris were afterwards found. The column, under Captain Rutherford of the 70th Regiment, arrived from Drury the same evening, and the next morning started off in pursuit of the enemy. Crossing the clearing where the fight had taken place, the bodies of the volunteers who had fallen were found laid out, partially stripped of their clothes, and frightfully tomahawked. A pole, on which a white haversack was fastened, marked the spot. The flying column reached the crossing place at Camerontown in time to see the last of the retreating natives escaping to the other side of the river in canoes, Captain Rutherford's force opened fire, and must have caused some loss to the enemy, as several Maoris were seen dragged out of the canoes and into the flax bushes on the opposite side. Having no means of crossing the Waikato in pursuit, the flying column, which had been joined by Jackson's company of Forest Rangers, returned to the Mauku.

The following is the official account of the affair:—

Mauku Stockade,
24 October, 1863.

Sir,—I have the honour to report that I started yesterday morning with a force to attack a body of the enemy who were shooting cattle on Mr. Wheeler's farm at the Ti-ti. An advance party of my force, under Lieutenant Percival, got close up to the enemy's position under cover of the bush. When discovered they were hotly pressed by the enemy and retired, skirmishing in good order on the main body, without loss. I then advanced. Having been joined by Lieutenant Norman with eight men, I drove the enemy through a strip of fallen timber on to the open ground beyond; but seeing that they wheeled around into the standing forest on my left flank, where they were largely reinforced, I deemed it prudent to retire. While re-crossing the fallen timber, the enemy, numbering from two to three hundred, charged us from the

THE WAIKATO WAR.   85

bush on the left, and after about ten minutes' very heavy firing at very short range (from ten to twenty yards) where both parties suffered severely, I, being out-flanked on both sides, retired into the forest on the right. The enemy did not venture to advance on us after we were under cover of the forest. I then re-formed my men and retired leisurely on the stockade. Our loss was 1 lieutenant (Percival) and 5 men killed, 1 man dangerously wounded; 1 lieutenant (Norman) and 1 private missing. The enemy's loss I believe to be about 16 killed and a large number wounded. Sergeant Hill and Private John Wheeler especially distinguished themselves by their determined gallantry under most trying circumstances. I have, etc.,

D. H. LUSK,

Lieut. commanding Mauku Volunteers.

N.B.—I omitted to mention that Mr. Norman on the right, and Mr. Percival on the centre, displayed great gallantry in endeavouring to stem the rush of the enemy, and fell fighting in front of their men.   D. H. LUSK.

Lieutenant John Spencer Percival was the son of Spencer Percival, Esq., for some years a leading member of the House of Commons, and grandson of Spencer Percival, First Lord of the Treasury, and Prime Minister in 1809, who was assassinated on May 11, 1812, by Bellingham, in the lobby of the House of Commons. Both Lieutenants Percival and Norman had, but a short time before their untimely deaths, arrived in the Colony from Victoria with the Militia Volunteers.

Not satisfied with the murders already committed, the natives, on Saturday, 26th October, made their appearance in the vicinity of Howick, and shot and tomahawked two boys, named Richard and Nicholas Trust, sons of Mr. Trust, who resided on Kennedy's farm. When the intelligence reached Auckland it caused the greatest excitement and consternation amongst the inhabitants. The enemy were evidently getting bolder, and had now made an attack on a settlement within a few miles of the city. The bugles at once sounded the alarm, and that same evening a force of 200 men, consisting of 100 of the Rifle Volunteers and 100 of the Volunteer Naval Brigade, embarked on board H.M.S. Miranda, which immediately steamed for the scene of the murder. The Rifle Volunteers were under the command of Major de Quincy, Capt. and Adjutant Mitchell, No. 2 Company; Capt. Clark, No. 6; Ensign Andrews, No. 3; and Ensign Batger, No. 5 Company. The Naval Brigade was in charge of Captains Daldy and Copeland and Lieutenant Guilding. Upon arrival the force skirmished through the neighbourhood where the natives had appeared, but the enemy, long before the Volunteers had arrived, had decamped through the bush towards the Wairoa. The force, not being prepared to follow, returned to Auckland.

The steamer Pioneer, together with several gunboats, having arrived on the Waikato, General Cameron made preparations for an immediate advance. Whilst steaming past the enemy's works at Mere Mere, on a reconnoitring expedition, the natives opened fire on the Pioneer from their two guns. One 14lb. weight, striking the bulwarks, passed through and embedded itself in a cask of beef that was on deck. The natives had been instructed to fire their

THE GUNBOAT "PIONEER" OFF MEREMERE, 1863.

THE WAIKATO WAR.   87

guns—one a 12-pounder and the other a 24-pounder—by an old Indian artilleryman. At the time of the war he was in the Waikato district, and was detained by the natives. He, however, managed to escape from the Maoris at Mere Mere to the British lines, and was enabled to give the General some reliable information respecting the enemy.

On Friday, the 30th of October, a strong force of 500 officers and men embarked on board the steamers Pioneer and Avon, both vessels immediately steaming up the Waikato River. When abreast of Mere Mere the natives opened a brisk fire from their two guns and small arms, but did no damage, the steamers continuing their passage. Upon arriving at a high bluff called Tapokau, 8 miles beyond Mere Mere, the troops were landed without opposition, and immediately commenced to throw up a redoubt. At about 3 o'clock the next morning one of the sentries, seeing a dark shadow moving in the fern, fired. A picket of the 40th, under Ensign Ducrow, at once advanced and patrolled for some distance round, but not discovering any signs of the enemy, retreated. Whilst so doing a heavy fire was suddenly opened upon them by the natives, who had been lying concealed among the fern and ti-tree. The troops, under cover of their earthworks, returned the fire, the position of the enemy being ascertained by the lightning-like flashes of fire that darted out in the gloom of night from the thick scrub. After keeping up the fusillade for about an hour the natives retired. The troops lost 1 private Royal Engineers killed; Captain Hon. Le Poer Trench. 40th Regiment, 2 privates, and 1 seaman wounded.

The natives finding that General Cameron, by the position he had taken up at Tapokau, had turned their stronghold at Mere Mere, which was consequently no longer tenable, at once retreated. On November 1 the General received information that the enemy had abandoned their position at Mere Mere, and a force of 500 men—consisting of 250 seamen under Commander Mayne, and 250 troops, detachments of the 12th, 14th, 18th and 70th Regiments, under Colonel Austin, of the 14th, at once moved forward and took possession of the deserted entrenchments, and threw up a redoubt. Captain Heaphy, of the Auckland Rifle Volunteers, who was on survey duty, accompanied the troops.

One of the Mauku Volunteers, named James Droomgould, on November 3 was shot and afterwards brained with the butt end of a gun by the natives who were prowling about the Mauku settlement. Droomgould at the time was in company with Felix McGuire, a corporal in the 1st Regiment Waikatos, engaged in collecting horses, when they were surprised by the enemy. They were both unarmed. Felix McGuire, hearing the shots fired, escaped to the stockade and gave the alarm. A force immediately marched out and brought in the body of Droomgould, but the enemy had decamped. About five months after the above occurrence a native was arrested for the murder of Droomgould. Some friendly natives swore they had heard him boast of having shot and brained one of the Mauku settlers at the time, and the noble savage being found guilty was sentenced to death.

It being rumoured that a number of natives had returned to their settlement between the Manukau Heads and Waiuku, an expedition was despatched on the 7th of November to capture them. The force embarked at Onehunga in the steamer Lady Barkly, Captain Hunt, and consisted of detachments of the Onehunga Naval and Rifle Volunteers, under Captain Parnell and Lieutenant Harris, accompanied by Dr. Weekes and Mr. Rice, Government Native Interpreter. The Lady Barkly arrived at Waiuku the next morning, and landed the expedition. Captain Lloyd, the officer in charge at Waiuku, arranged to join the expedition with 30 of his men. Accordingly, after dark that evening, the force marched out of Waiuku towards Awhitu, the native settlement at the Manukau South Head. The Onehunga detachment took one route, the Waiuku another; the two corps to join at a place agreed upon, viz., at Pehiakuru, a native settlement. On the march no natives were seen, and the two corps having joined, resumed their route towards Awhitu. Before starting from Waiuku, news arrived that the natives had crossed the Manukau to North Head, and cut down the signal staff that was erected on a rock adjoining the main land called Paratutae. The natives accomplished this daring feat at night time, and, as it were, in the very face of a party of Militia who were specially detailed to protect the flagstaff. The night being dark and windy the sentry did not hear the natives cutting down the staff. From Pehiakura the expedition struck a path that led them down to the west coast, which they followed for some distance, Mr. Mactier, an Awhitu settler, acting as guide. Some few miles before reaching the South Head, a deep gorge in the cliffs was reached. The expedition passed through this, and moved up on to the high land through several of the settlers' cultivations, and then down into the Awhitu Valley, at the mouth of which was situated the native settlement. Upon arriving at the village it was found deserted, but Maori foot-tracks denoted that the enemy was not far off. One of the Maoris who was reported to have assisted in cutting down the flagstaff had six toes, and as a natural curiosity would have made the fortune of a Barnum. The tracks of "six-toed Jack" were discernable, but he, with the other natives, was no doubt concealed in the dense and tangled forest that clothed the precipitous sides of the valley, and from some ambush was probably narrowly watching the movements of the expedition.

The Lady Barkly, having steamed along the shore from Waiuku, arrived at Awitu, re-embarked the expedition, and returned to Waiuku, passing on the passage the deserted homesteads of Messrs Logan, Graham, Featon, and Garland. Arriving at a creek called Rangiriri the steamer anchored, and a party went on shore to launch a large war canoe that was lying in a shed by the side of the creek. The canoe was over 70 feet in length, was elaborately carved, and would carry 150 men; its estimated cost was about £500. This celebrated specimen of Maori marine architecture was afterwards conveyed to England by one of the men-of-war. The canoe having been launched was taken in tow by the Lady Barkly to Waiuku. The next day the expedition marched out again, and surprised several natives with arms in their possession. Lead and bullet moulds were also found in their whares. They were taken prisoners, but afterwards released, as it was stated that they were friendlies. Bad weather setting in, the Lady Barkly, with Captain Parnell's detachment, steamed back to Onehunga.

A few days afterwards, news arrived in Onehunga that the natives were at the Awitu settlement in considerable numbers. Captain Parnell again started with a detachment of his Naval Volunteers in the Lady Barkly. The vessel at some distance passed the settlement, and steaming round a point, landed a party at Graham's to march overland and attack the settlement in the rear; the Lady Barkly to steam swiftly back and land a party on the beach to take the natives in front. The steamer arriving at the appointed time opposite the Awitu settlement, at once landed her shore party under Captain Hunt, who, extending his men in skirmishing order, rushed the settlement. The natives, however, retreated into the bush. The party under Captain Parnell shortly afterwards arrived and the bush was scoured, but was too dense to get at the enemy. The force then re-embarked on board the Lady Barkly and returned to Onehunga.

The troopship Himalaya, 3570 tons, Captain Lacy, arrived in Auckland harbour November 14th, with the 50th Regiment, consisting of 793 rank and file and 37 officers, under Colonel Waddy.

Queen Street wharf, Auckland, presented a scene of great bustle and excitement on Monday, November 16th. A large force of nearly 900 men were under orders for the Thames. The troops embarked on board H.M.S.s. Miranda and Esk, and the horses and baggage on board the s.s. Corio. The gunboat Sandfly, Captain Marks, also accompanied the expedition. The force consisted of detachments of the 12th and 70th, 1st Regiment of Waikato Militia, with 50 of the Defence Force under Captain Walmsley, and 100 of the Auckland Naval Volunteers, under Captain Daldy—the whole being under the command of Colonel Carey, 18th Regiment. The troops as they marched down to the place of embarkation were enthusiastically cheered by the crowds of citizens who thronged the wharf, the Auckland Navals having at their head the indispensable fiddler, who scraped away with great energy. The force having embarked, the transports steamed away down the harbour; but the weather coming on very rough the expedition anchored in the Waiheke Channel and remained there, owing to the tempestuous weather, for a week. On the Monday morning, a week from the date of embarkation, the expedition arrived at the Thames and landed at Pukorokoro without opposition, although several lines of earthworks had been thrown up by the enemy for the purpose of opposing the landing of the troops. The natives had but just retired, for the fires in the whares were still burning. After much pulling and hauling, in which the Auckland Navals displayed great zeal, the whole of the troops, horses and baggage were safely landed, and a redoubt was thrown up called the Miranda. The object of the expedition was to occupy the country between the Thames and the Queen's Redoubt, and so prevent the natives having free access to the Auckland district. As soon as possible, Colonel Carey advanced his force and opened communication with the Queen's Redoubt, having thrown up and garrisoned three redoubts, viz., the Miranda, the Esk, and the Surrey, communication being established by means of signal staffs, the Surrey communicating with the Queen's Redoubt. In those days the military ardour of the Auckland citizens was at its highest pitch; everyone capable of bearing arms was a soldier, and the apathetic Volunteer of these piping times of peace has but a faint idea of the enthusiasm that prevailed when grim-visaged war displayed its wrinkled front.

RANGIRIRI, FROM THE WAIKATO, 1863.

CHAPTER XXIV.

The natives, when they retreated from Mere Mere, fell back upon their entrenched position at Rangiriri, on the river bank, about 13 miles above Mere Mere. The enemy's works consisted of a line of entrenchments, with a double ditch, across the narrow ridge which divides the Waikato River from Lake Waikare, and in the centre of the works at the highest point there was a strong square redoubt with a high parapet, very similar in construction to the redoubts thrown up by the troops. On the 18th General Cameron proceeded up the river in the Pioneer, and reconnoitred the enemy's position, which he determined to attack without delay. Accordingly, on the morning of the 20th of November, the head-quarters of the 40th Regiment, consisting of 19 officers and 300 rank and file, under Colonel Leslie, Major Bligh, Capt. and Brevet Major Bowdler, Captains Hon. Le P. Trench, Cooke, Clarke, and Hines, embarked on board the steamers Pioneer and Avon, and steamed up the Waikato River. The Pioneer and Avon had in tow four gunboats. The steamers and gunboats were under the command of Commodore Sir William Wiseman, Bart., and Commanders Sullivan, H.M.s. Harrier; Mayne, H.M.s. Eclipse; and Philmore, H.M.s. Curacoa. The Avon was in charge of Lieut. Easther. At the same time a force of 28 officers and 723 rank and file marched from Mere Mere to attack the enemy's position in front. This force consisted of the following detachments:—

Royal Engineers.—2 officers and 13 rank and file, under Colonel Mould, C.B., and Captain Brooke.

Royal Artillery.—3 officers and 51 rank and file, under Captain Mercer, Lieutenant Pickard, and Assistant S.S. Temple, with two Armstrong guns.

12th Regiment.—4 officers and 108 rank and file, under Capt. Cole.

14th Regiment.—9 officers and 175 rank and file, under Colonel Austen and Captains Strange and Phelps.

65th Regiment.—10 officers and 376 rank and file, under Colonel Wyatt and Captain Gresson.

A party of seamen, with a 6-pounder Armstrong, in charge of Lieut. Alexander, H.M.s. Curacoa, also marched with the force.

General Cameron, C.B., commanded the troops, with the following staff: Major McNeill, A.D.C.; Lieut. St. Hill, A.D.C.; Col. Carey, C.B.; Col. Gamble, D. Qr.-M.G.; Lieutenant-Colonels Sir H. Havelock, V.C., and P. M. O. Mouatt, C.B. and V.C. Capt. Lacey, of the troopship Himalaya, also accompanied the staff.

The country between Mere Mere and Rangiriri is open undulating fern land, and presented no serious obstacles to the advance of the troops. The force, unmolested on the march by the natives, arrived in front of the enemy's position at Rangiriri at about 3 o'clock in the afternoon. The steamers Pioneer and Avon, with the gunboats, also arrived at about the same time, but owing to the strength of the current and the strong wind blowing, they were unable to take up their proper positions. This unforeseen occurrence caused considerable delay to the General, who, however, commenced shelling the enemy's works with Capt. Mercer's two Armstrong guns and the 6-pounder under Lieutenant Alexander, the troops in the meantime being halted under the brow of a hill about 600 yards from the enemy's advanced works. Some distance up the stream a party of natives crossing in a canoe became a fair target for Lieutenant Alexander's 6-pounder, who fired a shell, which burst right on the canoe, splitting it into pieces, and leaving the occupants who were not killed struggling in the water. After shelling the enemy's position for nearly two hours—two out of the four gunboats assisting—although the fire, owing to the nature of the enemy's earthworks, was not so effective as was expected, General Cameron gave the signal for the assault. The storming party consisted of detachments of the 65th Regiment, and advanced in the following order: No. 1 Company, under Lieutenant Toker, with scaling ladders and planks, accompanied by Captain Brooke and 10 men of the Royal Engineers in the centre; No. 2 Company on the right, under Captain Gresson; and No. 10 Company on the left, under Lieutenant Talbot. No. 9 Company, about 100 strong, under Lieutenant Pennyfather, formed the support.

Upon the bugles sounding the advance, the storming-party, led by their officers, rushed forward through the thick ti-tree scrub that lay between them and the enemy's rifle-pits. Under a heavy fire the ladders were planted, and the storming-party, followed by their supports, burst into the enemy's works and drove them out of the first line of rifle-pits. In the advance Captain Gresson fell, a ball having fractured his right arm; several men were also killed and wounded. Driven out of the first line of defence, the natives hastily fell back and made a desperate stand in the second line. The storming party, being reinforced, immediately with great gallantry swept over into the second line of entrenchments, dislodging the natives. At the rear of the rifle pits was the main position of the enemy, consisting of a square redoubt with parapets about 20 feet high. Numbers of the Maoris, after having been driven from their rifle pits, fled into the redoubt, whilst a great many attempted to make their escape through Lake Waikare swamp, but suffered severely from the fire of a party of the 65th under Lieutenant Pennyfather, which pursued them. The outer works having been captured, the troops attempted to storm the redoubt, but owing to the shortness of the scaling ladders were unable to gain the parapet in sufficient numbers to ensure success. The natives meanwhile kept up an incessant fire on the stormers, who were reluctantly compelled to fall back under cover of the captured earthworks, after losing many brave men. The 40th at this time had landed from the Pioneer and Avon, and a party under Captain Clarke, attacking a line of rifle pits on a ridge in rear of the enemy's position, dislodged the natives, who lost heavily. The 40th were supported by a detachment of the 65th, which had moved round from the front attack. General Cameron then gave an order which I believe to be unparalleled in annals of warfare. He directed Captain Mercer, with a detachment of his artillerymen, 36 in number, to assault the enemy's position. At the time over 600 British infantry were lying under cover—as brave men as ever marched on to a battle field. Captain Mercer

THE WAIKATO WAR.

immediately obeyed the command of his General, and the brave little band, armed each with a sword and revolver, rushed under a murderous fire to the assault. Sergeant-Major Hamilton gained the top of the parapet and discharged his revolver amongst the natives. He was severely wounded in the right arm, which was subsequently amputated. The Artillery, however, were driven back with the loss of their officer and several men. Captain Mercer fell before reaching the redoubt, a ball having struck him in the mouth, cut away part of his tongue and shattered his jaw—it was a mortal wound. Although a very strict disciplinarian, and on that account not over popular with many of his men, the service, when he fell, lost a man devoted to his profession, a brave soldier and an expert artilleryman, and one who could ill be spared by his country.

Commander Mayne, of H.M.s. Eclipse, with 90 seamen, was the next ordered to make an assault, but they, like the Artillery, were compelled to fall back from the heavy fire kept up by the natives. Mr. Watkins, midshipman, and several men reached the top of the parapet and were shot. Watkins, H.M.s. Curacoa, was shot through the forehead, and fell back into the trench at the foot of the redoubt amongst a crowd of soldiers and sailors who were there protected from the fire of the natives, the shots passing over their heads.. Staggering to his feet, Mr. Watkins asked for a drink of water, and directly fell back dead. In the assault Commander Mayne was severely wounded. Captain Mercer for some time lay on the ground where he fell; the spot was particularly exposed to the fire of the enemy, every one passing being struck. At length Lieutenant Pickard and Sergeants Houston and Mackay, under the heavy fire that was kept up, managed to drag their captain under cover, where he was immediately attended to by Assistant-Surgeon Temple. For assisting his commanding officer under a heavy fire Lieutenant Pickard afterwards received the Victoria Cross. It being at this time dark, General Cameron decided not to make any more attempts to capture the enemy's position until the next morning. The troops were accordingly disposed round the enemy's position so as to prevent their escape; but notwithstanding the precautions taken by the General, numbers of the natives, with most of their wounded, managed during the night to escape through the swamp to Waikare Lake. Amongst the wounded who got away was the chief Te Wharepu, who, although wounded in six places, had, with his blanket wrapped tightly round his bleeding wounds, encouraged his countrymen to continue the fight. During the night the natives kept up a continual fire, all the while shouting and yelling, especially when a shower of hand grenades was thrown over amongst them by the men in the trench outside the redoubt. The wounded were collected and carried on board the Pioneer, where they were attended to by the Regimental surgeons. The dead soldiers and Maoris lay stiff and stark where they fell in the outlying earthworks and on the hillside in front of the redoubt. Shortly before daybreak a party of the Royal Engineers, under the direction of Colonel Mould, C.B., commenced to mine under an angle of the redoubt with the intention of blowing up a part of the parapet so as to make a breach. Before the mine was ready, shortly after daybreak, the natives ceased firing and hoisted a white flag as a signal of surrender.

CHAPTER XXV.

Mr. Gundry, Interpreter to the Forces, upon communicating with the enemy, ascertained that they agreed to surrender unconditionally. The chiefs in command at the time of the surrender were Te Piori and Ti-ori-ori. The chief Rewi was not present. After some hesitation they gave up their arms, 175 in number. The number of natives that surrendered was 185. The troops immediately took possession of the redoubt, and had scarcely done so when a large body of natives were observed some distance off, who, seeing that Rangiriri was in the hands of the General, began to retire. Mr. Edwards, interpreter with the troops, was sent by General Cameron to ascertain who they were. He returned with the intelligence that it was a force of natives under William Thompson, who himself was desirous of surrendering, but his men would not. William Thompson sent to the General his mere or chief's greenstone as a sign of his desire for peace. He, however, retired with his men, in number about 400. The number of natives defending Rangiriri has been estimated at over 600 men, of whom about 100 men were killed and wounded and 185 taken prisoners; total killed, wounded and taken prisoners, about 285 men. The remainder escaped. The troops suffered severely, the casualties amounting to 2 officers killed, 13 wounded; 37 men killed, 80 wounded; total, 132 killed and wounded. The prisoners were sent to Auckland under a strong escort and placed on board H.M.s. Curacoa, but were shortly afterwards transferred to the hulk Marion, which had been fitted up for their reception, Captain Krippner of the Waikato Militia being in charge. Eventually the prisoners were forwarded to Kawau, from which place, one dark night, they made their escape.

When the prisoners were being marched through Otahuhu en route to Auckland a large number of soldiers' wives and settlers assembled, hooting and hissing them, and would have handled them rather roughly if they had not been prevented by the escort.

Most of the dead natives who were lying in the rifle pits were buried where they had fallen, the parapet being thrown over on top of them. The soldiers who were killed were buried in separate graves alongside the native church, Archdeacon Maunsell reading the service for the dead. Close by the soldiers' graves a large mound testifies to the last home of a number of the enemy, who were buried in one pit. The following is General Cameron's official account of the engagement:—

Head Quarters Camp, Rangiriri,
November 24th, 1863.

Sir,—I have the honour to report to your Excellency that on the morning of the 20th instant I moved from Mere Mere (with the force as detailed) up the right bank of the Waikato River, with the intention of attacking the

THE WAIKATO WAR.

enemy's entrenched position at Rangiriri, in which operation Commodore Sir William Wiseman, Bart., had arranged to co-operate with the Pioneer and Avon steamers and the four gunboats.

The troops under my command and the steamers and gunboats arrived near Rangiriri at the same hour—3 p.m.

The enemy's position consisted of a main line of entrenchments across the narrow isthmus which divides the Waikato River from Lake Waikare. This line had a double ditch and high parapet, and was strengthened in the centre (its highest point) by a square redoubt of very formidable construction. Behind the left centre of the main line, and at right angles to it, there was an entrenched line of rifle pits parallel to the Waikato River obstructing the advance of the troops from that direction. On a reconnaissance being made on the 18th, I had determined on landing a force in rear of the position simultaneously with attacking it in front, with the view of turning and gaining possession of a ridge 500 yards behind the main entrenchment, and thus intercepting the retreat of the enemy.

With this object 300 men of the 40th Regiment were embarked in the Pioneer and Avon, to land on a preconcerted signal at a point which I had selected.

Unfortunately, the strength of the wind and current was such that the Pioneer and Avon were unable to reach this point, notwithstanding the persevering efforts of Sir William Wiseman and the officers and men under his command. This same cause deprived us of the assistance of two of the gunboats. After shelling the position of the enemy for a considerable time from Capt. Mercer's two 12-pounder Armstrongs and the Naval 6-pounder under Lieutenant Alexander, R.N., in which the two gunboats joined, and it being now nearly 5 o'clock, I determined not to wait any longer for the landing of the 40th from the steamers, and gave the word for the assault. This was brilliantly executed by the troops, who had to pass over a distance of 600 yards in the face of a heavy fire—the 65th Regiment leading and escalading the enemy's entrenchment on the left.

After passing the main line of entrenchments the troops wheeled to the left towards the enemy's centre, and came under fire of the line of rifle pits facing the Waikato River. This they at once stormed and carried, driving the enemy before them to the centre redoubt, which they now defended with desperate resolution.

While the troops were forcing their way over the parapet of the main line, as already described, I was glad to perceive that the 40th were landing sufficiently near the point I had indicated to enable them to carry and occupy the ridge in rear, and to pour a heavy fire on a body of the enemy who were driven by them from that part of the position, and fled by the Waikare Swamp. In this part of the attack they were joined by a portion of the 65th Regiment detached from the main body, after the latter had passed the main line of entrenchment. The troops who carried the main line being still checked by the fire from the centre redoubt, two separate assaults were made on this work—the first by 36 of the Royal Artillery, armed with revolvers, and led by Captain Mercer; the second by 90 seamen

RANGIRIRI—STRONGHOLD OF THE MAORIS, CAPTURED NOVEMBER, 1863.

of the Royal Navy, armed in a similar manner, and led by Commander Mayne, under the personal direction of Sir William Wiseman.

Both attacks were unsuccessful, on account of the formidable nature of the work, and the overwhelming fire which was brought to bear on the assailants. An attempt was also made by a party of seamen, under Commander Philmore, to dislodge the enemy with hand grenades thrown into the work.

It being now nearly dark, I resolved to wait the return of daylight before undertaking further operations, the troops remaining in the several positions they had gained, in which they almost completely enveloped the enemy. Shortly after daybreak on the 21st the white flag was hoisted by the enemy, of whom 183 surrendered, unconditionally gave up their arms and became prisoners of war.

The exact strength and loss of the enemy I have been unable to ascertain, but they must have suffered severely. We buried 36 bodies, and there is no doubt a large number were shot or drowned in attempting to escape across the swamp of Waikare Lake.

Their wounded must have been removed during the night, as there were none among the prisoners. Our loss, necessarily severe in carrying so formidable a position, testifies to the gallantry of the troops I have the honour to command; and also, I am bound to say, to the bravery and determination of its defenders. I enclose a list of casualties. Your Excellency will observe that it includes a large proportion of officers, most of those who led in the different attacks being severely wounded.

It will afford me the highest gratification to report to the Right Honorable the Secretary of State for War and to His Royal Highness the Field Marshal Commanding-in-Chief the admirable conduct of the troops engaged on this occasion, and to bring to their special notice the names of those officers and men who more particularly distinguished themselves.—I have, etc.,

            D. A. CAMERON,
               Lieut.-General.

His Excellency Sir George Grey, K.C.B.

The following list contains the names of the officers who were killed and wounded. Those to which is affixed an asterisk shortly afterwards died of their wounds:—

OFFICERS KILLED.

Lieut. Murphy, 1st Battalion 12th Regt.
Mr. Watkins, Midshipman H.M.s. Curacoa.

OFFICERS WOUNDED.

Lieut.-Colonel Austen, 2nd Battalion 14th Regt., wound of thigh, severe.*
Capt. Mercer, R.A., gunshot wound of face, dangerous.*
Capt. Brooke, R.E., wound of finger, slight.
Capt. Gresson, 65th Regt., gunshot fracture right arm, very severe.
Capt. Phelps, 2nd Battalion 14th Regt., gunshot wound, abdomen, dangerous.*

MAORI PRISONERS CAPTURED AT RANGIRIRI, 1863.

THE WAIKATO WAR.

Commander Mayne, R.N., H.M.s. Eclipse, gunshot wound, left hip, severe.
Lieut. Downes, H.M.s. Miranda, gunshot wound, left shoulder, severe.
Lieut. Alexander, H.M.s. Curacoa, gunshot wound, right shoulder, severe.
Lieut. Hotham, H.M.s. Curacoa, gunshot wound, right leg, severe.
Lieut. and Adjutant Lewis, 65th Regt., gunshot wound, left arm, severe.
Lieut. Chevalier, 65th Regt., wound of left leg, severe.
Lieut. Talbot, 65th Regiment, gunshot wound of jaw, left shoulder, and chest, dangerous.
Ensign Ducrow, 40th Regt., gunshot wound of left knee-joint, very severe.*

Officers.		Men.	
Killed	2	Killed	37
Wounded	13	Wounded	80
Total	15	Total	117

The bodies of the officers killed in the field and of those who shortly afterwards died of their wounds were removed to Auckland and buried in the Church of England cemetery, Symonds-street. The graves lie in a cluster, and are carefully looked after by the officers of Her Majesty's ships of war on the station.

CHAPTER XXVI.

With the fall of Rangiriri was destroyed the power of the Lower Waikato tribes. The flower of their fighting men had fallen at Koheroa and Rangiriri, or were taken prisoners of war, and the remnant that escaped retreated to the Upper Waikato, where Rewi and his Ngatimaniapotos had decided to make a stand against the troops. Rewi did not aid in the defence of Rangiriri, on account of his objecting to the position. He was in favour of making a stand at Taupiri, about 15 miles above Rangiriri, where the high ranges and deep gorge presented a natural fortress that might have been rendered almost impregnable. Being, however, over-ruled, Rewi withdrew his men, and left the Lower Waikatos to fight their own battle at Rangiriri.

General Cameron, immediately after the capture of Rangiriri, threw up a redoubt, and pushed forward an advanced post at Armitage's, a few miles further up the river. The Governor, Sir George Grey, at this time received the following letter from the chiefs who had escaped from Rangiriri requesting him to liberate the prisoners that had been taken:—

Ngaruawahia, November 23, 1863.

Oh Friend Governor.—Salutations. This is to say to you. The fight has been fought and some are dead; some live. Restore to us Waikato. Let it suffice for you the men who are dead. Restore to us those who live. Enough.

From your friends,

Pene Te Wharepu.
Pene Pukewhau.

From all the Chiefs of Waikato.
To the Governor, Sir George Grey.

An answer was sent to the above letter by the Hon. Mr. Fox, the Premier, to the effect that the Governor would hold no communication with them whilst they continued in arms, but, upon their giving up all their guns, powder, and all their arms, communications would be opened with them, but not without.

On the 7th of December, General Cameron had moved forward and taken up a position about seven miles past Rangiriri, at Rahuipukeko—not far from where the Huntly coal mines are now being worked. At this part of the river the country is flat for some distance on each side. A few miles further on the river passes through the Taupiri Gorge, and runs swiftly between high wooded ranges, the highest part being the Peak of Taupiri, which rises 800 feet above the stream. From this spot a magnificent view is obtained of the Waikato district, which lies stretched like a panorama

THE WAIKATO WAR.

before the spectator. At the foot of Taupiri was the sacred burying-ground of the natives, and on the opposite bank stood the Mission Station of the Rev. Mr. Ashwell, nestled amidst a grove of peach trees. Far away to the southward, like a dark cloud, the giant Pirongia rears its lofty head. To the eastward, the Mangawara and Komakarau streams wind their silent course till they are lost in the distance.

On December 8th the British flag was flying on the King's flagstaff at Ngaruawahia, the headquarters of the Maori King. Early that morning General Cameron had made a reconnaissance in the Pioneer, and found the place deserted. He immediately returned to Rahuipukeko, and having embarked a force of 400 men, consisting of detachments of the 65th and 40th Regiments, under Colonel Wyatt of the 65th, returned and took possession of Ngaruawahia, unmolested. Upon landing, it was evident from the rifle pits and a half-finished redoubt that the natives had at first intended to make a stand, but the position being bad for defence—a neck of land at the junction of the Waipa and Horatiu rivers—they had wisely abandoned the idea, and retreated further inland. The next day the post at Ngaruawahia was strengthened by a reinforcement of 250 men of the 40th Regiment, under Colonel Leslie. At Ngaruawahia King Potatau the 1st was buried, but upon the capture of Rangiriri, the Ngatimaniapotos took the bones of the old king up, and carried them away, although the fact at the time was not known even by some of the Lower Waikato natives themselves, for the General, upon his arrival, found a letter addressed to the officers of the army, signed "W. Barton," requesting that the whares might not be destroyed, and that the grave of Potatau might be held sacred. A sentry was accordingly posted over the regal tomb. William Barton, the writer of the letter, was a native Wesleyan missionary living at Whata Whata, some few miles up the Waipa.

On December 9th the chief Pene Te Wharepu forwarded the following unique letter to the Governor:—

Te Kauri, December 9th, 1863.

Oh Friend, the Governor,—Salutations. Your letter has reached me. William Te Wheoro brought it to me. It is right. Yes, the Queen's flag is over us. Yes. I am pleased at it. Now let us talk. The first letter you wrote I have not seen. This ends my letter, from

Pene Te Wharepu.

The writer of the above letter, Wharepu, was the fighting chief of the Lower Waikatos, who made a most heroic stand at Rangiriri. As an earnest of his desire for peace, Wharepu forwarded his grand-daughter, a girl of 12 years of age, as a hostage to the General; but the brave Wharepu dying of his wounds a day or two afterwards, the girl was liberated.

. . . . .

The steam transport Lady Jocelyn arrived in Auckland Harbour on Thursday, December 10th, with the Head Quarters of the 43rd Regiment, consisting of 21 officers and 646 rank and file, under Lieut.-Colonel Booth.

CHAPTER XXVII.

Soon after noon on Friday, December 11th, Captain Jackson, with Ensign Westrupp, and his corps of Forest Rangers, started from his camp at Papakura, to reconnoitre the country towards the Wairoa and Hunua Ranges, Mr. Alexander Hill acting as guide. On the road to the Wairoa they discovered newly-made tracks of natives leading in the direction of the ranges. The trail was diligently followed up; the force bivouacking for the night in the forest. All the next day (Saturday), the tracks were visible, leading the corps towards the ranges, in the vicinity of Paparata. Captain Jackson pushing forward on the Sunday morning, December 14th, came upon the enemy in their encampment and surprised them. The natives, about 40 strong, were, there is little doubt, the same party that had been plundering and murdering the settlers in the Wairoa and adjoining district, evidently clearing out with their spoil. Captain Jackson, as it were, caught them red-handed; heretofore they had been surprising and murdering defenceless men, women, and children; this time they were surprised themselves, a fatal volley being poured into them whilst they were cleaning their guns and engaged in various other occupations, little suspecting the presence of the Forest Rangers. After the first volley the rangers closed on the natives with their revolvers, when those of them who had not been shot fled hastily through the bush. With the enemy were several women, who assisted in getting away the wounded. The natives lost 7 or 8 men killed, and several wounded. Captain Jackson collecting what he could conveniently carry of the plunder that the natives had left, consisting of 3 flags, rings, watches, and articles stolen from the settlers, returned to Papakura camp. The following is Captain Jackson's version of the affair:—

Papakura, December 14, 1863.

Sir,—I have the honour to report for the information of the Lieutenant-General Commanding, that in accordance with your instructions, I started on Friday, the 11th inst., at 1.15 p.m., with a force of my company of Forest Rangers, on an expedition towards the Wairoa River. At 6.30 p.m. on that day I camped on the Hunua River, and started from thence at 4.30 next morning; at 6.30 we struck native tracks which appeared to be quite fresh; at 10.30 a.m. we found a camping-ground, which was capable of accommodating 30 or 40 natives. One of the fires here was still hot. At 4.30 p.m. we got to another camping-ground, the fires of which were quite hot; we had evidently gained a day's march on the enemy. I continued our march until 6.15 p.m., when, finding we had overrun the track, I camped for the night. On Sunday, December 13th, I broke camp at 5.30 a.m. and turned back to re-examine the path, and found tracks diverging to the left. I then posted some men to look out for smoke, which we soon discovered rising out of the ranges. We went very quickly towards it, and by using great caution succeeded in surprising the enemy about 8.40 a.m. We had got between their sentry and their camp.

When about twelve or fifteen yards from the enemy, I halted my men on an eminence, to give them breath, and gave orders that they should first attack the enemy with their carbines, and then rush them with their revolvers. The Maoris were then cleaning their guns. The surprise was complete. After our carbines were discharged, the enemy, apparently expecting we had only empty pieces, turned upon us with their guns and tomahawks, etc., but the revolvers soon sent them to the right-about. Several of the enemy who were wounded by the discharge of the carbines were assisted away by the women, who were very busy removing arms, dead and wounded. I saw two or three natives hit who were immediately helped away by women. I had directed my men not to fire at the women, and I am happy to say they did not, though it is very possible that some of the women and children may have got hurt in the affray, but I only know of one instance—a woman, I believe, was wounded in the leg by a stray shot. The affair lasted only four or five minutes. I saw three dead men taken off, and four of their dead were left in our hands. Two of the natives, when surrounded, endeavoured to stab my men, one using a bowie knife and the other a large carving knife, but the revolver made short work of them. One native at great risk returned and attempted to carry away a small tin box, but a bullet made him drop it and run off. Many of those who escaped were wounded. Had my party been larger, I think I could easily have surrounded the enemy and taken them all prisoners. None of my men were hurt, as only those of the enemy who were on the outskirts of their camp could find time to load and fire on us, and they were just as likely to hit their own men as mine. I estimate the number of the enemy to have been over 40 men. One of the natives, before he died, told me there were 28, and on being asked again said there were 28 double, holding up two of his fingers. He also said his tribe was the Ngatipaoa. He would not tell his own name, but said the man next him was a chief named Matariki. The scene of the engagement was in the ranges, about five miles north of Paparata. The natives retreated in an easterly direction. One of the sentries I had posted informed me, some time after we had left the place, that a broad track led easterly from near where he was posted, and that he saw a man on horseback go up it. The enemy appeared to have plenty of provisions; we found a good deal of tea and sugar and some flour; there was abundance of fern-root, three or four iron pots had meat in them, and a good quantity of pork was hanging up. In the box which the native tried to secure, mentioned above, were three flags, one a large red flag on which was embroidered a white cross and star and the word "Aotearoa" in white letters. It is made of silk and is neat and handsome. Another flag is a large red pendant with a white cross; the remaining flag is a handkerchief, of the Union Jack pattern. The other spoils are a double-barrelled gun, a large horse pistol, and a smaller pistol, three or four cartridge boxes, a great deal of property which had belonged to settlers, such as scarlet hangings, fancy window blinds, small workboxes, etc., some papers belonging to Mr Richardson of Wairoa, and a coat belonging to Mr. Johnson, of the same place, several articles which had been stolen by the natives from Mr. McDonald at the time Trust's children were murdered near Howick. I therefore conclude these natives were of the party who committed those murders. One of my men has two small packets of hair, I think European. They are evidently relics. He will give them up to anyone who may claim them. We could not bring away much of the "loot," as we were heavily loaded with our arms, blankets, etc., but I think I brought away sufficient to prove the character of the party we fell in with. We destroyed several packages and tins of gunpowder, and threw a number of bullets into the creek.

I have great pleasure in reporting that my men behaved with great coolness and courage. There was no firing at random. I am anxious to bring to your notice the brave and cool conduct of Ensign Westrupp, who was foremost in the attack, and made every shot of his revolver tell; also of Private John Smith, who had a severe hand-to-hand struggle with a powerful native.—I have, etc.,

WM. JACKSON,
Captain Commanding Forest Rangers.

Lieutenant-Colonel Nixon,
Commanding Movable Column.

CHAPTER XXVIII.

Now that the troops had advanced well into the King Country the transport of stores to the front became an important part of the operations against the natives. To meet the sudden and increased demands on the commissariat department a large force had to be detached from the strength of the General's army for the transport of stores.

The Land Transport Corps, which hitherto had only to travel as far as the Queen's Redoubt, was largely reinforced, Captain Bishop, of the 2nd Battalion 18th Regt., being in command. This corps was in the Imperial pay, and was composed of volunteers both from regulars and Militia. As a distinguishing badge they wore a red band round their cap. To supplement the land force a Water Transport Corps was raised, Captain Breton, who arrived from Sydney in command of the Pioneer, being in charge. The duties that this corps had to perform were very arduous, they having to row large flat-bottomed boats loaded with stores from the Mangatawhiri Creek as far as Rangiriri—a distance of about 20 miles—against the swift current of the Waikato. From Rangiriri to the camp at Rahuipukeko the boats were towed by horses, the river at that season of the year—December—being very low, and obstructed with large snags dangerous to a steamer. From Rahuipukeko to Ngaruawahia the river had a deeper channel, enabling the Pioneer to convey the stores to headquarters. Colonel Gamble superintended the formation of the Transport Corps, Commissary-General Jones being the officer in command of the Commissariat Department. Colonel Gamble also organised an efficient store department for the colonial forces, Militia and Volunteers, at the head of which was Colonel Kenny, a retired officer from Her Majesty's service, with Messrs Reid, Ed. King, and George P. Pierce as chief clerks or superintendents, Mr. R. J. Feltus, A.R.V., No. 1 Company Commissariat Issuer, being travelling clerk in charge of stores in transitu. At the commencement of the war Mr Feltus, whilst on duty, happened to be with the escort under Captain Ring, when they were attacked by the natives near Martin's farm, and received several slight wounds.

The first meat contractors were Messrs Walters and Scarrott, and the contractor for the supply of groceries was Mr Ralph Simpson, who at every camp occupied by the troops had a canteen, where could be obtained, during canteen hours, wines, spirits and beer, and almost everything that a soldier would require from a needle to an anchor.

At Putataka, Waikato Heads, a large depot was formed for the reception of military stores. Workshops were erected for fitting and repairing the steamers on the Waikato. This post, called Port Waikato, was garrisoned by a strong force of Regulars and Waikato Militia; and with the large number of workmen employed in building the substantial stone wharf and erecting large stores and workshops, presented a busy aspect. Vessels, sailing and steam, arrived here from Sydney with Government stores, and owing to the good depth of water were enabled to discharge their cargoes direct on to the wharf or quay in close proximity to the sheds. The largest vessel that crossed the bar and anchored in the river during the war was H.M.S. Eclipse, drawing about 18 feet of water.

The blacksmith's shop at Port Waikato presented a scene of great activity: the iron plates and machinery for a new stern wheel steamer had arrived from Sydney, and were fitted up under the direct supervision of Mr James Stewart, C.E., of Auckland. This vessel, designed by Mr. Stewart, was much smaller than the Pioneer, and was to draw, if anything, less water, but like her larger sister was to be a stern wheeler, and was to act as a gunboat, and also, when required, to tow two large barges that were being built for her. To get this steamer ready as soon as possible, the clang of the blacksmith's hammer was heard at Port Waikato day and night.

As if Nature favoured the advent of steam on the Waikato, a seam of good coal cropped up out of the range on the proper left bank of the river, near the Taupiri Gorge. The General immediately took advantage of Nature's gift, and a party of miners, under the superintendence of Mr W. Rowe, arrived from Auckland, and opened the seam. The miners in their operations were assisted and protected by a covering party of soldiers. Huts and tents were erected, and a coaling station formed. The river channel at that point was deep enough to allow the Pioneer and Avon to come close up to the bank, and the coal seam cropped out some distance above, on the side of the range.

The majority of the men who volunteered for the Water Transport Corps, were, as may be imagined, those who had been used to a sea-faring life, and accustomed to boats and rowing. They were a rough-and-tumble lot, and many are the wild stories told of their escapades. The boats' crews (8 and 12 oars) used generally to sweep up against the stream to the chorus of a sailor's chanty song, "I'm bound away" or "Ye rolling rivers" usurping the canoe chant of the natives. When the boats' cargoes consisted of rum, large puncheons of real commissariat, 30 o.p., then it was a field day, and the passage was generally a tedious one. Boat accidents are of daily occurrence and were then: all sorts of stores fell overboard, sometimes even a cask of rum reached not its proper destination, but a soft bed amidst the tangled weeds and rank vegetation on one of the numerous islands that dot the river Waikato. For some time afterwards the boat from which the cask was lost always somehow stopped near the scene of the sad mishap. Rumour hath it that to this day in the swamp by the river side, not very distant from Mere Mere, there lies a large puncheon of commissariat. Amongst the men in the Transport Corps were several who had fought in the American Civil War, and the following strange incident is perhaps worth recording. Two of the Transport Corps, who had been in the American Civil War, were relating their experiences to each other. One had been in the Federal Navy and the other in the Navy of the Confederates. On comparing notes, it transpired that they had both been in the same naval engagement as adversaries, the ex-federal transport corps man having been one of the crew of the frigate that destroyed the Confederate gunboat in which was his companion, who was taken prisoner. Victor and vanquished, both Englishmen, had met again on the Waikato, brothers in arms under their own flag. Such are the fortunes of war. Amongst a large body of men there are always to be found some who by a peculiarity in their manner come prominently before their fellows. Many will still remember Lieutenant Fraser, Waikato Militia, attached to the Water Transport Corps, who by his brusque manner and a free use of strong adjectives, earned for himself the soubriquet of Bully Fraser. Another oddity was the voluble Lieutenant Lomax, of the 1st Waikatos, of slight figure, and long Dundreary whiskers that he was everlastingly twiddling about. "I'm Lomax, sir, Lieutenant Lomax, by gad!"—which emphatic exclamation after some doubtful yarn, generally annihilated his audience, who at once, meekly and without argument, accepted his asseverations as the truth, the whole truth, and nothing but the truth. Entering one day the tent of Major St. John, the gallant Lieutenant espied on the table two half-crowns, which taking up, he thus quaintly expressed himself, "Majar! Lomax is in a state of impecuniosity, by gad! Lomax will borrow five shillings from the Majar, by gad!" And wishing the Major good morning, Lomax took his departure, by gad. After the war, Lomax left the colony, by gad, and is reported to have returned to England, where, walking along Oxford-street in London one day, he was accosted by a sergeant of a Light Cavalry Regiment, who asserted that Lomax, by gad! sir, had deserted some few years before from his regiment, and Lomax, by gad! sir, had to accompany him to inquire further into the matter, by gad!

CHAPTER XXIX.

The New Zealand Ministry of the day thought, when General Cameron took possession of Ngaruawahia, that the time had arrived for peace to be made with the natives. It was therefore arranged that the Governor, Sir George Grey, should proceed to Ngaruawahia and interview those chiefs who were inclined to submit to the Queen's authority. On the appointed day a carriage and horses were ready to convey His Excellency on his journey. But the Governor changed his mind and decided not to go. The Ministry at once waited upon the Governor, urging him to proceed on his journey. The result was that the carriage and horses were ordered back again. His Excellency, however, when about to step into the carriage, again altered his mind and would not go. The Ministry begged His Excellency to reconsider his determination, and after some time Sir George agreed once more to go, and again, at the last moment, finally resolved not to go; the carriage and horses were consequently sent back to the stables. The fickleness displayed by Sir George Grey upon this occasion can perhaps only be satisfactorily accounted for by himself. In all probability he was trying to please the Ministry against his own inclination, and was consequently unsuccessful in the attempt. Looking back from this period of time, it is not very plain to see what good Sir George Grey could have done if he had gone on his journey, for the natives that most desired peace had already been conquered, the Ngatimaniapotos and others being still full of fight, and showing a bold front. Any overtures of peace to them at that time would most likely have done more harm than good, and it is reasonable to suppose that that was the private opinion of His Excellency the Governor at the time.

On Saturday, December 26th, the township of Onehunga was a scene of great bustle consequent upon the arrival of 300 rank and file of the 50th Regiment, under Colonel Waddy, who marched from Auckland and embarked on board the steamers Alexandra and Kangaroo, en route to Raglan. Two days afterwards 250 of the Waikato Militia also embarked in the s.s. Alexandra for the same destination. This force was commanded by Colonel Haultain with the following officers: — Captain Freer, Lieutenants Abbott, Johnson and Storey, and Ensigns White and Speedy—Dr. Stuart, Medical Officer.

General Cameron did not remain long at Ngaruawahia, for after establishing a strong post at that important position, he moved forward to Whata Whata, and thence on to Tuhi Karamea, where he established his headquarters on January 1st. The River Waipa, being narrow and having sharp bends, was not navigable by the Pioneer, but the little Avon was enabled to do good service in transporting stores to headquarters from Ngaruawahia.

THE WAIKATO WAR.

The force under Colonel Waddy at Raglan having advanced over the ranges towards the Waipa, communication was successfully opened with the headquarters camp at Tuhi Karamea without opposition from the natives. The Militia and Volunteers had now once again to leave Auckland and take the field. On Thursday, January 7th, a force of 150 men marched from the Albert Barracks for Papakura and Drury. This party consisted of 100 of the Auckland Militia, under Captain Brophy, Lieut. Morrow and Ensigns Kelly, Nation and Horne, and 50 of the Rifle Volunteers, under Major Campbell, Lieuts. Waddel, LeRoy and Tabuteau, and Ensigns Brighton, Tole and Batger.

The next day, January 8th, two large transports arrived in Auckland harbour with troops, viz., the s.s. Australian from Rangoon, with the headquarters of the 68th Regiment Light Infantry, under Lieutenant-Colonel Morant, and the ship Chariot of Fame, from Queenstown, with 510 rank and file consisting of Army Hospital Corps and drafts for the Royal Engineers and the different regiments.

It having been known that for some time the natives of Tauranga had been aiding the Waikato tribes, which they were now joining in large numbers, it was decided to despatch a strong force to Tauranga for the purpose of retaining the attention of the natives in that district, and diverting them from the scene of operations in the Waikato. Tauranga, a settlement on the East Coast, in the Bay of Plenty, about 146 miles by sea from Auckland, possesses a good harbour which can be entered by vessels of large size in almost any weather. The settlement at the time of the war consisted only of two or three stores, the trade being principally with the natives. On January 20th, Colonel Carey, with a force of about 700 men, embarked in Auckland for Tauranga, where they landed without opposition and formed an entrenched camp.

CHAPTER XXX.

At early dawn on January 28th, the troops broke camp and commenced the march from Tuhi Karamea for the enemy's position at Paterangi. The column consisted of nearly 3000 officers and men, who were about seven hours on the march, the force being delayed through having to cross several creeks, over which the engineers had to construct rough pontoons, and it was noon before General Cameron arrived in front of the enemy's stronghold. Although the natives were in strong force they did not molest the troops, but allowed them to take up a position at Te Rore by the river side, where General Cameron, close by the ruins of a house belonging to Mr. John Cowell, that had been fired by the natives upon the advance of the soldiers, fixed his headquarters. A redoubt was thrown up on each side of the river, and a post was also established at Ngahinapouri, between Tuhi Karamea and Te Rore. The native position was very formidable, consisting of three large redoubts connected with strong lines of rifle pits, and held by about 3000 warriors—over twenty different tribes being represented. Upon the arrival of the troops the natives swarmed on the parapets of their works, and here and there, one, probably a chief, could be seen dancing about and waving his shawl, evidently haranguing his dusky followers. The engineering skill displayed by the natives in the construction of their works was of the highest order, and was a matter of much wonder to General Cameron and his officers, who could scarcely believe that a savage race without any education in military tactics could have designed and so thoroughly carried out the details of such a complete system of defence. Forming a cordon outside their trenches, the natives had a chevaux de frise made of sharp-pointed ti-tree stakes. Within the lines of the enemy was the homestead of Mr. Macfarlane, who was married to a native woman, and had resided amongst the Maoris for many years. Mr. Macfarlane was not interfered with by the natives, and he remained with his family at his house during the operations of the troops. Upon the arrival of the forces the hitherto solitary fern hills of Te Rore became imbued with life, and a large canvas town sprang into existence. The steamer Avon, Lieutenant Mitchell, R.N., steamed up to the landing place at Te Rore with stores, and made almost daily trips between Ngaruawahia and the front. The transport corps with their teams moved up from Whatawhata on the left bank of the river under strong escort. Owing to the many times the stores had to be unloaded and then loaded, first into drays, then boats, then shifted into steamer, then again steamer and drays, it was with the greatest difficulty that the commissariat could supply the troops at headquarters.

The extreme end of the enemy's works at Paterangi was about three miles distant from the headquarters' camp at Te Rore, and Colonel Waddy, C.B., of the 50th, with 600 men, moved forward and took up his position within 1,500 yards of the enemy's entrenchment. An Armstrong gun was also placed in position, which at intervals fired shell into the native works. At night strong pickets were thrown out in front of the British lines, and occasionally shots were exchanged with the enemy's sentries in the fern. The sailors under Lieutenant Hill, H.M.S. Curacoa, had their camp close to the landing place, and these jolly tars, to relieve the monotony of camp life, had by some means contrived to obtain a set of cricketing materials, and on fine afternoons the stumps were set up and play commenced as earnestly and unconcernedly as if there were no such thing as a Maori foe within a few hundred yards of them. Watching the game with a sang-froid peculiarly his own, smoking a cigar, oftener a cigarette, sometimes might have been seen Von Tempsky, who was, with his own and Captain Jackson's Forest Rangers, with headquarters, and invaluable as scouts to the General. The Rangers had most perilous duties to perform. If the troops advanced, the Rangers scoured the country in front. Did the General desire any particular and specially dangerous duty performed miles away from the camp, the Rangers did it, frequently lying out for two or three nights in the open with a bundle of fern for pillows, and the stars for blankets. A few biscuits and a ration of rum and water very often constituted the commissariat, yet to many such a life was fascinating and had a peculiar charm. Von Tempsky, or Von as his men loved to call him, was the beau-ideal of a Forest Ranger; of a wiry form, rather above the middle height, keen eyes, high cheek bones, and sharp features; a forage cap with oak leaf band sat jauntily on the side of his head, over a mass of dark curling hair hanging almost to his shoulders. Often, instead of his regulation coat, he wore a blue jumper thrown open at the neck, military trousers with thin red stripe, and knee boots or gaiters; round his waist a red silk sash, with revolver and sword belt. In his trousers was a pocket or case to hold a bowie knife, in the use of which he was an expert. Von Tempsky, trained in the Mexican war, believed in the knife, and instructed his company how to use it effectively against an enemy, especially when thrown with precision. It was a saying amongst the troops that Von Tempsky could scent out a native if he was a mile away. As an illustration of his keenness in ferreting out a party of natives while lying in ambush, the following anecdote will perhaps not be amiss, although the occurrence took place some time after the Waikato war. When General Chute made his memorable march through the bush round Mount Egmont to Taranaki, Von Tempsky, then Major, with his Forest Rangers marched with the column. Whilst passing through the dense bush, Von Tempsky suddenly left the track with his men, and disappeared in the forest. The troops thought that he had taken a wrong path: but very soon was heard the sound of sharp firing, which lasted but a few seconds, and then appeared in front of the column, forcing his way through the tangled supple-jacks, Von Tempsky, a sword in one hand, a revolver in the other, the smoke still hovering about one of the barrels; and between his teeth he held his knife, dripping with the blood of a native. Von Tempsky had detected and destroyed an ambuscade that was laid by the natives for the advancing troops.

On February 1st Lieutenant Mitchell was fired at by a party of natives and mortally wounded. He expired at Ngaruawahia two days after. At the time Lieutenant Mitchell was standing with Mr. Foljambe, midshipman, on the

MAJOR VON TEMPSKY.

bridge of the Avon, whilst on her passage down the Waipa. Some natives who were seen in the fern on the river bank were fired at; they returned the fire, one of the bullets striking Lieutenant Mitchell. Shortly after the above affair the Avon struck a snag not very far from Ngaruawahia, and sank near the river bank. This accident, occurring at the time it did, was a most serious mishap—the troops at headquarters largely depending on her for supplies. Orders were at once sent down to Port Waikato to get the new steamer ready with all speed, the retention of the General's position in front of Paterangi depending, in a great measure, on her arrival up the river at once. At this time the Colonial Defence Force, under the command of Colonel Nixon, arrived at Te Rore to co-operate with the troops in the field, the country being open and suitable for the use of cavalry.

FIGHT AT WAIARI, MANGAPIKO RIVER, NEAR TE RORE, FEBRUARY 11th, 1864.

CHAPTER XXXI.

About 1,000 yards on the south-east, from the advanced post of the troops, the Mangapiko stream winds its way through the country, its banks being heavily clothed with dense high scrub, making it difficult to penetrate. At this place the soldiers were in the habit of going to bathe. On Thursday, February 11th, at about 3 o'clock in the afternoon, a party of the 40th Regiment left the camp for the bathing place; they were accompanied by a small covering party of some 20 men of the same regiment, the whole party being under the command of Lieutenant Simeon. The bathing party had no sooner reached the bank of the stream than a sharp volley was fired into them by a party of natives, who lay concealed on the opposite bank. The covering party immediately returned the fire, and a sharp fusillade commenced on both sides. The sound of the firing being heard at the advanced camp, reinforcements to the number of 200 men of the 40th and 50th Regiments were despatched to the scene of action, the whole under command of Lieutenant-Colonel Havelock. The troops, separating into two detachments, wound round to the rear of the place, where the natives lay in ambush, and owing to the dense character of the fern and ti-tree, they accomplished the intended movement, and came upon the natives suddenly, close to an old native earthwork, called Waiari, the scene of former native wars, but at this time almost hidden with the heavy growth of scrub. Captain Jackson, of the Forest Rangers, and Captain Heaphy, of the Auckland Rifle Volunteers, who was attached to the troops as field surveyor, happened at the time to be at the advanced camp, and marched with the supports to the scene of action, where they were soon hotly engaged. Taking cover under the shelter of the old earthworks, the natives made for some time a determined resistance, but were eventually driven away after the 40th Regiment had lost several men killed and wounded. Capt. Jackson, in advancing through the fern, came suddenly upon a native with a double-barrelled gun, who at once took aim, but the piece missed fire, and Captain Jackson shot him with his revolver. Captain Heaphy here gained the coveted Victoria Cross; under a heavy fire and at great personal risk he attended a wounded soldier. The escape of Captain Heaphy was miraculous, his clothes being riddled with bullets, one of which struck the buckle of his revolver strap, and the Captain after the fight, unbuttoning his coat, showed to the writer the course the ball had taken after it had struck the buckle which it broke—right round the Captain's waist was a red seam as if he had been slashed with a whip, the bullet having circled half round his body. Some time after the fight had commenced, a small reinforcement of 20 men, a detachment belonging to Jackson's and Von Tempsky's Forest Rangers, arrived on the scene from the camp. Captain Von Tempsky and his men were ordered to cross the river and penetrate the dense scrub on the opposite side, where a number of natives were concealed. The manner in which the brave Von Tempsky and his handful of men carried out this order will for ever redound to the credit of the Colonial Forces. Without a moment's hesitation they struggled across the stream, and dripping wet plunged into the high fern and ti-tree and rushed on the natives. A most determined hand to hand struggle here ensued, every pop, pop of a revolver denoting the fall of an enemy. Here in the scrub by the Mangapiko stream, several Victoria Crosses were earned but never received. The natives, not able to cope with their adversaries, retreated, leaving in the hands of the Rangers eight dead, whom they laid out side by side on the trampled fern. The Forest Rangers in this brilliant exploit only had two or three men wounded. Mr. C. De Thierry, interpreter to the 50th Regiment, who was present, viewed the bodies and recognised several that had been previously employed in Auckland and Newmarket. The sun had now fallen behind the ranges, and the dark mantle of night would soon fall upon the scene of strife, so the recall was sounded, once, twice, three times, before the firing slackened, a body of natives having come out of the pa at Paterangi to reinforce their comrades, but they were checked by the fire of the 40th skirmishers, who were thrown forward to stop them. . Haste was made to collect the dead and wounded. Private Thompson, of the Forest Rangers, was with a soldier carrying one of the wounded on a stretcher, when a ball struck the soldier, causing him to fall, and the weight of the wounded man coming suddenly on Thompson, upset him, and the three went down in the fern. In obedience to orders, the troops returned to camp, the Forest Rangers forming the rear guard, the natives still occasionally firing a shot at the troops from their lairs in the fern.

The casualties on the part of the troops, considering the nature of the engagement, cannot be considered as heavy. They consisted of five men killed and six wounded, of whom one died afterwards. The natives on the other hand suffered severely, losing over forty men killed and about thirty wounded.

The morning after the fight, Mr. De Thierry was instructed by General Cameron to proceed to the pa, which he did with a flag of truce. As soon as the white flag appeared, firing stopped on both sides. Arriving at about 200 yards from the pa, the natives waved their hands to Mr. De Thierry to stop, and four of the Chiefs came to meet him and hear his communication, which was to ask them whether they would prefer to take their dead away or leave them to be buried by Bishop Selwyn. The Chiefs replied that they would fetch their dead away, and a party of about twenty natives afterwards accompanied Mr. De Thierry back to the camp for the bodies which were laid out in a line. On the way to the camp, Mr. De Thierry noticed a party of natives lying in the fern, evidently watching for Bishop Selwyn, who was riding down to the enemy's position, but upon Mr. De Thierry informing him that there was an ambuscade on the road, the Bishop replied that he did not believe that the natives would fire at him. However, at the request of Mr. De Thierry, the Bishop turned back. He had no sooner done so, than the natives opened fire at him, but the distance was too far for the bullets to take effect, and the Bishop put spurs to his horse and galloped back to camp.

One of the natives who came with Mr. De Thierry, named Topi, amongst the bodies recognised that of his son, a lad of about 14 or 15 years of age, and he requested that he might be allowed to tangi or cry, after the native custom, over him. His request was granted, and hugging the lifeless form to his breast Topi cried bitterly.

Bishop Selwyn read the funeral service over the graves of the soldiers who were killed; and the natives, under a flag of truce, collected the bodies of their

THE WAIKATO WAR.

slain, most of which they took away to their pa. A few, doubtless slaves, they buried in old potato pits near the scene of the fight. The number of Maoris engaged at Mangapiko was estimated, according to their own account, at 150. The dense scrub concealing their strength made it difficult to judge; the native account is, however, probably right. A redoubt was afterwards thrown up at Waiari, near the scene of the engagement, and occupied by the troops.

The following is Col. Havelock's official account of the affair:—

Camp before Paterangi,
12th Feb., 1864.

Sir,—Having been directed by the Lieut.-General Commanding to report on the successful skirmish of yesterday, on both banks of the Mangapiko River, I have the honour to state that at about 2.30 p.m., on an alarm that a bathing party had been suddenly fired on from an ambush by apparently 100 Maoris detached from the Paterangi Pa, the inlying pickets of the 40th and 50th Regiments at this camp turned out promptly and hastened to the scene, being reinforced immediately by parties of both regiments as fast as the men could seize their arms.

The Maoris retired along the left bank, and a sharp running fight soon commenced between them and the foremost pursuers. Finding themselves so readily met, they took post, while endeavouring to gain their pa, on the site of an ancient entrenchment called Waiari, where the high mounds and deep ditches of an old fortification, densely overgrown with thick cover, gave them, together with their intimate knowledge of the ground, great advantage. On reaching the level plain under Paterangi, after crossing the Takoutu stream, I found that the pursuit and fight had gone to my right; but as there were threats of large bodies sallying out to cut off those of our men whose eagerness had carried them farthest to the front, I collected every available soldier of both regiments and formed them up in a chain of skirmishers to watch this flank.

Soon after, a considerable party under Captain Trench (40th) having assured our left and rear, I moved rapidly down to where our leading men were hotly engaged and pressed. They were commanded by Captain Fisher (40th) who had hastened here earlier with a few men. Captain Heaphy, Auckland Rifle Volunteers, and Captain Jackson, Forest Rangers (both accidentally on the spot), had lent their services, and reinforced him with some 30 men of the 40th and 50th. These parties, that which I myself brought up and one under Ensign King (40th), united, had now the happiness to come full on the main body of the Maoris retreating towards Paterangi. We turned them back to the shelter of the ancient earthwork above mentioned, which is singularly placed in a double loop of the Mangapiko.

Major Bowdler's party of 40th, who had moved down the right bank, were firing on the front of the Maoris from across the river. Our arrival on their rear effectually hemmed them in and sealed their fate.

After much hot firing we were able to dash across the river into the entrenchment, over a bridge formed of a single plank. The banks are here from 40 to 60 feet high, precipitous, and densely wooded.

A series of hand-to-hand encounters here took place between the Maoris crouching secreted in thick bush and our men, who displayed if anything too keen an eagerness to dash at and close with their lurking enemies whenever

MAJOR CHAS. HEAPHY.

visible. This forwardness cost some valuable lives, but the punishment inflicted on the Maoris was sharp and telling, and read them a severe lesson.

At the time, some 20 men of the Forest Rangers (both companies) arriving from the headquarters camp, materially assisted in hunting out and destroying the enemy. Eventually, every Maori that could be discovered being either killed, wounded or made prisoner, the work of removing our wounded (most difficult on account of the narrowness of the planked bridge) and of securing their dead commenced.

Two large parties of the enemy now approaching through thick bush endeavoured to intercept this. It became necessary to throw Captain Fisher's party, with which were Lieutenant Simeon and Ensign King, again on the right bank, where they most steadily covered this operation under a sharp cross-fire.

Finally, near dark, all our wounded having been removed, and as many as possible of the Maori dead brought in, the skirmishers were gradually withdrawn, file by file, across the plank bridge, and the troops moved slowly, taking every advantage of ground, towards camp.

This very successful affair cost the Maoris twenty-eight men killed (counted) and two wounded and prisoners in our hands. Both these are said to be chiefs. Our loss was five killed and six wounded (one since dead).

The effect on the Maoris of their insidious attempt at ambuscade being thus promptly met, and signally and completely frustrated with their heavy loss in dead, cannot but be salutary.

It becomes my pleasing duty, as senior officer accidentally on the spot, to report that nothing could have been better than the behaviour of the men and officers engaged. Where the forwardness of all was distinguished, it is enough to name the officers present as per footnote.* But I would beg specially to bring to your notice Adjutant-Surgeon Stiles, 40th Regiment, to whose assiduity in caring for the wounded in the most exposed situations, and under sharp fire, their safe and early removal to camp is mainly attributable.

Captain Heaphy, Auckland Rifle Volunteers, took charge of a party and ably directed it. In gallantly assisting a wounded soldier of the 40th who had fallen into a hollow among the thickest of the concealed Maoris, he became the target for a volley at a few feet distant. Five balls pierced his clothes and cap, and he is slightly wounded in three places. Though hurt himself he continued to aid the wounded to the end of the day.

Captain Jackson, Forest Rangers, gave great assistance, and Captain Von Tempsky, when I directed him to relieve the soldiers who had been skirmishing for hours, covered the extreme rear of our march with much coolness and judgment.—I have, etc.,

H. M. HAVELOCK,
Lieutenant-Colonel, Deputy-Adjutant, Quarter-Master General.

*Brevet-Major Bowdler, 40th Regiment; Captain Hon. F. LeP. Trench, 40th; Captain Fisher, 40th; Lieutenant Simeon, 40th; Ensign King, 40th; Captain Doran, 50th; Lieutenant Leach, 50th; Ensign Campbell, 50th.

CHAPTER XXXII.

Although the new steamer being put together at Port Waikato was not nearly completed, the demand for her services up the river was so urgent that it was decided to launch her as she was, a mere shell. The vessel was accordingly launched in the presence of the Hon. Thomas Russell, Defence Minister, and named the "Koheroa." After she was launched she unfortunately swung on to the rocks, but a gang of men working all night got her clear again. The engines and stern wheel being in position, a crew of 24, consisting of 12 men belonging to H.M.S. Eclipse, and 12 of the Auckland and Onehunga Naval Volunteers, were placed on board, the vessel being in charge of Lieutenant Coddington, H.M.S. Eclipse, and Lieutenant Turner, who arrived from Auckland in charge of the volunteers. Steam having been got up, the Koheroa started on her passage up the river. Carpenters were placed on board for the purpose of fixing the deck and strengthening the vessel as far as possible. On crossing the flats at Kohanga, near where the Avon grounded when she first entered the river, the Koheroa took the ground and stuck hard and fast, the tide ebbing at the time. Suddenly, with a loud report, the iron plates amidships burst asunder; the vessel having no strengthening band, the strain on the iron rivets had been too great, and they had broken. Great excitement at once prevailed on board amongst the crew, and numbers of officers who were proceeding in her up the river. The ship's boat, with a crew, at once rowed back to the heads for assistance, which arrived after dark with the flood tide. The aperture or rent was patched up, and when she floated, the unfortunate Koheroa steamed back to the Heads. A heavy timber belt was then bolted fore and aft on each of her top sides. Fresh plates were bolted on, and another start was made, this time with more success. Upon the Koheroa passing the military posts at Tuakau, the Bluff and Mere Mere, the men stationed in the redoubts turned out and greeted her with lusty cheers. At Mere Mere Commodore Sir William Wiseman came on board and proceeded in her up the river. The numerous native settlements passed looked melancholy and deserted, and the cultivations that but one short twelve months before had been luxuriant with maize, wheat, potatoes and kumeras, were already overgrown with weeds: but the peach, with its branches loaded with luscious fruit, still kissed the stream as of yore, tempting the Commodore and party to stop the vessel, when a supply of fruit was obtained. On the third night after leaving Port Waikato, the Koheroa arrived at Te Rore with thirty tons of commissariat stores, and the General's position was assured. Had a delay of another few days occurred he would have been compelled to fall back. Stores now accumulated rapidly at the front, the Koheroa arriving regularly from Ngaruawahia almost every other day. Orders were issued that the steamer was to anchor for the night at Ngahinapouri if she made that port at dusk, and not to proceed to the front, as it was expected that the natives would attack her. This, however, they did not do, although a party of the enemy were seen in the fern by the river bank one day watching her. The crew stood to their arms, but no shots were exchanged. A covering party of soldiers from Te Rore protected her when she neared the camp. All sorts of rumours were afloat at headquarters concerning the expected attack on the enemy's position, and there was great excitement among the troops. The night was even stated when the assault was to take place. But the rumours had no foundation in fact, and were no doubt circulated to reach the enemy's ears, for instead of assaulting the Maori position, General Cameron marched with a strong force past Paterangi toward Te Awamutu and Rangiaowhia, the granary of the Maoris in the Waikato. From these places the enemy had been drawing their supplies, and a long string of horses laden with food could frequently be discerned from the British lines entering the enemy's position.

At 11 o'clock on the night of the 20th of February, the night being very dark, a force, consisting of about 1000 men, paraded in silence and marched towards Te Awamutu, a half-caste named Edwards acting as guide. Von Tempsky's Forest Rangers formed the advance guard, and Captain Jackson's Rangers the rear guard. With the troops was a detachment of seamen and marines—the Artillery mounted as cavalry, and the Colonial Defence Force, under Colonel Nixon, General Cameron in command. After leaving the British outposts, the column had to pass not very far from the enemy's works, and the chiefs could be plainly heard warning their men to be on the alert, somewhat in the following terms: "Be careful, the soldiers are watching us. Take care and let not sleep overcome you. Be ready to man the pits. Be silent!" The strictest silence was observed on the part of the troops as they marched past, but the peculiar dead sound that a large number of men make when marching, especially on a still night, was no doubt detected by the quick ears of the Maori sentinels, for long before daylight the formidable positions at Paterangi were tenantless. Early the next morning Captain Saltmarshe, of the 70th Regiment, reported to Colonel Waddy, who was left in command at Te Rore, that he believed the native positions at Paterangi were abandoned. Colonel Sir H. Havelock, with 100 men of the 70th Regiment, advanced cautiously towards the position on one side, whilst Colonel Waddy skirmished up on the other with the inlying picket. Not a native was seen, and this stronghold of the natives was occupied, like Mere Mere, without being assaulted. Two hundred men of the 40th Regiment, under Major Blyth, were left in possession of the pa. In the centre of the works there was a deep well, and the natives had left behind them large quantities of potatoes. Mr McFarlane, who was still living in the immediate vicinity of the pa, informed Colonel Waddy that the natives during the night had evacuated their works and gone towards Rangiaowhia.

CHAPTER XXXIII.

Early on the morning after the General had marched, a large convoy of provisions started from Te Rore for Te Awamutu, escorted by the 50th Regiment under Brevet Colonel Weare; a detachment of Royal Artillery and sailors with two six-pounder Armstrong guns and one Naval six-pounder also accompanied the convoy.

General Cameron arrived at Te Awamutu at daybreak on the 21st, and immediately pushed on to Rangiaowhia, which he found nearly deserted. The few natives who were in the place were completely taken by surprise, and, refusing to lay down their arms, fired on the Mounted Royal Artillery and Colonial Defence Force, who were sent on in advance of the column. The natives were quickly dispersed, and the greater part escaped; but a few of them, taking shelter in a whare, made a desperate resistance until the Forest Rangers and a company of the 65th Regiment surrounded the hut, which was set on fire and the defenders either killed or taken prisoners.

Several casualties occurred amongst the troops. Our loss was 2 killed and 6 wounded; about 12 natives were killed and 12 taken prisoners. In attempting to dislodge the natives from the whare as mentioned above, the brave and respected Colonel Nixon fell mortally wounded, a ball penetrating his chest, injuring the lungs. One of the Defence Force, Private McHale, dismounted and endeavoured to burst open the door of the whare, but was shot and dragged inside by the natives; another of the Defence Force, Corporal Alexander, was killed, and two wounded, viz., Corporal Dunn, who received a ball in the thigh, and Private Brady, slightly in the hand. Finding it difficult to dislodge the natives from their lair, the Troopers set fire to the whare, which, with its occupants, was consumed by the flames. The buckles alone indicated the remains of the unfortunate Trooper who had been dragged inside the whare previous to the conflagration.

On the morning of the 22nd the General discovered that the natives in force had taken up a strong position blocking the road between Te Awamutu and Rangioawhia on the site of an old pa called Haeirmi. He determined to attack them immediately, and at 1.30 p.m. advanced on their position with a force of 1000 men and two 6-pounder Armstrong guns. The General's skirmishers, consisting of companies of the 50th and 70th Regiments, being pushed forward, soon came into contact with the enemy's pickets, who were posted some distance in front of their position. These were driven back, and when within 500 yards the Armstrongs opened fire on their works. After a few rounds, General Cameron ordered Colonel Weare, with the 50th Regiment, to carry the position at the point of the bayonet, having the 65th in support and the 70th in reserve, while the Cavalry, consisting of 31 of the Royal Artillery and 38 of the Colonial Defence Force, were formed up on the right behind the brow of a hill, ready to pursue the enemy. The Forest Rangers, 72 strong, were well up in front, and had the honour of charging with the 50th, and entered the enemy's works by their side. The storming party, although exposed to a heavy fire, carried the works in splendid style, the natives falling hurriedly back before the leading files could reach them with the bayonet, and retreating through a swamp in the direction of the Maungatautari-road.

The number of natives defending the position at Haeirini was estimated at about 400, and their loss in killed and wounded at over 30, besides several prisoners. As they were retreating, the Cavalry pursued them for some distance, cutting off a few stragglers. The casualties on the part of the troops consisted of 2 killed and 16 wounded, amongst whom were Ensign Doveton of the 50th, Corporal E. B. Gilmer and Thomas Little of the Defence Force, and Private James Taylor of the Forest Rangers. Corporal Little afterwards died from the wound which he received in the thigh.

The following is Colonel Weare's official account of the attack on the Maori position at Haeirini:— Rangiaowhia, 23rd February, 1864.

Sir,—I have the honour to report for the information of the Lieut.-General commanding the Forces, that with reference to his instructions conveyed to me personally for storming the enemy's works on the 22nd inst., I proceeded to carry out his instructions in the following manner:—The enemy's works could only be approached by a narrow road, hemmed in on either side by high fern, through which it was impossible for the men to advance in line or skirmishing order, and necessitated the position being stormed with only a front of four deep, until within a few yards of the trench and rifle-pits. This compelled me to advance the whole regiment in a column of four at the double over some 350 to 400 yards under a very severe and concentrated fire from the enemy, most trying to troops in that formation. I ordered a small storming party of 20 men, under Lieut. White, 50th Regiment, to break cover in the first instance, to endeavour to draw out the first fire of the enemy; this party was almost immediately followed up by the storming party, consisting of Nos. 1 and 10 Companies 50th Regiment under command of Captains Johnson and Thompson respectively, and these three officers entered the enemy's works at the head of their men, at the same time closely followed by the remainder of the regiment.

The nature of the ground and formation left little for the commanding officer to do but to place the men in the first instance and leave the officers commanding companies to fight their men; and I am proud to say officers and men nobly did their duty under very trying circumstances, and while exposed to a fire that must have caused a very large increase to the list of casualties had it not been for the dense dust raised by the men doubling, which partially concealed them.

I beg to bring to the notice of the Lieut.-General commanding the Forces the names of Captains Johnson and Thompson and Lieut. White, 50th Regt.

The medical officers for the regiment, Drs. Davis and Dempster, accompanied the regiment into action, and shared their lot, attending to the wounded as they fell.

I much regret to say that Ensign Doveton, 50th Regiment, fell dangerously wounded by the side of Captain Thompson while gallantly performing his duty.—I am, etc., H. E. WEARE,
Colonel Commanding 50th Regiment.

To the Assistant Military Secretary.

HEADQUARTERS OF GENERAL CAMERON, AT PUKERIMU, WAIKATO.

CHAPTER XXXIV.

Wednesday, March 2nd, 1864, was the day on which the first steamers ascended the rapid Horatiu river; on that day the Koheroa, accompanied by the Pioneer with Sir William Wiseman and a detachment of the 65th on board, steamed up the river as far as Kirikiriroa, where the town of Hamilton West now stands. At that time there were merely a few native huts, which were found deserted. The steamers anchored for the night, and at daylight the next morning the Commodore, Sir William Wiseman, and the detachment of the 65th Regiment under Captain Bulkley, went on board the Koheroa, Lieut. Coddington, of H.M.S. Eclipse, in charge. The Koheroa then proceeded up the river, leaving the Pioneer at anchor. After steaming against the strong current for some thirteen miles to Pukerimu, close to where Cambridge now is, the anchor was dropped and Mr. Boultain, R.N., and Mr. O'Meara, surveyor, with Captain Bulkley and a few soldiers, went on shore and ascended the hill on the left bank of the river (proper right bank); at this spot the steamer's party were then only about 21 miles in a direct line from the General's advanced post, but the country round was swarming with natives, and the enemy's position at Maungatautari could be plainly seen. While Messrs Boultain and O'Meara were taking a rapid survey with their instruments, the cry was raised that the natives were coming, and, looking over the country on the other side of the river, several natives on horseback were seen. The survey party immediately stopped operations and hurriedly descended the steep hill to the river bank, and scrambling into the boats returned on board the Koheroa. Word was passed to up anchor, but, owing to the foul bottom, it had caught amongst the rocks, and it was some time before it could be lifted—the party on board expecting every minute to be fired on by the natives, who, however, fortunately did not appear, and the steamer drifted stern first for some distance rapidly down the stream. Passing through the rapids, one of the boats alongside was crushed against the cliff which rises abruptly from the river, and floated away in pieces, the men who were in the boat at the time having a narrow escape from death. After passing through the Narrows the steamer's head was got round and she proceeded at a quicker speed back to the Pioneer. The natives in the meantime had lighted large fires, vast columns of dense black smoke rising up from near where the Koheroa had anchored, evidently a signal by the natives that the pakeha had invaded that part of their territory. The Koheroa having joined the Pioneer, both steamers returned to Ngaruawahia. The object of the expedition was successful; good soundings of from 8 to 20 feet having been found all the way up. Military posts were shortly afterwards established at Kirikiriroa and Pukerimu, without opposition from the natives. The troops detailed for the above service consisted of detachments of the 18th and 70th Regiments, numbering about 400 men. At Kirikiriroa, Ensign Martin, of the 70th Regiment, was accidentally drowned whilst bathing. The above force having junctioned with the General's forces (who had marched from Te Awamutu), the whole proceeded to reconnoitre the enemy's position at Maungatautari, where the natives were discovered in full force. The troops were halted about 1,200 yards from the position, when the Maoris hoisted a blood-red flag on a flag-staff—the same flag, no doubt, that had been flying at Paterangi. Skirmishers were thrown forward towards the pa, and halted at about 400 yards, the natives opening fire, without effect, upon them. The General, advancing to the front, took a good survey of the position. The bugles then sounded the recall, and the force returned to camp, the Defence Force capturing a number of horses.

Orderly duty in time of war is the most arduous and dangerous work that the soldier is called upon to perform. Sometimes singly, or at most in parties of two or three together, the orderlies have to keep up communication between the posts of an army in the enemy's country. Sometimes in the dead of night they have suddenly to mount and leave a strongly entrenched post for some other camp miles away, across swamps, rivers, and surrounded by enemies who may strike at them any moment; every clump of scrub or bush may conceal the enemy, and they ride, as it were, with their lives in their hands. Whilst performing orderly duty between Pukerimu (Cambridge) and Te Awamutu—a distance of about 18 miles—Sergt. Kenrick, of the Defence Force, and a civilian named Macarthy, escaped from an ambush laid by the enemy in a way that deserves more than a passing notice. Returning from Pukerimu to the General's headquarters at Te Awamutu they proceeded about six miles on the road, and while passing a spot where the fern grew high and thick, a party of natives, about 30 in number, suddenly rose up and fired a volley at the two troopers. Sergeant Kenrick's horse was wounded in seven places, and that of Macarthy fell dead. Macarthy, extricating himself from his fallen horse, ran after Sergeant Kenrick, whose horse still fortunately held on. The natives instantly left their ambush and started in pursuit, when Sergeant Kenrick, seeing his companion's predicament, immediately turned his horse, and taking steady aim at the foremost of Macarthy's pursuers, fired. The native—a tall, ruffianly-looking fellow—staggered back, and the rest of the natives halted. In an instant Macarthy jumped on behind Sergt. Kenrick, and the brave animal, although severely wounded, brought them safely within a mile of the camp at Te Awamutu, and then dropped exhausted. For the coolness and courage he displayed in saving his comrade's life, Sergeant Kenrick afterwards received a commission in the Colonial Forces, and was recommended for the Victoria Cross, which, however, for some reason, was not awarded—probably because he did not belong to the regulars.

A few days after the above incident, Lieutenant-Colonel McNeil, on the staff of General Cameron, whilst proceeding along the same road, attended by a single orderly named Vosper, belonging to the Colonial Defence Forces, was fired upon by a party of natives who had secreted themselves in a clump of bush not far from Ohaupo (a native village then held by a detachment of the 40th, and situated between Te Awamutu and Pukerimu). The sudden fire of the natives so startled the horses that Private Vosper was thrown from his seat. Lieutenant-Colonel McNeil succeeded in arresting his fall, and, quickly remounting, they got safely away amidst a shower of bullets that was fired after them. For this service Lieut-Colonel McNeil received the Victoria Cross.

CHAPTER XXXV.

A number of natives under Rewi and other chiefs having taken up a position and thrown up strong earthworks at Orakau, a spot situated about five miles from Rangiaowhia and three miles in a south-east direction from Kihikihi, Brigadier-General Carey, in command of the British advanced forces, determined to dislodge them. At this time a portion of the Waikato Militia had been moved up to the front and assisted in the operations that were about to take place. The siege and capture of Orakau was one of the most important episodes in the Waikato war, on account of the desperate and prolonged defence made by the natives who, for three days and two nights, kept a large force of British troops at bay.

FIRST DAY.

Before daybreak on the morning of Thursday, the 31st March, a force, consisting of detachments of the Forest Rangers under Captain Von Tempsky, 65th Regiment under Captain Bulkley, and 40th Regiment, the whole numbering about 300 men, under Major Blyth, started from Te Awamutu towards Kihikihi under the guidance of Mr Gage, interpreter. The forces marched about six miles beyond Orakau to get in the rear of the enemy's position. At 6 o'clock another column, numbering 600 men and two 6-pounder Armstrong guns, under the command of Brigadier-General Carey, moved forward to dislodge the enemy at Orakau. On the road they were joined by a detachment of the 65th Regiment and a company of the Waikato Militia under Colonel Haultain. A third body of troops, consisting of detachments of the 65th and Waikato Militia, under Captains Blewitt and Gower, also marched to Orakau, advancing through the bush to the north-east of the village. The disposition of the troops was excellently planned, and the enemy's position was completely surrounded.

The main body under Brigadier-General Carey advanced to the village, driving in a few Maoris who hastily retreated; the troops still advancing, were fired upon by a body of natives who had taken up a position in a masked pa. The 18th Regiment, under Captain Ring, and Forest Rangers being in front, at once charged the Maoris, a company of the 40th under Captain Hinds furnishing the supports. The natives retired from their position, and the troops suddenly found themselves confronted by a strong post and rail fence, behind which was a deep trench and parapet, the strength of the position being concealed by a grove of peach trees and high flax bushes. As Captain Ring advanced to the assault with the 18th and Forest Rangers the natives opened upon them a heavy fire, mortally wounding the brave Captain Ring and killing and wounding eight others. The storming party checked by the heavy fire fell back, but the supports under Captains Hinds and Fisher coming up, another rush was made

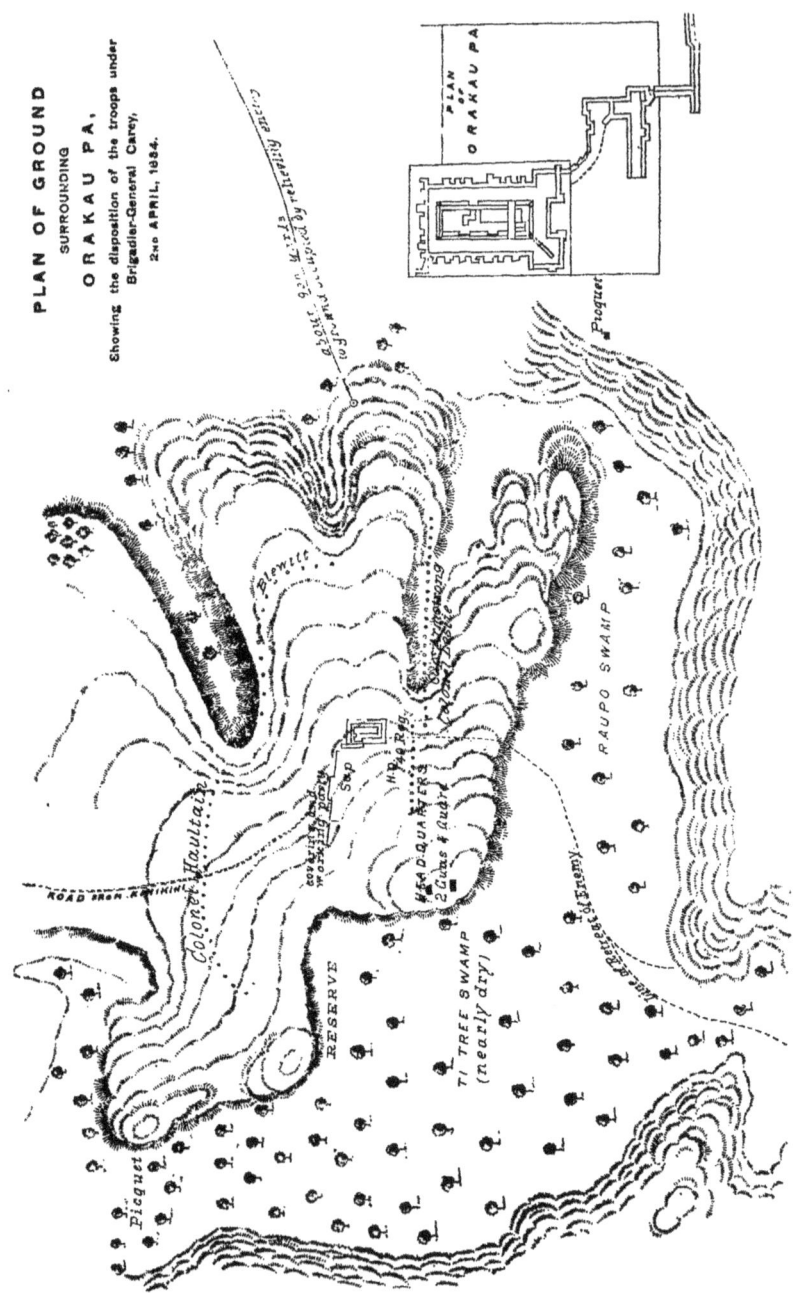

at the position, which also proved unsuccessful, Captain Fisher, who led the attack, being severely wounded. The troops again falling back, the two 6-pounder Armstrongs under Lieutenant Carre were brought forward and commenced to play on the enemy's works, which turned out to be far stronger than was at first suspected. Major Blyth with his force at this time arrived and took up a position at the rear of the pa, the other columns under Captains Blewitt and Gower also marched on the ground from Rangiaowhia.

Seeing that any further attempts to carry the enemy's works by assault would entail a heavy loss of life, and the position being now completely surrounded, Brigadier-General Carey gave orders for a flying sap to be commenced. Some gabions that were on the way from Te Awamutu were brought into requisition and a number of soldiers were detailed to go into the swamp on the south side of the pa and make gabions. Whilst this was being done, an irregular fire was kept up on both sides, and Brigadier-General Carey sent back to headquarters for reinforcements; these, consisting of detachments of the 12th, 18th, 70th, and Captain Jackson's Forest Rangers, arrived during the evening, and brought the number of troops surrounding the native position to close on 1500 men; the number of natives under Rewi defending the pa was estimated at about 300 men. The flying sap under the direction of Lieutenant Hurst, of the 12th Regiment, was pushed forward the whole night long, the gabions protecting the soldiers from the fire of the natives. So passed the first day's operations against Orakau.

SECOND DAY.

Friday morning, the 1st of April, found the natives still defending their position and the flying sap every hour getting nearer and nearer to their works. During the morning several men were wounded, owing in a great measure to their raising their heads above the gabions to get a shot at the natives. A large number of the enemy appeared on the ranges in the direction of Rangiaowhia with the object of reinforcing their comrades in the pa, but they were kept in check by a party of the 65th, the Forest Rangers, and a company of the Waikato Militia. They did not attempt to reach the native position, but satisfied themselves by firing heavy volleys at too great a distance to do any mischief. Friday went, the sap still drawing nearer and the natives firing intermittent volleys the whole day, which were briskly responded to by the troops. During Friday night the natives mustered up sufficient courage to attack the working party in the trenches; they could be plainly heard shouting, and one, doubtless a chief—perhaps Rewi himself—urging his men to attack the soldiers. About 20 or 30 young braves made the attempt; rushing out of the pa they clambered on the top of the gabions in front of the sap, but they no sooner showed themselves than the Waikato Militia under Captain Herford, Commissariat Transport Corps, who were guarding the trench, fired a volley into them and they fell back in confusion to their pa. The remainder of the night passed away quietly, broken only by the sharp crack of the rifle and intermittent flashes of flame that lit up the darkness of night like lightning after each discharge of the firearms. All the while figures in shirt and trousers were busy pushing forward the sap.

MAJOR MAIR.

THE WAIKATO WAR.

THIRD DAY.

On Saturday morning, April 2nd, the sap was close up to the enemy's works; under the shelter of the gabions the working party had escaped any serious loss; all had gone well. It was expected that the natives would have surrendered, seeing that they were so closely invested, and no chance of escape—but they did not—no white flag appeared—and the firing on both sides was kept up, although on the part of the natives slacker than it had been at first. At noon, General Cameron and staff arrived from Pukerimu, and the escort, a detachment of the Defence Force, under Captain Pye and Lieutenants Macpherson and Hutchinson, accompanying them, brought a quantity of hand grenades. The sap was now only some twenty yards from the palisading in front of the pa, and one of the 6-pounder Armstrong guns was placed in the sap and opened fire with grape, whilst numbers of hand grenades were thrown over into the enemy's position, and a heavy rifle fire from all sides was opened on the pa. The bugles at this time suddenly sounded "cease firing," and Messrs. Mair and Mainwaring, interpreters to the forces, were requested to go as near as possible in the sap to the enemy's position, and summon the natives to surrender. Major Mair went forward alone, and was answered by one of the chiefs, who said (translation): Friends—This is the word of the Maori —they will fight on, for ever! for ever! for ever! Firing was immediately resumed, and a soldier working in the sap, throwing his cap over into the enemy's trench, rushed after it, followed by about twenty of the Waikato Militia, Forest Rangers, and Regulars, led by Captain Herford. The party succeeded in getting into the trench; but the attack not being followed up, it being premature, the natives poured into the brave little band a deadly volley, which killed and wounded half their number. Captain Herford received a severe wound in the eye, from which he afterwards died. Ensign Chater, of the 65th, was shot through the side. Privates Armstrong and Levitt, of the Waikato Militia, were killed, and several others wounded. The natives, having discharged their pieces, ran into another trench out of sight, enabling the party to get back to the sap with their dead and wounded. On another side of the pa an attempt was made to get into the enemy's works by a party of 65th and Waikato Militia, but it likewise proved unsuccessful.

At four o'clock in the afternoon the sap was within a yard or two of the enemy's trench, and showers of hand grenades were thrown over amongst the natives, under the direction of Sergeant McKay, of the Royal Artillery. At this time, on the south side of the position, and under the brow of a hill leading up to the enemy's works, were posted the 40th Regiment, under Colonel Leslie, for the purpose of preventing the escape of any natives who might attempt to retreat that way. Many of the 40th men were, at the time, cutting ti-tree on the edge of the swamp and making gabions; and at one spot for some distance there were only three or four men, the line of sentries having been removed to enable the fire from an Armstrong gun to be directed in that quarter on the enemy's works. Here a road was cut out of the steep embankment, and the two or three soldiers stationed along it suddenly heard the rush of men coming through the scrub, and immediately a large number of natives who were escaping from the pa jumped across the road and plunged into the high ti-tree and

ORAKAU PA, TAKEN BY BRITISH TROOPS, APRIL 2nd, 1864.

scrub that lined the edge of the swamp close to the road. Several of the 40th men, attempting as well as they could to stay the crowd of natives rushing across the road, got severely wounded. The working party in the sap becoming aware that the natives had escaped from the pa, the bugles sounded cease firing. The men crowding on the parapets, fired a volley after the fugitives, and the Forest Rangers leading the way ran at the double round the edge of the swamp with the intention of cutting off the natives. The whole force, Regulars and Militia, mixed together without order or formation, with loud shouts rushed in pursuit. The Mounted Artillery, under Lieutenant Rait, galloping round the edge of the swamp, cut off the natives as they came out on the other side. The Defence Force also arrived at the same time, and numbers of the unfortunate wretches were cut to pieces. Driven back into the swamp, the remnant of the natives got away out in another direction and retreated across the Puniu River, being all the time hotly pursued by the Forest Rangers and some of the infantry. The pursuit ended at the river, several natives being shot whilst in the act of crossing. The chief Rewi escaped, although it was reported that he was amongst the killed, and a reward of £10 was offered for his body. The natives had no water in the pa, and must have suffered terribly from thirst; perhaps as much as anything it was the cause of their retreating when they did.

That Saturday night, 2nd of April, 1864, the sun went slowly down and set in the far west, and then a dark shroud, the pall of night, fell upon the scene of blood and strife that had been raging for three days and two nights; and with the setting of the sun also set for ever, never to rise again, the glory and the pride of the Waikatos. Their braves were lying stark and dead in the Orakau swamp, and the remnant, in small bands, were dragging their weary limbs across country as fast as they could, and did not stop until far out of the reach of pursuit they laid their weary limbs down in some friendly whare to rest. The natives in their retreat suffered severely, 101 dead bodies being found the next day outside. Only the bodies of twenty natives were found in the pa, notwithstanding the heavy fire to which they were exposed for three days and two nights; the remaining bodies were found in the swamp, and a day or two after several more bodies were found—doubtless to this day the bones of some remain. Total loss of natives in killed, wounded and prisoners about 130. During the retreat of the natives many interesting incidents occurred, the most noteworthy, perhaps, being the following: In the pa with the natives were several women, and in the fight one or two were killed and wounded. One woman with a child under her arm escaped with the natives and made towards the bush near the pa. She was seen by Mr. Charles De Thierry, interpreter to the 50th, who was present at the fight. Thinking that she was a man, the woman having scarcely any clothing on, Mr. De Thierry went after her with a revolver. Seeing herself pursued, the unfortunate woman, who had been shot through the breast, went down on her knees and begged that her life and that of her child might be saved. Mr. De Thierry assured her that she should be safe, and brought her out of the bush on to the road. Here a ruffianly half drunken soldier belonging to the Transport Corps made an attempt to bayonet her, but was kept back by Mr. De Thierry, who very properly threatened to shoot the coward if he advanced a step. Mr. De Thierry escorted the woman safely into camp, where she was cared for, and ultimately recovered from her wound, severe as it was. In gratitude to her deliverer, the woman gave Mr. De Thierry her little boy, which he kept for some time, and, dressing him up in a miniature suit of soldier's clothes, he was the observed of all observers in the camp. Mr. Mair, interpreter, also rescued a woman from death. One Maori, refusing to leave the pa, stayed by himself holding a white flag, and was saved from instant death by the exertions of Captain Greaves. Several other Maoris' lives were also spared, and the men taken prisoners. The loss on the part of the troops amounted to 68 killed and wounded. No sooner had Orakau fallen than the natives hastily abandoned their last stronghold at Maungatautari and retreated back into the interior.

The following is the official account of the capture of Orakau:—

Camp Te Awamutu, April 3, 1864.

Sir,—I have the honour to state, for the information of the Lieutenant-General commanding the forces, that about mid-day on the 30th ult. it was reported to me by Lieutenant-Colonel Haultain, commanding the Kihikihi Redoubt, that natives were seen in force at the village of Orakau, about two and a-half to three miles distant from his post.

I immediately rode over and made a reconnaissance. Found that the natives were engaged building a pa, and as it was then too late in the day to attack at once, I returned to this camp and made arrangements to march on the enemy's position during the night. Captain Baker, 18th Royal Irish (Deputy Assistant Adjutant-General), fortunately found two men in the camp—Messrs. Gage and W. Astle—whom from their local knowledge I at once engaged as guides, which circumstance enabled me to determine on a combined movement. My plan of attack was to advance with the main body along the dray road to Orakau; to detach a force of 250 men under Major Blythe, 40th Regiment, who would take a circuitous route through a somewhat difficult country, crossing and re-crossing the Puniu River, and, marching on my right flank, to take the enemy's position in reverse; and thirdly, to draw a force of 160 men from Rangiaowhia and Haeirini under Captain Blewitt, 65th Regiment, who would march across to the enemy's position on my left, the three bodies of troops arriving, if possible, simultaneously before the enemy's stronghold shortly before daylight.

At midnight Major Blythe, 40th Regiment, marched with 250 men, with directions to take the road to the right, to cross and recross the Puniu River, and to gain the rear of the enemy's position before daylight, halting there until he should hear my attack, and then to dispose of his force so as to cut off the retreat of the enemy.

The road from Rangiaowhia to Orakau I found on inquiry to be very difficult, being intercepted by deep swamp and thick bush. However, having every confidence in Captain Blewitt's energy, I directed that officer, who commands at Rangiaowhia, to march during the night and endeavour to form a junction with me before daylight on the proper right of the enemy's position, bringing with him 100 men.

At three o'clock on Thursday morning, the 31st, I marched with the main body along the dray road to Kihikihi, taking on Lieutenant-Colonel Haultain

THE WAIKATO WAR. 135

and 150 men from that post, and then proceeded by the same road to the village of Orakau, which I reached without opposition as the day dawned.

The enemy, evidently taken by surprise, opened fire on the advance guard—composed of 120 of the Royal Irish and 20 of the Forest Rangers, gallantly led by Captain King, 18th Royal Irish, and supported by 100 of the 40th Regiment, who immediately rushed forward to the attack in skirmishing order.

The position being found very strong, an earthwork with strong defences, deep ditches with posts and rails outside, and nearly covered from view with flax bushes, peach trees, and high fern—this party were forced to retire; but it at once re-formed, and, being reinforced by another company of the 40th Regiment, again tried to take the place by assault, but with no better success. Here Captain Ring, 18th Royal Irish, fell mortally wounded, and Captain Fischer, 40th Regiment, severely so, besides four men killed and several wounded. On Captain Ring's falling, Captain Baker, 18th Royal Irish (Deputy Adjutant-General), most gallantly galloped up, dismounted, and, calling for volunteers, again endeavoured to carry the place by assault. This also failed.

Finding that there was no chance of taking the pa in this manner, from the immense strength, and other men having fallen, I determined to desist from this mode of attack; and having heard that both Major Blythe, 40th Regiment, and Captain Blewitt were at their appointed posts, I decided on surrounding the place and adopting the more slow but sure method of approaching the position by sap, which was shortly after commenced under the very able direction of Lieutenant Hurst, 12th Regiment, attached to the Royal Engineers Department. At this time Lieutenant Carre, Royal Artillery, endeavoured to effect a breach in the enemy's works, but could make no impression upon it.

A further supply of entrenching tools and gabions (which latter had most fortunately been prepared at the neighbouring posts for service at headquarters on the Horotiu) were immediately ordered up with the men's blankets, food, etc., and every possible precaution taken by the proper disposition of the force to prevent the escape of the enemy.

During the afternoon a reinforcement of some 150 or 200 of the enemy, from the direction of Mangatautari, appeared in sight, evidently determined on relieving the place. They advanced to a bush situated about 900 yards in rear of our outposts, but seeing that it was scarcely possible to break through the line formed by our troops, they halted and commenced firing volleys, at the same time exciting the men in the pa to increased energy by dancing the war dance, shouting, etc.

The wounded were sent on to Te Awamutu and Kihikihi. The sap was pushed forward vigorously, and the troops so posted as to prevent any possibility of escape by the natives during the night.

Heavy firing was kept up by the enemy on the troops both in the sap and around the place during the day and night, causing but few casualties, the men contriving to cover themselves in temporary rifle pits, dug out with their bayonets and hands.

A reinforcement of 200 men, under the command of Captain Inman, 18th Royal Irish, reached me from headquarters during the afternoon.

THE WAIKATO WAR.

Having reported my proceedings to the commander of the forces in the morning, I was glad to receive a reinforcement sent by him (148, of 12th Regiment) and guided by Captain Greaves, Deputy-Assistant Quartermaster-General, which arrived about daylight on the morning of April 1, and which enabled me to relieve the men in the sap more constantly, and therefore to carry on the work more quickly. Captain Greaves ever afforded me material assistance in the duties of his department. This day was spent in working at the sap and making rifle pits around the pa, few casualties occurring. Captain Betty, Royal Artillery, arrived during the day and assumed command of the Royal Artillery, which enabled Lieutenant Carre to render some assistance to Lieutenant Hurst in constructing the sap, he having been at it without intermission.

During the night a few of the enemy were perceived trying to effect an escape from the pa, but, being immediately fired upon, returned to their earthwork. I omitted to mention that Captain Betty, Royal Artillery, threw some well-directed shells at he Maori reinforcements in the bush and on the hills, which evidently disconcerted them considerably.

At an early hour on the morning of the 2nd April, Lieutenant-Colonel Sir Henry Havelock, Bart. (Deputy Assistant Quartermaster-General), arrived with the hand grenades, which were at once thrown into the enemy's position with great effect by Sergeant McKay, Royal Artillery, who thus rendered good and gallant service at great personal risk, under a galling fire.

About noon I ordered Captain Betty, Royal Artillery, to have a six-pounder Armstrong gun carried into the sap, an entrance having been made. It opened fire on the enemy's work, destroying the palisading, making a considerable breach and silencing in a great measure the fire of the enemy on the men engaged at the head of the sap.

The commander of the forces, with his staff, etc., arrived on the ground at this time, and witnessed the remainder of the operations.

Colonel Mould, C.B., Royal Engineers, coming up with General Cameron, gave his able assistance towards the completion of the sap into the enemy's work.

As it was known that women and children were in the pa, the enemy was called upon to surrender previous to the concentrated fire of the Armstrong gun and hand grenades on their work. They were told that their lives would be spared, and if they declined they were requested at least to have compassion on their women and children, and send them out. They replied that they would not do so, but would fight to the last. The pa was then carried. The enemy, effecting his escape from the opposite side of the work, dashed through a space from which the troops had been thrown back under cover, to enable the gun to open. They were, however, speedily followed up, and suffered a severe loss during the pursuit of nearly six miles, Lieutenant Rait, Royal Artillery, with his troopers, and Captain Pye, Colonial Defence Force, with a small detachment, having headed them and kept them back until the infantry came up. I regret to say that in the pa and in the pursuit some three or four women were killed unavoidably, probably owing to the similarity of dress of both men and women,

THE WAIKATO WAR. 137

and their hair being cut equally short, rendering it impossible to distinguish one from the other at any distance.

The troops were recalled about sundown, and bivouacked round the enemy's late position.

At an early hour this morning I caused diligent search to be made for the killed and wounded of the enemy. Their loss was considerable, amounting to 101 killed, besides 18 to 20 reported by native persons as buried in the pa; 26 wounded and taken prisoners, and 7 unwounded taken prisoners. In addition to this number, the natives were seen to be engaged carrying off dead and wounded early in the morning at the most distant point of pursuit, and fresh tracks showed that they had been similarly occupied during the night.

I beg to bring to the special notice of the Lieutenant-General commanding the forces the gallant bearing of Captain Baker, 18th Royal Irish (Deputy Assistant Adjutant-General), during the whole of the operations, but more especially on the occasion already mentioned of the fall of that brave and lamented soldier, Captain Ring.

Also, the determined bravery of Captain Herford, Waikato Militia, who was very severely wounded (loss of eye), and the gallantry of Lieutenant Harrison, Waikato Militia, both of whom remained at the head of the sap nearly the whole time, keeping down the fire of the enemy by the well-directed balls of their own rifles. Likewise of Sergeant McKay, Royal Artillery, who, as before mentioned, under a galling fire, threw, with the greatest precision and coolness, hand grenades from the sap and from the lodgment made in the outer work of the enemy into his stronghold.

The wounded received the greatest possible attention on the field from the senior medical officer, Dr White, 65th Regiment; ably seconded by Assistant-Surgeons Spenser, 18th Royal Irish, Jules, 40th Regiment, and Tilston. R.N., until the arrival of Dr. Mouat, C.B., V.C., the P.M.O., who left nothing undone in providing for their comfort, etc.

I trust the conduct of the officers and men under my command during this long operation of three days and two nights, without cover and constantly under fire, may meet with the approval of the Commander of the Forces.

The casualties on our side—16 killed and 52 wounded, of which I enclose a return—are, I regret to say, severe.

GEORGE J. CAREY,
Brigadier-General.

The Assistant Military Secretary, Headquarters.

WIREMU TAMEHANA.

CHAPTER XXXVI.

Simultaneously with the occupation of the Waikato district by the troops, the preliminary arrangements for the permanent occupation of the country were made. The surveyors followed close on the heels of the military, taking flying surveys of the country around, and fixing upon eligible sites for townships. Oftentimes the survey parties were exposed to great danger, frequently working some miles away from British posts unprotected from the numerous small bands of natives that continued to hover about the neighbourhood of their former homes. It being desirable to ascertain how far beyond Te Rore the Waipa was navigable, Lieutenant Rayner. of the Commissariat Transport Corps, was ordered to proceed up the river in charge of two boats. A number of the enemy being in the vicinity of the river rendered the task a dangerous one. It was, however, successfully performed, the men pulling with muffled oars, and the spot where now stands the township of Alexandra was fixed upon as one of the frontier posts, to be occupied by the Waikato Militia. The telegraph was also pushed rapidly forward: this department was under the supervision of Colonel Gamble, Deputy Quartermaster-General, and was efficiently worked by Lieutenant Burton, Deputy Assistant Quartermaster-General, and his two able assistants, Corporals Brodie and Butcher, of the Royal Engineers. The telegraphists were selected from the men of various regiments, and soon became able operators.

When the natives retreated from their last stronghold at Maungatautari and fell back, it was considered advisable by the Governor, Sir George Grey, that communication should be opened with their leading chief, Wiremu Tamehana (William Thompson). The natives being sullen after their severe defeats. and making no overtures for peace, rendered it a difficult and dangerous task to reach Tamehana, who, with a large number of his followers, was reported to be in the vicinity of Mata Mata. At this time one of the members of the House of Representatives, Mr George Graham, who was well known to Tamehana and many of the Waikato chiefs, came forward and volunteered to go by himself and interview him, with the object of inducing the chief to make peace. The offer of Mr Graham was accepted by the Governor, and although he was strongly advised by many of his friends, amongst whom was the late Bishop Selwyn, not to attempt so hazardous an undertaking, he determined to go, and accordingly started upon his important errand.

The following extract from the "Waikato Handbook" gives an interesting and full account of Mr. George Graham's journey and interview with William Thompson, which resulted in that important chief agreeing to lay down his arms and make peace:—

Going up the Waikato, Mr George Graham stopped a night at the Narrows Redoubt with his son, Mr W. A. Graham, who was at the time engaged survey-

SURRENDER OF WM. THOMPSON, 1865.

ing the town of Hamilton East, and military farm sections surrounding. The next day he went on to Tamahere, where the neutral chief, Te Raihi Toroa a Tai, cousin of Tamehana, and his wife Riria Raihi, with their followers, were residing. After advising Mr Graham to no purpose to return, Raihi and Riria agreed to accompany him. Tamehana at this time was supposed to be across the Maungakawa Mountains at a settlement in the Matamata Valley. The Maungakawa ridges were lined with hostile natives in such force that it was deemed necessary that the troops should stand to their arms from three o'clock a.m. till daylight in anticipation of an attack. The track Mr. Graham had to take to reach Tamehana led across these mountains, necessitating his meeting these armed natives on his way. For some miles after leaving Tamahere the track was over level country, crossing some swamps and creeks till it reached the base of the Maungakawa range. In crossing one of the creeks Mr Graham was ahead and his horse commenced plunging in the mud, which was rather deep. Te Raihi paused at the moment and his horse kicked Mr. Graham severely on the ankle, which commenced to swell and became so painful that he had to dismount. His native companions did their utmost to relieve the pain by applying cold water from the creek. They considered it a bad omen, and asked him to desist from going further, as at the top of the spur they had to pass over was encamped the main body of hostile natives. Mr Graham with great difficulty remounted his horse and pushed on up the hill. On nearing the summit the ground was so steep that Mr Graham had to dismount, but his ankle was so swollen that he could not put his foot to the ground. Riria Raihi came to his assistance, and although Mr Graham was no light weight took him on her back and pikaued him to the top, where he found himself immediately surrounded by armed Kingite natives, one of whom recognised him, having worked in his employ in the building of the old barrack wall at Auckland. He told Mr Graham that they were made aware of his coming by the "Southern Cross" newspaper, which they got the day after issue. They carried him into their camp and treated him with great kindness, sitting up with him all night and pouring from calabashes a continual stream of water on his ankle, using an ointment of their own manufacture, which greatly subdued the pain. They nevertheless requested him not to proceed any further, as his mission was useless. Mr Graham replied that he had made up his mind to see Tamehana, and from him alone would he receive his answer. In the morning he again pushed on, the natives permitting him to pass, no doubt in respect for the motive which actuated him and the determination displayed in coming alone and unarmed into their strongest camp. Nothing further happened till he met Tamehana at his settlement in the Matamata Valley. Here an earnest discussion took place between them, which lasted a day and a night, resulting in the admission of the force of Mr Graham's arguments by Tamehana, who agreed to go with him and make peace. He said, "You have persuaded me, Graham; let us go at once, and do not lose sight of me now or let me go or you will see me no more." At once the horses were saddled, and, although scarcely yet daylight, they started on their return. Passing through the several settlements in silence, Tamehana took

WILLIAM THOMPSON NEGOTIATING WITH GENERAL CAREY. 1865.

no notice of his people's exclamations, and invitation to stop and partake of their food. On arrival at the summit of Maungakawa his armed warriors crowded round him and tried to alter his determination; but he rode through them without saying a word, and commenced the descent into Waikato. On seeing this a number of leading chiefs had their horses brought to them and followed their chief down the hill. Arriving at the foot of the hill, Mr. Graham despatched a letter to his son at the Narrows to send General Carey to meet them at Tamahere. On receipt of the despatch the General and his staff came with all speed to the Narrows and proceeded to Tamahere. In the meantime a hasty preparation was being made by the Tamahere natives to receive their guests. Breakwinds of ti-tree and flax were erected, in the centre of which was hoisted the British ensign. The women were busy cooking everything they could lay their hands on, their limited supplies being supplemented by some flour and sugar from Mr. W. A. Graham's survey camp. At Tamehana's special request the General limited his party to a few officers, amongst whom were Majors Blewett and Brett; Mr Mainwaring, R.M. of Waikato, also was present. Arriving at the settlement where the preparations were being made, some time elapsed without any sign of Tamehana's party, and the General began to get impatient at the delay. However, a messenger arrived from Mr Graham to say that the scouts had returned to Tamehana with a report that the General was bringing an army of soldiers, at which Tamehana was inclined to fly. Word was sent to Mr Graham that such was not the case, only a few principal officers being present. Tamehana still wavered, and his chiefs tried to induce him to return with them; but Mr Graham spoke strongly to Tamehana, saying he had not feared to come alone into his camp, relying on his knowledge of Tamehana, and the Maoris being a brave but not a murdering people; and, further, offered to stay with the party of chiefs as hostage and let Tamehana go on and meet the General. This decided the question, Tamehana saying, "Come on, we will go together; I can trust in you." And the party advanced slowly. All this time messengers from both sides kept coming backwards and forwards. By this means the General was made aware of the near approach of the coming chief. When about half-a-mile distant the General and party walked forward to meet Tamehana. Owing to the luxurious growth of koromiko and flax, fern and other scrub, the parties had reached within 300 yards of each other before coming in view. At a turn of the track they hove in sight, Mr Graham and Tamehana in front, and about sixty chiefs following in Indian file, all mounted. Tamehana, on seeing the General, dismounted, which was a signal for all his party to do the same. Tamehana then came forward, evidently much excited, but with silent dignity, taking off a gold-band cap (which he had accepted from Mr Graham at Matamata, and worn through his tribes on the way in token of his ultimatum decided upon), he advanced to the General, stooped slowly down, and laid his taiaha at the General's feet. This was his surrender. The General picked up the taiaha and held out his hand to the chief, which Tamehana convulsively grasped, the General saying, "Tamehana, by your valiant acts you have proved yourself and people a brave race, and by your coming in to-day and making peace you will have won the goodwill and respect of every man. To make war is often easier than to make peace. You caused your people to go to war; you have now ended it by making peace. Let this be for ever an end to our fighting." Tamehana replied, "I and my tribes will fight no more. The fighting is at an end in Waikato as far as I and my influence go." The General then shook hands with all the chiefs accompanying Tamehana, and the united parties retired, walking to the settlement, and were received by loud welcomes from the natives waiting to receive them, the women waving their shawls and garments, and calling "Haeremai! Haeremai!" etc. Tamehana and the General walked to the place of honour, and Tamehana seated himself under the ensign. Food was then served up, the General and Tamehana eating together. Afterwards it was suggested that some document should be signed by Tamehana, which resulted in a sheet of paper being handed to him, on which he wrote: "I have made peace, as witness my coming into the presence of my antagonist (hoariri) the General. The laws of the Queen shall be the laws of the King. Signed, Wiremu Tamehana Te Waharoa." This important document was written on the fly-leaf of a private letter, no other writing material being obtainable at the time. Major Brett afterwards handed the pen to Mr. Graham to keep in remembrance of the event. Though simple, the effect was the same as if it had been more elaborate, for peace was then made. Tamehana's surrender made the Native King's cause utterly hopeless. The Waikato war was ended, the troops withdrawn, and peaceful settlement there has extended its operations unimpeded to the present day. The General being anxious to return to Te Awamutu that night, the proceedings were brought to a close early. On parting with the General, Tamehana emphatically urged him, unless it came from his own lips, to heed no rumour that any further attack would be made on the positions of Europeans in Waikato. The General accepted his assurances, and he and his party rode away.

CHAPTER XXXVII.

The Waikato tribes had no sooner been dispersed, and their positions captured, than their allies at Tauranga began to menace the troops under Colonel Greer, stationed at Te Papa. On Saturday, April 2nd, a force of 300 or 400 natives made their appearance in front of the British outposts, and opened fire on the sentries. A 12-pounder Armstrong was immediately run forward, and opened fire on the enemy with shell. After a few rounds the natives retired a distance of about three miles to some earthworks they were busily employed in throwing up at a place called Pukehinahina (Gate Pa). The land at this part formed a narrow neck, having a swamp on one side and a river on the other. At this time the natives were not molested, but allowed to continue their defensive works. General Cameron and staff arrived in H.M.S. Esk on Thursday, April 21st, and took command of the forces at Tauranga. The flying column, 300 strong (being detachments from 12th, 40th, 65th, and 14th Regiments), under Major Ryan, 70th, also arrived.

A tribe of friendly natives, the Arawas, residing at Maketu, a few miles along the coast south of Tauranga, having been threatened by a neighbouring hostile tribe (Ngatiporou), Major Colville, with a detachment of the 43rd Light Infantry and Waikato Militia, was despatched from Tauranga to their assistance. An ambuscade having been laid by the enemy about two miles from the fort on the river bank, near Waihi, Major Colville, Ensign Way of the Waikato Militia, and Private Key, 43rd, who were in a canoe, had a miraculous escape. Whilst paddling across the river the natives opened fire at a distance of about fifty yards, but without effect. Quickly paddling to the bank, Major Colville and his companions jumped ashore and made for the bank, followed by a yelling crowd of Maoris, who had crossed the stream in pursuit. Under cover of the bush, Major Colville's party got safely back to camp. Major Colville at once returned with a party of 50 men under Captain Smith, 43rd Light Infantry, to attack the natives who had crossed the river, but upon arrival found that they had recrossed and lined the opposite bank in force, and at once opened fire on Captain Smith's men, who briskly replied, the range across the river being about 400 yards. A reinforcement, consisting of 30 men under Captain Harris, 43rd, and Ensign Way, 3rd Waikatos, with 14 men of the Forest Rangers under Major Drummond Hay and Captain MacDonnell, and a number of the Arawas, having arrived, Major Hay was ordered to cross the river with the Rangers and Arawas. This was done, but the Arawas refusing to advance on the enemy, the party were compelled to return. At dusk the troops retired, Major Colville leaving a strong force of Arawas to guard the crossing-place at Waihi, and watch the movements of the enemy.

Casualties on the part of the troops—Captain MacDonnell and four privates, wounded. The enemy's loss could not be ascertained.

K

The following is the official report:—

Fort Maketu, April 21, 1864.

Sir,—I have the honour to report to you an engagement with the East Coast natives at Waihi, two miles from the fort at Maketu, in which about 110 men of the force under my command were engaged.

An ambuscade was laid near the fort at Waihi this morning, and at least 50 rebels opened fire on Ensign Way (3rd Waikato Regiment), Private Key (43rd Light Infantry), and myself, when we were crossing the river at 10 a.m. in a canoe.

The rebels were certainly not above 50 yards distant at the time, and I consider our escape as most providential and wonderful. They pursued us across the ford on our jumping out of the canoe into the water, and followed us, yelling and firing, till we got into the bush and escaped.

On arrival at the fort I immediately ordered out a party of 50 men of the 43rd Light Infantry and 3rd Waikato Regiments under the command of Captain Smith, 43rd Light Infantry, to drive the enemy across the ford. We found on arrival that the enemy had re-crossed the river, and had established themselves about 400 yards distant on that side, and kept up a constant fire from the sandhills and bush around, which we returned with interest.

Finding the enemy mustering strong, I sent for a further reinforcement of 30 men, under the command of Captain Harris (43rd Light Infantry) and Ensign Way (3rd Waikatos). Major Drummond Hay and Captain MacDonnell also arrived with the Forest Rangers (14 men), and a number of the friendly Arawa tribe also joined. I requested Major Hay to cross the river with his Rangers and all the native allies.

This he did, but as very few of the natives would follow him, he was reluctantly compelled to retire, after remaining engaged for some time.

My orders are so very stringent not to go far from the settlement of Maketu, that I was compelled to content myself with lining the side of the river and firing at 400 yards and more at the rebels.

The East Coast natives, apparently 300 strong, are now concentrating themselves at the position they occupied to-day, and I hear they are receiving further reinforcements. I have therefore requested Major Hay to attack them across the river in the morning if he can induce the native allies to follow him.

At dusk I withdrew my men and returned to the fort, leaving a strong party of natives to protect the village of Waihi and give the alarm in the event of any rebels coming on.

My best thanks are due to Captains Smith and Honourable A. E. Harris, 43rd Light Infantry, for the able manner they led their companies into action. Also to Ensign Way, commanding the detachment of 3rd Waikatos.

I have the honour to announce the list of wounded (four privates), which I am glad to say is but small, considering we were under fire for between six and seven hours. Besides the enclosed, Captain MacDonnell, of the Forest Rangers, was slightly wounded in the hand.

I consider I am strong enough to hold the settlement provided more ammunition is sent me as soon as possible, as I expect to be engaged again to-morrow.

From the nature of the country, and from our being unable to cross the river, it is impossible to estimate the loss of the enemy. They were, however, seen carrying off killed or wounded men on several occasions during the day.— I have, etc.,

J. M. COLVILLE,
Major 43rd L.I., commanding at Maketu.

The next day, according to instructions from Major Colville, Major Hay advanced towards the enemy's position with Captain MacDonnell's Forest Rangers and a force of friendly natives. The enemy were found in considerable force, and after a few hours' desultory firing, Major Hay retired. That night the enemy crossed the river. The friendly native picket posted to give the alarm failed to do so, and the next morning some 600 natives were entrenching themselves in front of Fort Colville, the British post at Maketu, and commenced sapping towards the redoubt.

On the morning of the 26th H.M.S. Falcon, accompanied by the gunboat Sandfly, Captain Marks, having on board Captain Jenkins, of H.M.S. Miranda, arrived off Maketu to relieve the beleaguered troops in Fort Colville. The Falcon anchored on the western side of Maketu, about 1200 yards from the enemy's position, and, swinging broadside on, commenced shelling the native earthworks, driving the enemy out on to the beach. Major Colville immediately left the redoubt and seized the works. The natives, unable to retire inland owing to the formation of the country, were compelled to retreat along the beach, and as they ran along the shore were followed by the gunboat Sandfly, which kept dropping every now and then a shell amongst them from the two Armstrong guns which she had on board. After retreating some miles the natives took up a position in an old pa, but the Falcon coming up, commenced firing into them, one shell bursting in the middle of about 30 natives, making sad havoc, and driving them away inland. The Falcon and Sandfly having cleared the coast, returned to Tauranga. The same evening the seamen belonging to H.M.S. Miranda, Esk, and Harrier were landed at Te Papa, to take part in the operations against the enemy's position at Gate Pa.

CHAPTER XXXVIII.

General Cameron having completed his dispositions for attacking the Maori position at Gate Pa, the 29th of April, 1864, was the day fixed upon for the assault which ended so disastrously to the British troops. On the night of the 28th, Colonel Greer, with the 68th Regiment—who carried one day's cooked rations and a greatcoat—marched from the headquarter camp, which was situated about 1,200 yards in front of the enemy's works, round to the rear of the enemy, so as to prevent his escape. Mr. Purvis acted as guide, and under cover of a feigned attack on the front of the pah, the movement was successfully performed, the 68th being in their assigned position by 2 o'clock on the morning of the 29th. At the time it was dark and raining, and the natives could be plainly heard shouting in their works—evidently unconscious that the 68th were posted in their rear. Before daylight Colonel Gamble, with a detachment of the Naval Brigade under Lieutenant Hotham, joined the 68th, leaving the detachment as a reinforcement for Colonel Greer. Colonel Gamble returned alone in safety to the headquarters camp.

Shortly after daybreak the artillery posted in front of the enemy's position —consisting of one 110-pounder Armstrong, two 40-pounder Armstrongs, two 6-pounder Armstrongs, two 24-pounder howitzers, two 8inch mortars, and six cohorn mortars: total, 15 pieces of ordnance—opened fire on the left of the enemy's works. The guns were manned by detachments of the Naval Brigade and Royal Artillery.

At 12 o'clock—the fire on the works having been kept up since it commenced—a breach was made in the left angle of the stockading which was erected in front of the enemy's rifle-pits. At this time the natives made an attempt to escape, but were driven back by the 68th, who were extended across the rear of the pa. The fire of the artillery was at times rather wild, many of the shells passing far over the enemy's works and endangering the men of the 68th, several of whom were slightly wounded from fragments of the bursting shells. The two 24-pounder howitzers (in charge of Captain Smith, R.A.) were well served, and contributed largely to making the breach in the enemy's works. The shells directed at the Maori flagstaff did no damage, owing to the fact of the staff being erected in rear of the pa instead of in the centre, as was at first supposed.

At 4 o'clock, the breach being large enough, a rocket was sent up as a signal for the assault. The storming party—consisting of the Naval Brigade and 43rd Regiment; in all about 300 men—were led by Commander Hay, of H.M.S. Harrier, and Colonel Booth, 43rd Regiment. The storming party (four abreast—two soldiers and two sailors), upon the signal for the assault, at once, with hurrahs and cheers, rushed at the double into the breach, under a heavy fire from the natives. At the same time the 68th Regiment, answering the cheers of the storming party, moved up closer to the rear of the pa, and at once opened fire. In a few minutes, the storming party, gallantly led by their officers, were in the centre of the pa, the natives falling back before their advance, and attempting to escape by the rear, were driven back by the tremendous fire that the 68th opened on them. The rifle-pits in the pa were mostly covered over with ti-tree and earth, and formed a network of concealed passages, the roof being raised a few inches above the parapet, so as to enable the natives to fire out on their assailants. In entering the breach the storming party lost most of their officers, who were shot down whilst cheering on their men. When the defenders of the pa were driven back by the 68th—the fire of which must no doubt have struck both friend and foe— the storming party, soldiers and sailors, without leaders and owing to the formation in which they entered the breach, mixed together, appeared at a loss to know what to do.

At this critical moment, instead of occupying the trenches which the natives abandoned, the stormers wavered. As the natives swarmed back into their works, some one, it is said, shouted out, "Retire! Retire!" but whether such was the case or not, the stormers at once, in a confused crowd, retreated. The natives having regained their pits, at once opened a murderous fire on the men pouring out of the pa. The reserves under Captain Hamilton arriving, endeavoured to rally and stem the retreating party. Captain Hamilton, R.N., rushing forward, had no sooner reached the second trench than he fell dead; and the whole force—storming party and reserves—hurriedly fell back to the nearest cover they could find outside the pa. Having rallied his men, General Cameron before dark took up a position about 100 yards from the pa and threw up a breastwork. Captain Jenkins, of H.M.S. Miranda, who led the supports—an officer of small stature—had a miraculous escape, he being at one time actually in one of the enemy's rifle-pits by himself, not being aware that his men had retired.

The natives, during the early part of the night, which was pitch dark, made a great noise, shouting to the troops to come on. At midnight they were silent, and Major Greaves, D.A.Q.M.G., creeping up to the works, believed the natives had gone. At 5 a.m. a sailor belonging to H.M.S. Harrier entered the pa, and reported that it was deserted. The troops at once advanced and took possession of the abandoned earthworks which the natives had left during the night, escaping in the darkness through the spaces left in the lines of the 68th Regiment.

When the troops took possession of the pa a sad spectacle presented itself. A correspondent who entered the pa the morning after the assault thus describes the scene:—"Three men of the 43rd Light Infantry were lying dead against the inner paling of the front face. On entering the pa, within a space of a few yards, the bodies of four captains of the 43rd were lying; and further on, in line with the others, Colonel Booth, of the same regiment, was leaning against the rear paling of the pa mortally wounded; officers of the ships of war were lying stark dead in the same line of trenches. As they lay alone they must have been in advance of their men, and fell nobly in the execution of their duty. Captain Hamilton, of H.M.S. Esk, and Captain Muir, of the 43rd, lay in the second trench of the pa, opposite the beach.

They fell, leading on their men. Captain Hamilton, of the 43rd, was lying against the fence, and breathed a moment after he was found. He had been mortally wounded, and having been left in the pa, lay there neglected amongst the enemy all night. Close by him were the bodies of Captain Utterton, of the 43rd, and Captain Glover of the same regiment. In the centre rifle-pit of the pa lay the body of Lieutenant Hill, of H.M.S. Curacoa, who was the senior officer saved from the wreck of the Orpheus on the Manukau bar. Poor Hill was shot through both cheeks and through the centre of his neck. He had lived long enough to bind up the wound in his face, for he had his pocket handkerchief tied around his head, covering the face-wound, when his body was found.. Colonel Booth was mortally wounded in the spine, but was able to speak when relieved from his perilous position. The dead body of a sailor lay in the second trench. There were several tomahawk cuts across the face, and the head was split in two by a tomahawk blow, the contents of the skull being cleared entirely out. The gunner of H.M.S. Miranda (Mr Watt) had his head severed from the crown to the lower jaw with one cut of a tomahawk—the cut passed right down through the centre of the nose. Captain Hamilton, of the Esk, lay dead with a gunshot wound in his temple, through which the brains were protruding. The bodies were not stripped or injured; they lay as they fell, and the tomahawk wounds were inflicted during the first encounter when the stormers entered. The watches, rings, money, and clothing of our dead were untouched. This was the finest act of the enemy during the struggle. No one expected it. No one could believe that exultant rebels would not satiate their passion for revenge by mutilating the helpless bodies, but thank God, it was not so. They had, it appears, made a law not to hurt the wounded or mutilate the dead that fell into their hands, and they kept their agreement. The dead and wounded were removed. The wounded Maoris were taken on stretchers into camp and attended to; one died the same night. Rewiti was wounded in seven places by bullets and had his legs broken. Others had severe gunshot wounds; one Maori had been cut in two by a shell, and the head, trunk and extremities were carefully gathered and placed in line with the remaining dead in front of the pa. Another native had his skull cloven by a blow of a cutlass given by the black sailor of the Miranda, who had already done good service during the war. Poor fellow, he fell dead in turn in the pa."

Colonel Booth, Commander Hay, Captain Hamilton, and Lieutenant Glover expired shortly after of their wounds, and were buried alongside their comrades in the Tauranga burial ground on the cliff overlooking the harbour.

Samuel Mitchell, captain of the foretop of H.M.S. Harrier, was recommended to the Admiralty for the Victoria Cross for bravely bringing Commander Hay, who was severely wounded, out of the pa.

Mr. Watt, gunner of H.M.S. Miranda, who was killed, had, before his death, cut down with his sword the native who shot Captain Hamilton, of H.M.s. Esk. One seaman belonging to the Curacoa ran after and bayoneted a native outside the pa in front of the 68th Regiment; whilst returning to his messmates he was shot dead.

The casualties on the part of the British were unusually severe, especially in officers, the 43rd Regiment alone losing their colonel, four captains, and one lieutenant killed, and one lieutenant and two ensigns severely wounded. Lieutenant Glover was shot whilst endeavouring to recover the dead body of his brother, Captain Glover. The Naval Brigade had nearly all their officers shot down. Most of the non-commissioned officers and privates who were killed and wounded fell outside the pa whilst rushing to the assault and when retiring. The total casualties amounted to 10 officers killed and 4 wounded; non-commissioned officers and privates killed 21, wounded 76; total killed and wounded, 111 officers and men.

OFFICIAL RETURN OF OFFICERS KILLED AND WOUNDED.
NAVAL BRIGADE.
Killed.

Captain Hamilton, H.M.s. Esk; Lieutenant Hill (late of Orpheus), H.M.s. Curacoa; Mr. Watts, gunner, H.M.s. Miranda.

Wounded.—Commander Hay (abdomen, mortally), H.M.s. Harrier; Lieutenant Hammick (shoulder, severe), H.M.s. Miranda; Lieutenant Duff (back, two places, severe), H.M.s. Esk.

43rd REGIMENT.
Killed.

Captain R. C. Glover (head); Captain C. R. Muir (tomahawk, right axilla); Captain R. T. Hamilton (head); Captain Edwin Utterton (neck); Lieutenant C. J. Langlands (chest).

Wounded.—Lieutenant Colonel Booth (spine and right arm, mortally); Lieutenant T. G. E. Glover (abdomen, mortally); Ensign W. Clark (right arm, severe); Ensign S. P. T. Nicholl (scalp, slight).

The natives who so bravely defended the Gate Pa belonged to Tauranga, of the Ngaiterangi tribe, and numbered about 400 men. The loss the natives sustained could not be exactly ascertained, but as they acknowledged to having over 30 men killed, if their casualties are put down at 60 killed and wounded, it will be not far out. Amongst the killed were several chiefs of note. One native taken prisoner belonged to the Bay of Islands, named Niko, of the Ngapuhi tribe.

General Cameron having sent word to the natives that they had his permission to come and bury their slain, twenty of the enemy arrived as a burial party. Mr. H. E. Rice, of the Native Office, attached to the General's staff as Interpreter, ably conducted what correspondence was required by the General with the natives. The burial party having collected their dead bodies, laid the common men in a row, and the chiefs and more important personages across their stomachs, and then covered them with earth. This was done in accordance with an old Maori saying, "Kati ano ia kia mate hei whariki ano aku rangatira"—it is well (or proper) that he should die to be a couch for my chiefs. The bodies of the leading chiefs who had been killed had been taken away when the natives retreated from the pa.

The official dispatch of General Cameron is as follows:—

Headquarters, Tauranga, May 5, 1864.

Sir,—It having been decided by your Excellency and myself, in consequence of information received from Colonel Greer, commanding at Tauranga, that reinforcements should be sent to that station, detachments were embarked without delay in H.M. ships Esk and Falcon, placed at my disposal by Commodore Sir William Wiseman, and by the 26th April all were landed at the mission station, Tauranga, to which place I had transferred my headquarters on the 21st April.

On the 27th April, I moved the 68th Regiment, under Colonel Greer, and a mixed detachment of 170 men under Major Ryan, 70th Regiment, towards the rebel entrenchments, of which I made a close reconnaissance.

It was constructed on a neck of land about 500 yards wide, the slopes of which fell off into a swamp on either side. On the highest point of this neck they had constructed an oblong redoubt, well palisaded, and surrounded by a post and rail fence—a formidable obstacle to an assaulting column, and difficult to destroy with artillery. The intervals between the side fences of the redoubt and the swamps were defended by an entrenched line of rifle-pits.

I encamped the 68th Regiment and Major Ryan's detachment about 1,200 yards from the enemy's position on the 27th, and on that and on the following day the guns and mortars intended to breach the position were brought up to camp, which was joined by a large force of sailors and marines, landed at my request from the ships of the squadron by Commodore Sir William Wiseman.

Having received information that, by moving along the beach of one of the branches of Tauranga harbour at low water, it was possible for a body of troops to pass outside the swamp on the enemy's right, and gain the rear of his position, I ordered Colonel Greer to make the attempt with the 68th Regiment, after dark, on the evening of the 28th, and, in order to divert the attention of the enemy from that side, I ordered a feigned attack to be made in his front.

Colonel Greer's movement succeeded perfectly, and on the morning of the 29th he had taken up a position in rear of the enemy, which cut off his supply of water, and made his retreat in daylight impossible, but was necessarily too extended to prevent his escape by night.

During the same night the guns and mortars were placed in position, and opened fire soon after daybreak on the morning of the 29th. I gave directions that their fire should be directed principally against the left angle of the centre work, which, from the nature of the ground, I considered the most favourable part to attack.

Their practice was excellent, particularly that of the howitzers, and reflects great credit on the officers in command of batteries.

About 12 o'clock, the swamp on the enemy's left having been reported by Captain Greaves, Deputy Assistant Quartermaster-General, practicable for the passage of a gun, a six-pounder Armstrong gun was taken across to the high ground on the opposite side, from which its fire completely enfiladed the left of the enemy's position, which he was thus compelled to abandon. The fire of the guns, howitzers, and mortars was continued with short intermissions until 4 p.m., when, a large portion of the fence and palisading having been destroyed, and a practicable breach made in the parapet, I ordered the assault.

150 seamen and marines, under Commander Hay, of H.M.S. Harrier, and an equal number of the 43rd Regiment, under Lieutenant-Colonel Booth, formed the assaulting party.

Major Ryan's detachment was extended as close to the work as possible, to keep down the fire from the rifle-pits, with orders to follow the assaulting column.

The remainder of the seamen and marines, and of the 43rd Regiment, amounting together to 300 men, followed as a reserve.

The assaulting column, protected by the nature of the ground, gained the breach with little loss, and effected an entrance into the main body of the work, when a fierce conflict ensued, in which the natives fought with the greatest desperation. Lieutenant-Colonel Booth and Commander Hay, who led into the work, fell mortally wounded. Captain Hamilton was shot dead on the top of the parapet while in the act of encouraging his men to advance, and in a few minutes nearly every officer of the column was either killed or wounded. Up to this moment the men, so nobly led by their officers, fought gallantly, and appeared to have carried the position, when they suddenly gave way and fell back from the work to the nearest cover. This repulse I am at a loss to explain, otherwise than by attributing it to the confusion created among the men by the intricate nature of the interior defences, and the sudden fall of so many of their officers.

On my arrival at the spot I considered it inadvisable to renew the assault, and directed a line of entrenchment to be thrown up within one hundred yards of the work, so as to be able to maintain our advanced position, intending to resume operations the following morning.

The natives, availing themselves of the extreme darkness of the night, abandoned the work, leaving some of their killed and wounded behind.

On taking possession of the work in the morning, Lieutenant-Colonel Booth and some men were found still living, and, to the credit of the natives, had not been maltreated; nor had any bodies of the killed been mutilated. I enclose a list of our casualties.

I deeply regret the loss of many brave and valuable officers who fell in the noble discharge of their duty on this occasion.

The 43rd Regiment and the service have sustained a serious loss in the death of Lieutenant-Colonel Booth, which took place on the night after the attack. I have already mentioned the brilliant example shown by this officer in the assault; and when I met him on the following morning, as he was being carried out of the work, his first words were an expression of regret that he had found it impossible to carry out my orders.

The heroism and devotion of Captain Hamilton and Commander Hay reflect the highest credit on the naval service.

The loss of the enemy must have been very heavy, although not more than twenty bodies were found in and about their position. It is admitted by the

THE WAIKATO WAR.

prisoners that they carried off a large number of killed and wounded during the night, and they also suffered in attempting to make their escape, as described in Colonel Greer's report.

In my reports to his Royal Highness the Field Marshal Commanding in Chief and the Right Honourable the Secretary of State for War, I have brought to their favourable notice the names of the officers who particularly distinguished themselves on this occasion.

Commodore Sir William Wiseman on this, as on every other occasion, co-operated with me in the most cordial manner, and I am much indebted to him as well as to the whole Royal Navy and Marines who took part in these operations, for their valuable assistance.—I have, etc.,

D. A. CAMERON, Lieutenant-General.

His Excellency Sir George Grey, K.C.B.

CHAPTER XXXIX.

In a few days nearly all traces of the struggle that had taken place at the Gate Pa were obliterated, the native trenches had been filled in, and a strong redoubt was thrown up which effectually prevented the enemy from making any advance from the interior on Te Papa, if they had been so inclined. From information received, Colonel Greer, with several companies of the 68th Regiment, together with the Colonial Defence Force, which corps had arrived at Tauranga a few days before, left headquarters camp at daybreak on the morning of 12th of May, and marched in the direction of the Wairoa, distant about eight miles. The route led the troops across an open country intersected with hills and dales, the land being rich and fertile. One creek had to be crossed, the water reaching to the men's waists. No natives were seen during the march, but when near Wairoa it was found that the Maoris had thrown up a strong line of rifle-pits. The Defence Force, in command of Captain Pye, were at once ordered forward to reconnoitre, and returned with the intelligence that the enemy's works were deserted. The troops at once moved forward and took possession of the position, which was on rising ground surrounded by trees, with a fresh-water stream running round its base. In the vicinity was a corn water-mill and extensive cultivations of potatoes, corn, pumpkins and melons. Leaving a detachment of 150 men to hold possession of the place, Colonel Greer, with his force, returned to camp. The next day the post was visited by His Excellency the Governor, who had arrived at Tauranga. He was accompanied by General Cameron and staff. After being held for a few days, the garrison at the Wairoa was withdrawn. On May 15 the Governor had a meeting with a large number of friendly natives. His Excellency expressed a desire for the two races to be at peace, and promised generous treatment to the natives in arms in case of surrender. The friendly natives promised to try and persuade the Ngaiterangi and other tribes fighting against the troops to give up their arms and surrender. The same evening Sir George Grey embarked on board the gunboat Sandfly, Captain Marks, and steamed at once for Auckland. The following day General Cameron and staff left Tauranga for Auckland in H.M.S. Esk. The Miranda and Falcon, with a portion of the Artillery and troops, also steamed for Auckland, leaving H.M.S. Harrier as a guard ship in Tauranga harbour. The sudden departure of the Governor, General Cameron, and a portion of the troops was on account of dispatches received respecting the attitude of the natives on the West Coast at Whanganui.

At this time the Arawas and a few Europeans, under the command of Major Drummond Hay and the Arawa chief Winiata, attacked and defeated at Te Awa Te Atua, near Maketu, the Ngatiporou, who suffered a loss of about 100 killed and wounded. In this engagement the Arawa chief Winiata was killed whilst leading on his men.

The month of May passed away quietly both in the Waikato and Tauranga districts. Colonel Greer was left in command at Tauranga, and in place of some of the troops which had been withdrawn a reinforcement of 280 of the 1st Waikato Militia arrived from Auckland. June arrived, and Colonel Greer received information that the Ngaiterangi were again collecting in force to attack the troops. On the morning of June 21, Colonel Greer, whilst reconnoitring the country in his front, came upon a large number of natives busily engaged entrenching themselves about four miles beyond the Gate Pa at Te Ranga. The force, under Colonel Greer, consisted of detachments of the 68th, 43rd, and 1st Waikato Militia—in all, about 600 men. The Maoris were estimated at about the same strength. A line of sentries in front of the native position was at once attacked by a party of skirmishers thrown forward by Colonel Greer, and driven back under shelter of their works. Colonel Greer having sent back to the camp for an Armstrong gun and 220 men, extended his men in front of the Maori position, and kept up a sharp fire on the natives, who vigorously replied. After the fusillade had been kept up for about two hours, the gun and reinforcement had arrived within a short distance of the attacking party. The troops, who had been with great difficulty restrained from rushing on the Maoris, now received the order to attack. The bugle sounded the advance, which was answered by the troops with loud cheers. The 43rd were burning to avenge the death of their comrades at the Gate Pa, and to wipe away the stain which had sullied the glorious laurels gained by the regiment in bloody battles long since fought in the Peninsula and on the burning plains of India. Before the last sound of the bugle had died away, the 43rd, 68th, and 1st Waikato Militia charged. A tremendous fire was poured by the natives upon the rapidly advancing line, but few casualties occurred, the fire of the natives being too high. Before the natives, numbers of whom fled after the first discharge, had time to reload, the troops were in the rifle pits, and a short but desperate struggle ensued. The natives, using their tomahawks and guns, fought with the greatest determination, but they were unable to resist the torrent of steel that swept upon them like a wave. From the time the bugles sounded the charge until the cheers of the soldiers denoted that they had carried the enemy's works was only a few minutes. The natives who had effected their escape were pursued for several miles by the Defence Force, who sabred many of the enemy. Numbers, however, escaped across gullies and swamps, where they could not be pursued. Most of the natives killed were bayonetted; sixty-eight bodies lay dead in the rifle pits, the flower of the Ngaiterangi tribe—they had dug their own graves.

The loss of the natives altogether was about 120 killed and thirty-seven wounded and taken prisoners. Several natives, however, doubtless perished in the swamps and gullies whilst retreating. Rawiri, a leading chief of the natives, was amongst the slain, also Pauri Tuaia, one of the leaders at the Gate Pa, Poihipi, a chief of the Whakatohea tribe, Bay of Plenty, and several other men of note. The casualties on the part of the troops consisted of thirteen non-commissioned officers and privates killed, and six officers and thirty-three non-commissioned officers and privates wounded—total killed and wounded, fifty-two. Officers wounded, 43rd: Captains F. H. Smith and H. Bernards; 68th: Captains H. W. J. Trench and T. Casement, Lieutenant H. J. R. V. Stuart, and Ensign W. H. F. Palmer. Captain Smith, 43rd Regiment, who led the line on the right, was wounded in two places, and was recommended for the Victoria Cross. Sergeant Murray, of the 68th Regiment, was also recommended for the Victoria Cross for saving the life of Corporal J. Bryne, V.C., 68th Regiment. Corporal Bryne had passed his bayonet through a native, who at once seized the bayonet with one hand and was about to tomahawk Corporal Bryne with the other, when he was killed by Sergeant Murray. Private John Smith, 68th Regiment, bayonetted a native, and before he could recover, his antagonist dealt him two severe wounds on the head with his tomahawk. Smith also had a gunshot wound in his left leg.

The behaviour of the 1st Waikato Militia was excellent, the men rushing to the charge led by Captain Moore with the greatest dash and enthusiasm.

A strong force of natives who had been hovering some distance in the rear of the rifle pits, instead of supporting their unfortunate brethren, retreated directly the rifle pits were carried by the troops.

The following is the official dispatch:—

Camp Te Papa, Tauranga,
June 21, 1864.

Sir,—I have the honour to report, for the information of the Lieutenant-General Commanding, that I marched out of camp with the following force, viz., three field officers, nine captains, fourteen subalterns, twenty-four sergeants, thirteen buglers, 531 rank and file, this morning at 8 a.m. I found a large force of Maoris (about 600) entrenching themselves about four miles beyond Pukehinahina (Gate Pa). They had made a single line of rifle pits of the usual form across the road, in a position exactly similar to Pukehinahina—the commencement of a formidable pa. Having driven in some skirmishers they had thrown out, I extended the 43rd and a portion of the 68th on their flanks as far as practicable, and kept up a sharp fire for about two hours, while I sent back for reinforcements, viz., one gun, 220 men. As soon as they were sufficiently near to support, I sounded the advance, when the 43rd, 68th, and 1st Waikatos charged, and carried the rifle pits in the most dashing manner, under a tremendous fire, but which was for the most part too high. For a few minutes the Maoris fought desperately, and then were utterly routed—sixty-eight men killed in the rifle pits. (The position was very favourable for their retreat, otherwise few could have escaped). The Defence Force pursued them several miles, but could not get well at them owing to the deep ravines with which the country is everywhere intersected. The majority pursued as long as they could keep the Maoris in sight. All did their duty gallantly. The 43rd were under the command of Major Synge, whose horse was shot; the 68th, under Major Shuttleworth; the 1st Waikato Militia under Captain Moore, and they each led their men well. It is impossible for me in this hurried report to do justice. I will therefore have the pleasure, in a supplemental report, to bring those to your notice who more particularly distinguished themselves.

I marched the men back to camp this morning. 107 Maoris were found, and carried up to the rifle pits, and we have brought in twenty-seven wounded and ten prisoners. Many more must have been killed in the ravines, whom we did not find. I enclose a return of killed and wounded, viz., 43rd Light Infantry: Killed, five men; wounded, two officers, thirteen men. 68th Light Infantry: Killed, eight men; wounded, four officers, two sergeants, eighteen men. Total, fifty-two killed and wounded.

I must not conclude without remarking on the gallant stand made by the Maoris at the rifle pits. They stood the charge without flinching, and did not retire until forced out at the point of the bayonet.

The name of the position which the Maoris occupied is Te Ranga.

I have thought this of sufficient importance to request Captain Phillimore to take my report up in the Esk.—I have, etc.,

H. H. GREER,
Colonel Commanding Tauranga District.

The Deputy Quarter-Master-General.

CHAPTER XL.

The capture of the Maori position at Te Ranga was the closing scene in connection with the Waikato War. The Ngaiterangi tribe surrendered unconditionally, and Sir George Grey promised them that not more than one-fourth of their lands should be confiscated.

It having been deemed advisable not to penetrate further into the interior of the country, the boundary marking the confiscated territory was drawn outside the posts already in the occupation of the military, and the troops were ordered into winter quarters. Along the frontier in the Waikato, redoubts were thrown up and strongly garrisoned, for although the Tauranga natives and Wiremu Thompson's tribe had surrendered, the Maori King Potatau II., with the chief Rewi and his Ngatimaniapoto tribe, still assumed a hostile attitude across the Puniu River—the confiscated boundary—but without powerful aid from their southern neighbours they were too weak to attack the troops with any chance of success. Te Awamutu, where but one short year before Rewi incited his men to destroy the Government Printing Establishment and Press, was the spot fixed upon for the headquarters of the military in the Waikato.

A wooden township of considerable size soon sprang into existence, and the bandsmen of the regiments having once again obtained their instruments, the hills and dales of the Waikato resounded with the inspiring strains of martial music. To relieve the ennui of garrison life a rough theatre was erected, where some capital amateur performances were given. These entertainments were graced by the presence of the fair sex, many of the officers having been joined by their wives. Balls and concerts were of frequent occurrence, and the races, under the able direction of Captain Baker, of the 18th Royal Irish, became an institution.

At Te Awamutu was the military prison, the triangles and cat-o'-nine-tails being often in request. As the winter passed away the regular troops were gradually withdrawn, and their posts occupied by the Waikato Militia, the different regiments being located in the districts where it was decided they should receive their land and serve the remainder of their military term, according to the conditions under which they had enlisted. The 1st Regiment of Waikato Militia, under Colonel Harrington, were located at Tauranga; the 2nd Regiment, under Colonel Haultain, at Alexandra; the 3rd Regiment, under Colonel Lyons, at Cambridge; and the 4th Regiment, under Colonel Moule, at Hamilton. The Forest Rangers had their land apportioned to them at Harapipi and Kihikihi. The Defence Force, who did good service during the war, were not allotted any land. This corps was raised before the Waikato Militia, but on the formation of those regiments a verbal promise was made to the men of the Defence Force that they should have the same land privilege as the military settlers. No record having been made of the promise it was afterwards ignored. At the present time the old members of the Defence

Force are petitioning the New Zealand Parliament to inquire into their longstanding grievance.

In recognition of the services performed by the forces, a vote of thanks was passed by both Houses of the New Zealand Legislature to General Cameron and the troops under his command; also to Sir William Wiseman and the naval forces who operated with the troops; to General Galloway and the colonial forces, for their gallantry in the field. General Cameron was made a K.C.B., and upon leaving Auckland for England was presented by the citizens with a very handsome sword, as a token of their appreciation of the services that he had rendered the colony at large, and the Auckland province in particular.

After the assault on the Gate Pa a newspaper published in Auckland, called the "New Zealander," in commenting upon the affair, accused the men belonging to the Naval Brigade of cowardice in deserting their officers and leaving them in the pa. The men forming the brigade having rejoined their several vessels, arrived in Auckland and demanded from the editor an apology, which was refused. A few days afterwards about 200 sailors, having obtained leave, assembled in front of the newspaper office, which was situated at the top of Shortland-street, and again demanded an apology, which was refused a second time. The men then declared their intention of pulling the edifice to the ground, for which purpose they had brought the necessary ropes and tackle. A number of sailors, entering the building, proceeded to carry their threat into execution. Ropes were passed through the upstairs windows, the purchase tackle rigged, and all made ready, when the newspaper people, seeing affairs looking so serious, agreed to apologise, which they did, and saved their establishment from instant demolition.

Referring to the engagement at the Gate Pa. Dr. Manly, of the Royal Artillery, was stated to have been the last to leave the enemy's works. He was so busily engaged in one of the trenches, binding up the broken arm of a soldier who was wounded, that he did not observe the assaulting column retiring. As soon as he discovered his dilemma he hastily ran out of the pa, and succeeded in reaching the British lines in safety.

Captain Jenkins, of H.M.S. Miranda, who in the attack on the Gate Pa found himself alone in a part of the enemy's works, was so situated on account of chasing a native up one of the trenches, which were constructed in zigzag fashion. Captain Jenkins, finding that he could not overtake the native, threw at him a telescope which he had in his hand just as the native was about to disappear round a corner of the trench. The telescope was afterwards discovered amongst the debris of the pa by Mr. Rice, interpreter to the forces, and forwarded home to its owner, who duly acknowledged the receipt thereof.

The following anecdote, in which Captain Jenkins was a principal actor, will not be amiss:—During the war, when H.M.s. Miranda was anchored in the Manukau. Captain Jenkins, coming on shore, went into the private parlour of the Royal Hotel, then kept by Mr. Hallimore, for some refreshment. Upon looking round he discovered one of the Onehunga Naval Volunteers lying stretched on the sofa, breathing heavily. Such a state of things was of course infra dig. in the presence of one of Her Majesty's naval officers, so the gallant captain at once stepped over to the sleeper and shook him rather roughly.

Christy, the name of the sleeper, after a few growls, uncoiled six feet of humanity and stood before Captain Jenkins, who, looking up fiercely at him, ordered him to leave the room. Instead of obeying this order, Christy, who had been imbibing, saluted the astonished captain with a tremendous volley of adjectives, that would have annihilated any officer but the one in question. Captain Jenkins, becoming excited, placed his hand on his sword hilt, but before he could draw it Christy darted forth a hand as large as a shoulder of mutton, and, grasping the handle, whipped it out of the scabbard and flourished it over the head of the astonished captain, and, in anything but choice language, threatened to cut off the owner's head, and so deprive Her Majesty of the services of a valuable officer for ever. At this juncture Captain Jenkins, seeing that affairs were looking serious, requested Christy to put down the sword and have a drink. This happy thought ended the dilemma in which Captain Jenkins found himself placed. Christy accepted the invitation, and, throwing the gallant Captain his cheese-knife, as Christy called it, drank to his health and prosperity in a glass of brandy. Many incidents that occurred during the war might be enumerated, but they would fill a volume of themselves.

The number of troops engaged in the Waikato War, amounting altogether to about 15,000, has been deemed by many as out of all proportion to the number required; but when the disturbed state of the country at that time is taken into consideration, the above number of troops was necessary to secure the protection of the settlers and to assert the supremacy of the Queen. The fact of so many soldiers being in the country deterred a number of native tribes from open hostility, and the power of the British, which had hitherto been but imperfectly understood, was made patent to all the tribes, both friendly and disaffected. The allegiance of the friendly tribes was strengthened, and the disaffected, to a great extent, deterred from overt acts—the Queen was acknowledged in a way that she had never been before. Of the 15,000 troops enumerated, 6000 were Militia, undrilled, and hastily collected after hostilities had commenced, and were only in a fit state to take the field when the war was nearly finished. If it had so happened that the powerful tribes in the Whanganui district had commenced hostilities and attacked the colonists whilst the Waikato War was in progress—which it was suspected they would have done—General Cameron would have been hard pushed for men; and at that time any serious reverse to the British arms would have driven a number of tribes, both north and south, into the ranks of the hostile army, and placed the position of the colonists in serious peril. These facts were known and considered by the Imperial Government before they decided to despatch the force they did to protect the colonists and uphold the supremacy of the Queen in New Zealand. The Government return of the number of natives in New Zealand at the time of the war in 1863 was put down at 38,807; of this number only some 1,500 resided in the South Island, the remaining 37,307 living in the North Island. Looking at the then strength of the Maoris it is reasonable to suppose that if they had been so minded they could have arrayed against the colonists in the North Island a force of at least 10,000, as their women, in time of war, were very active, performing commissariat duties, and many of them fighting as savagely as the men.

Several years after, when the Imperial troops had left the colony, the success that attended the operations of the Colonial Forces, under Colonel Whitmore, against certain native tribes, was no evidence as many have thought that the first struggles with the natives could have been fought as well, or better, with Colonial troops than Imperial. At the time of the Waikato War the conditions were different, and whilst according every praise to Colonel Whitmore and his men for their bravery, it must be borne in mind that it was on account of what the Imperial troops had before done that enabled the Colonial Forces afterwards to do what they did.

The expenses incurred by the colony in the Waikato War amounted to no less a sum than £3,000,000, besides numerous other expenses charged to the colony on War Account by the Imperial Government. It was thought at the time that the sale of the lands confiscated would meet the above debt, as may be seen by the following extract from the Colonial Treasurer's speech delivered on the second reading of the Loan Bill:—

"If we take the total area of land in the rebel districts, it will be found that it amounts to eight and a-half million acres, and we have obtained information from persons well acquainted with the districts and the quality of the land, that one half of it will be available for settlement; therefore we have for settlement 4,250,000 acres. If we deduct from that the quantity required for the location of European settlers and natives, there will be a balance of three millions for sale, reserves, and for the preservation of the territory of those loyal natives who may not be desirous of disposing of their lands. I said there was a balance of 3,000,000 of acres, and supposing we set apart 500,000 acres for roads and reserves, and 1,000,000 for land that may be retained by the loyal natives, it would not be desirable, if it were even possible, to dispose of this land at once; but by bringing it into the market judiciously, it appears that 1,500,000 acres, economically dealt with and properly sold, will realise, at the very least, £2 per acre, and £3,000,000 will be obtained at the time these arrangements are completed."

When the intelligence reached England that the lands of the rebellious natives were about to be confiscated, those no doubt well-meaning but misinformed individuals presided over by Samuel Gurney, M.P., and styling themselves the "Aboriginal Protection Society," at once took active steps to prevent it. An influentially-signed memorial was presented to the Duke of Newcastle, Her Majesty's Principal Secretary for the Colonies, stating that they regarded with the utmost alarm, &c., &c., the passage of such a Bill through the Legislature of New Zealand and humbly praying that his Grace would advise Her Majesty to withhold the Royal assent from the Bill. If the so-called Aborigines Protection Society, instead of interfering with affairs that they knew very little about, had formed themselves into a society for the protection and amelioration of the starving poor in London, some good might have resulted from their labours and much valuable time and annoyance to the colonists of New Zealand saved.

THE WAIKATO WAR.

It will be sufficient to say that Her Majesty did not withhold her consent, for the Bill became law and the lands were confiscated. The price obtained for the land when sold did not, however, fetch near the estimated amount, and the major portion of the debt was afterwards generously written off by the Imperial Government.

If anything, the Maoris were treated too generously, for the broad and rich lands of the Ngatimaniapoto, who had been actively engaged in hostilities from the commencement of the war, were not touched. Neither was the extensive district owned by Wiremu Thompson; and the Ngaiterangi at Tauranga, where a large number of our soldiers' lives had ben sacrificed, were promised that only one fourth of their lands should be confiscated. The principal portion of the land confiscated comprised the Lower Waikato district, and the natives belonging to that part were repeatedly offered large tracts for settlement, but persistently refused to accept any without they could have back again the whole, preferring to remain as exiles with the Ngatimaniapoto. A short time back, however, they accepted from the Government, at the hands of the Hon. Mr. Whitaker, a valuable block of land suitable for all their requirements at Onewhero.

The losses that the settlers sustained during the war were to some extent mitigated by the Colonial Government, but the effects of the war were severely felt for several years afterwards on account of the great stagnation in trade that ensued.

The settlement and cultivation of the Waikato by the Military Settlers did not progress so satisfactorily as could have been wished. The majority of the men, as soon as their military term had expired, sold land for what they could get, many 50-acre lots changing hands at as low a figure as £5. The same land at the present time is worth more than that per acre.

The loss of the troops—Imperial and Colonial—in the Waikato War, including the Gate Pa and Te Ranga, from July, 1863, until July, 1864, amounted to 110 officers, non-commissioned officers, and privates killed; and 460 officers, non-commissioned officers and privates wounded—total killed and wounded, 570 men. To this number must be added about 100 (including 18 settlers who were murdered by the natives) who met with their deaths by drowning, sickness through exposure in the field, and various other causes incidental to a campaign. The casualties on the part of the natives it is difficult to ascertain, but if their loss is put down at 800 killed and wounded it will not be over the number. In addition to the above, 220 prisoners were taken by the troops, making altogether a total estimated loss on the part of the Maoris of 1,020 killed, wounded, and taken prisoners.

The majority of the soldiers who fell were young men in the prime of life, their ages averaging from eighteen to thirty years. The bones of these once brave men lie scattered over the country, and when gazing on the well-trimmed cemetery grave, or the rough mound, unpaled and overgrown with fern, on some bleak hillside, that marks their resting-place, let us bear in mind that it is not the living, but the dead, who gained the victory.

THE END.

The Poverty Bay Massacre.

Expeditions Against Te Kooti.

A PROLONGED WARFARE.

CHAPTER I.

ESCAPE OF MAORI PRISONERS FROM WAITANGI, CHATHAM ISLANDS—TE KOOTI SACRIFICES HIS UNCLE TO THE GOD OF THE WINDS.

At the conclusion of the fighting in the Poverty Bay and Hawke's Bay districts in the year 1886 the New Zealand Government deported a number of natives taken prisoner during the several engagements to Waitangi, Chatham Islands, distant from Wellington about 400 miles. It was here that Te Kooti first comes prominently before the public. Te Kooti was sent into exile, charged with holding communication with the enemy. He at the time was supposed to be a loyal native, but was charged with being a bad character and dangerous to the peace of the district, and on these counts he was found guilty by a not over-friendly European tribunal, and transported with the rest. For several years Te Kooti owned and sailed a schooner called the Henry, trading between Poverty Bay and Auckland, where at that time he was well known. He afterwards sold the schooner to Capt. Read, and then became mixed up in the affairs that eventually led to his deportation. An Auckland phrenologist, who is said to have examined Te Kooti's head, said that he had acquisitiveness, strong cautiousness, mechanical and inventive talent, and great secretiveness, making him guarded and shrewd. Altogether the phrenologist did not think him such a bad sort of fellow. Te Kooti is generally regarded as having been a wild, untutored savage, but although possessed of strong animal passions, like the majority of his race, from his intercourse with the Pakeha he was more civilised than perhaps the majority of the people. Te Kooti belonged to the Rongowhakaata tribe, living in the Poverty Bay district. He was not tattooed, as was generally believed, nor was he a chief. His iron force of character pushed him forward as a leader over the people he was connected with, despite the fact that among them were chiefs of high rank. All alike succumbed to the magnetism with which Te Kooti seemed to be endowed. For two years the prisoners had been on the Chatham Islands and were supposed to have become reconciled to their lot. Consequently a small guard under Capt. Thomas was considered sufficient to look after the prisoners, and the question was raised in the House of Representatives as to the advisability of granting an amnesty to the prisoners and returning them to their several tribes in New Zealand. Te Kooti, however, prematurely solved the question by heading a revolt and escaping with the whole of his companions, with the exception of two or three, who, strange to say, preferred to remain behind. On the 4th of July, 1868, the schooner Rifleman (Captain Christian), which had just arrived from Wellington, was lying at anchor off the township; the ketch Florence was also at anchor a short distance off. Capt. Christian was on shore, and the Rifleman was in charge of the mate (Mr. W. A. Payne), when Sergt. Elliott, of the Armed Constabulary guard, put off in a whaleboat, manned with about fourteen Maori prisoners, to take Government stores brought by the Rifleman on shore. The township of Waitangi wore its usual quiet aspect, and there was no suspicion of the scene that was about to take place. Having obtained a plough from the schooner, Sergt. Elliott rowed back to the shore, and had no sooner landed than the prisoners commenced hallooing and shouting, and at the same time he heard the report of fire arms. During the sergeant's brief absence the Maoris on shore had mutinied, and with a sudden and preconcerted rush disarmed the guard and taken possession of the redoubt. In the struggle that ensued they killed one of the guard (Michael Hartnell), who had made a desperate resistance. Capt. Thomas was seized, handcuffed, and marched to the Customhouse, where he found Capt. Christian tied up. Sergt. Elliott and the rest of the constables were also secured and tied up. The guard having been disposed of, the township was then looted and everything valuable taken possession of by the Maoris, who were now complete masters of the situation. Te Kooti had given the most explicit orders that no violence was to be used, and, with the exception of Hartnell, neither Captain Thomas, his men, nor the inhabitants were injured. Sergt. Hartnell was killed by Tamihana Teketeke, who had a personal animus against him. Wi Piro, another desperado, who was afterwards killed at Te Pononga, Taupo, assisted in the murder. A Mrs. Fougene had a bag in her house containing 300 sovereigns which she, with great presence of mind, placed in a kettle of water that was boiling on the fire. In this way the prize escaped the clutches of Te Kooti. The Government boat was taken possession of and a number of armed natives pulled off to the "Rifleman," but they were ordered off by Mr. Payne, who pushed two or three of them back into the boat again; but other boats full of Maoris arriving, they swarmed on board, took charge of the schooner and made Mr. Payne, the steward, and crew, consisting of three seamen, prisoners under threat of instant death in case of any resistance on their part or attempt to escape. Mr. Chudleigh, a Chatham Island settler, made a gallant attempt to save the situation by going on board and paying out the cable. He had nearly succeeded when he was seized and almost hanged, till Te Kooti made his men desist. The boats were kept constantly going to and fro until the whole of the Maoris had embarked to the number of 298 souls, comprising 163 men, 64 women, and 71 children. Te Kooti, the organiser and ringleader of the revolt, arrived on board in the last boat that came off from the shore. The crew of the ketch Florence were then ordered on shore, her anchor was lifted and the vessel was left to drift on to the beach. At the same time the Rifleman's sails were unfurled, the anchor tripped, and Mr. Payne, under penalty of death in case of refusal, was ordered to navigate the schooner to Poverty Bay. The canvas swelled out to the breeze, and the "Rifleman," crowded like a slave ship, forged through the sea, and by sunset Chatham Island was a blue haze on the horizon. Te Kooti secured from the Redoubt 49 stand of arms, a quantity of ammunition, over 4,000 rounds—and £500 in cash, which had been sent to pay the officer and men, besides all the stores on board the "Rifleman," consisting of, amongst other articles, 17 tons of flour, 6,200lbs. of sugar, and 5 barrels of ale. After the departure of the "Rifleman," Captains Thomas and Christian were released by the inhabitants, and they endeavoured to launch the ketch Florence, which had beached hard and fast, with the idea of taking her to Wellington; but the attempt failed, a native being drowned in the effort. On Thursday, July 9th, there having been a head wind for two days, a considerable amount of quarrelling ensued amongst the Maoris, who began to waver in their faith as to the mana or power of Te Kooti, who had given out that he was a prophet chosen of God. How could that be if the winds were angry and refused to assist him? After all, he was really no chief but only a common man of no rank, like the most of them on board. Te Kooti, however, proved equal to the occasion, for, with all the solemnity of a tohunga or priest, he informed his companions that to propitiate the God of the Winds, a sacrifice must be made and one of their number thrown overboard. When that was done, all would be well. To the astonishment of all, Te Kooti pointed out his own uncle, who was on board, as the Jonah to be sacrificed. This uncle, Mohi, had opposed Te Kooti throughout, calling him "a tangata kino"—bad man. The unfortunate man was immediately seized and dragged on deck, where his hands and arms were securely lashed together, and, amidst his heartrending screams for mercy, and struggling violently, he was pitched over the side of the vessel. For some time he was seen struggling in the waves, then he suddenly disappeared. Shortly afterwards the wind changed and the good ship "Rifleman" sped gaily on her course.

MAJOR R. BIGGS.

CHAPTER II.

TE KOOTI LANDS AT POVERTY BAY, DEFIES CAPT. BIGGS AND DEFEATS A FORCE UNDER CAPT. WESTRUP.

On Sunday, July 12, 1868, Percy Porter and one or two other Europeans who had a contract building woolsheds, were strolling along the beach at Whareongaonga, some few miles south from Turanganui, Poverty Bay, when they saw in the offing a large schooner making for the land. When a short distance from the shore the vessel dropped anchor, crowds of people were noticed on the deck of the schooner, and it was a matter of great speculation on the part of Porter and his companions as to who the new-comers could be. Their speculations were, however, soon set at rest, for several boats were lowered from the schooner and speedily filled with natives, who hastily pulled for the shore, when it was found that the strange vessel was the Rifleman, with Te Kooti and the escaped Chatham Island prisoners. The Maoris having landed and brought on shore a large quantity of stores and ammunition, the schooner tripped her anchor and stood out to sea again. The news soon spread throughout the Poverty Bay district that the prisoners deported to the Chatham Islands had returned and that one Kooti, as he was then called, was their leader. The greatest excitement prevailed all along the coast, and various were the surmises as to how and in what way they had escaped, for at first it was but a rumour. Some said that a French whaler had brought them, others that the prisoners' friends had chartered a vessel to bring them back. The only thing certain was that they had returned and were camped a few miles from Turanga (Gisborne), and native messengers were despatched by the different chiefs in the district to convey the news far and near.

> Now to the four centres of the earth,
> With the swiftness of a shooting star,
> Is spread the news . . . . .

At this time Capt. Biggs was the Government officer in charge of the Poverty Bay district, and upon receiving intelligence of the landing of the Chatham Island prisoners, he at once took steps to recapture, if possible, the fugitives before they could retreat to the mountain fastnesses of the Urewera country. The European force at the disposal of Capt. Biggs consisted mostly of cavalry and was small, numbering only about 50 men, badly armed. To make matters worse, there were no arms or ammunition in store. Notwithstanding, Capt. Biggs called his squad out for service, and interviewed the leading friendly chiefs for assistance. The chiefs, however, in view of the want of arms and ammunition, advised a different line of action to that contemplated by the Capt. They pointed out the risk that would be run in attacking Te Kooti, who was known to be well supplied with arms and ammunition, and proposed instead that they should go and meet the fugitives and ask them to return with them as guests. Then when once they were scattered about amongst their own people, it would be possible to suddenly disarm them. You can then, said the chiefs, pick out the most criminal and let the others go peaceably to their different districts. Whether the advice, if acted upon, would have been successful is perhaps doubtful, for Te Kooti was too wary a bird to be caught napping. It is idle, however, to speculate upon that now, for Capt. Biggs rejected the proposition of the friendly chiefs, and mustering his small troop of cavalry, started off to suggest to Te Kooti the advisability of his at once laying down his arms and ammunition and surrendering himself and companions to Her Majesty the Queen as represented by the Government of New Zealand. In negotiating with Te Kooti, Capt. Biggs selected Paora Kati, a chief who had been a fellow-prisoner with Te Kooti at Chatham Islands and had been released by the Government a few months before, to act as emissary, as he was a chief of high rank and would probably have great influence over Te Kooti. Capt. Biggs, as might have been expected, failed in his mission, for he was coolly informed by Te Kooti that the arms and ammunition they had were given to them by a new God who was going to deliver them from the Pakehas, who would be all destroyed, and the best thing that the Capt. could do would be to make himself scarce before the new God made a start upon him and his men. Being too weak to enforce his demands, and plainly seeing from the attitude of Te Kooti that under the circumstances discretion was the better part of valour, he turned about and galloped back with his troop to Turanganui and, posting patrols at the different crossings that led into the interior, awaited events. Te Kooti got through Capt. Biggs' lines at night, at Whareongaonga, and moved slowly towards the Urewera mountains, which loomed up in the distance like a dark cloud and formed the backbone of that part of the island. On his march he was daily joined by numbers of restless and disaffected natives, so that very soon he had a considerable number of followers. About a week after Te Kooti had landed, Colonel Whitmore arrived at Turanganui in H.M.S. Rosario from Napier with a small detachment, consisting of 2 officers and 32 men, as a reinforcement to the settlers, but found on his arrival that the bird had flown and was by that time in the mountains. In the meantime Capt. Westrup started with a detachment of volunteers via Te Arai to intercept Te Kooti on his march to the Urewera country. After travelling through a wild and mountainous country for two days, Capt. Westrup pitched his camp and waited for a reinforcement of friendly natives that was supposed to join him at that spot. Te Kooti was known to be in the vicinity, for the smoke from his camp fires could be plainly seen in the ranges. On the 19th July a few natives joined Capt. Westrup's party and brought the intelligence that Te Kooti intended to attack them on the following day. The force lay under arms all night surrounded by double sentries. At the first dawn of day, smoke, evidently issuing from numerous camp fires, could be plainly discerned rising with the morning mist from the ravines below. Captain Westrup's party were on the alert and waited for the attack which they knew was soon to take place. The hope of receiving reinforcements had now vanished; the friendly native supports had evidently never started or else had turned back or gone over to the enemy with their arms and ammunition. The scene was wild and picturesque in the extreme. The country was hilly, and on the left front, where the Whakapunake range stands out in bold relief, huge ranges piled on range, the tops of which melting away in the distance were shrouded in dense clouds of mist that lay heavy on the spurs and deep groves. A hill rising up and connected with the main range by a narrow ridge offered a good position for defence, and Lieut. Wilson, with 20 volunteers and 12 friendly natives, was ordered to take possession of it. The movement had barely been effected when a crowd of Natives suddenly emerged from the edge of the bush. In front of the Natives was Te Kooti, clad in a long white robe and holding his hands above his head. He seemed to be engaged in prayer or in showering curses on the heads of the Pakeha. Having finished his prayers, or curses, Te Kooti dropped his hands, which was a signal for his followers to pour a volley into Westrup's party, who lay on the ground under cover of the dense flax and fern with which the spur was covered. The fight now commenced; Westrup's men extended in skirmishing order, kept well under cover, and only fired when a chance of having a pot shot at one of the enemy occurred. Te Kooti's men, who seemed reckless in the expenditure of their ammunition, sent shower after shower of bullets that went pinging overhead or hurtling through the flax and fern which concealed Westrup's men. All the while they kept up a great shouting and hallooing. By a judicious movement Capt. Westrup occupied an eminence to the right of the Natives who, as soon as they observed what was taking place, tried hard to gain the same vantage ground, but were kept in check by the superior fire of their adversaries. The fire from Te Kooti's men was wild and unsteady, and so the fight went on hour after hour. Several of the enemy were seen to fall, and a few casualties had occurred amongst Westrup's party, but nothing serious. At 4 p.m. Te Kooti, having no doubt received reinforcements, increased his fire, and made a demonstration as if to make a rush, and it was plainly to be seen that he was gaining ground. Westrup's party, not being supplied with bayonets, were powerless to charge, and the enemy becoming bolder every minute, Capt. Westrup ordered his detachment to retreat—a rather difficult operation under the circumstances and one requiring a large amount of coolness. The order was carried out successfully, the men falling back gradually from spur to spur and checking any attempt on the part of Te Kooti's men, who followed closely up, to rush—which with much shouting and yelling they seemed anxious to do. A vigorous, well sustained rush on the part of Te Kooti's men at this time would, no doubt, have resulted disastrously for Westrup and his party, but the spirit was wanting, and darkness fast falling over the ranges, Westrup's men found cover amidst a storm of bullets in an old Maori fortification. It being now too dark to continue operations, the Natives gradually ceased firing at their foes and retired. From their position Westrup's party could plainly see numerous fires and hear sounds of firing and shouting from the position they had occupied in the morning. Te Kooti and his men were looting their camp and shooting their pack horses. Fortunately for Capt. Westrup he had with his party a faithful Native guide named Hori Kakapanga, who during the night succeeded in enabling the detachment with the wounded to escape from the clutches of Te Kooti. Capt. Westrup lost in this affair only two men killed and several wounded, very slight casualties under the circumstances. Te Kooti must have suffered pretty severely, for during the day numbers of his men were seen to fall.

CHAPTER III.

TE KOOTI ESTABLISHES HIMSELF IN THE UREWERA COUNTRY AND AMBUSCADES COLONEL WHITMORE.

Great was the consternation in Auckland and Wellington when the news arrived that the Chatham Island prisoners had escaped and were at large in the Poverty Bay district. Crowds thronged the streets of both cities earnestly canvassing the important event which it was thought might unsettle numbers of Natives who had been quiet for years and cause many other Maoris who were wavering in their allegiance to again take up arms and endeavour to wipe out old scores. The Government at once despatched from Wellington to the Chatham Islands the s.s. Stormbird to learn full particulars as to the escape of the prisoners and the fate of Capt. Thomas, his guard, and the inhabitants. The escape of the prisoners could scarcely have happened at a worse time, for the Government had still on their hands a lingering and costly war on the West Coast, in which the Natives under the ferocious Titokowaru were having decidedly the best of the fighting. The Imperial troops had all left the colony with the exception of the 18th Regiment, and they were not under any circumstances allowed to take the field. The only corps the Government had was a small force of Armed Constabulary, and a few local volunteer cavalry who were unable to cope with the enemy on the West Coast without engaging a fresh foe in a distant and rugged part of the country. Four years had elapsed since the Waikato war, and the thousands of trained men who had taken part in that campaign had long since been disbanded and were now scattered in all directions, although many were still in the colony. In Auckland the military spirit that had sprung into existence and been developed during the progress of the war in the Waikato, was fast dying out and was but a mere ember that would take a considerable amount of fanning to produce any sparks. Rich gold had just been discovered in the Thames ranges, and gold, gold, was the absorbing topic of the day—the magnet that was drawing crowds to that one spot from all parts of the colony. Those ready and willing to bleed for their country were few in number. The Government had neither the means nor the inclination to engage in a fresh war; they were sick of fighting, and longed for peace almost at any price, and so the urgent appeals for reinforcements from the East Coast were almost unheeded. No. I Division A.C. Force, 100 men, under Major James Fraser, had been taken from the Wairoa and sent to Opotiki, leaving Poverty Bay and Wairoa defenceless, one man being left at Wairoa in charge of ammunition. This state of affairs exactly suited Te Kooti, who, having passed the Hangaroa stream, had now firmly established himself in the almost inaccessible ravines and ranges of the Urewera, from whence he could swoop down

MAJOR-GENERAL SIR G. S. WHITMORE.

TE KOOTI EXPEDITIONS.

like a bird of prey upon almost any part of the East Coast from Napier to Opotiki. The Urewera Natives received Te Kooti and his followers with open arms; they were Hauhaus to a man—a superstitious religion that enjoined the extermination of all Europeans and a belief that the angel Gabriel with his legions would protect and fight with them against their enemies. The priests of the order claimed to have the gift of tongues and power to work miracles. Marriage was proclaimed of no account and men and women were enjoined to live together promiscuously. Te Kooti said he had a divine message from God, and that he was commanded to set the Israelites free from their bondage. He adopted the Old Testament, especially the Psalms of David, as his special creed, and cut out the New Testament altogether. He never accepted the Hauhau creed, which was originated by Te Ua, of Taranaki, and spread like wildfire through the country. The Urewera were all Hauhaus, when Te Kooti landed, but he afterwards induced them to adopt his religion. Te Kooti had a strong force at his back, which he believed was able to cope with any force that might be sent against him. One great drawback to him when on the move was that he had hundreds of camp followers in the shape of women and children who considerably hampered his movements, although many of the women could and did handle a gun as well as most of the men. The women also loaded the guns, cooked, and attended to the sick and wounded. There being no signs of any fresh reinforcements from either Wellington or Auckland, and the Volunteers at Turanganui objecting to march into the Urewera country and leave their own district unprotected, Colonel Whitmore determined to start after Te Kooti with the men he had brought from Napier. On the 6th of August Colonel Whitmore crossed the Hangaroa with a mixed force of Constabulary and Natives numbering in all about 130 men. At this point the pack horses that accompanied the column were sent back and three days' rations were served out to each man. The trail to be followed led the expedition through a wild and rugged country. Many times the column could only advance in Indian file, the river had to be crossed and recrossed knee deep, steep precipices had to be climbed, and the cold was intense. At night the men lay on the ground in their blankets despite falling snow, and the expedition suffered severely. In the distance the glare of Te Kooti's camp fires could be seen. On the afternoon of the 8th Colonel Whitmore was close to the enemy's position, and the column proceeded with great caution, expecting any moment to fall into an ambush, for which the country was peculiarly favourable. The men were tired, ragged, and footsore and for the most part more fit for hospital than to engage in a deadly struggle with a foe like Te Kooti. At 3 p.m. the advance guard entered the gorge on the banks of the Ruakituri river. They had no sooner done so than a heavy musketry fire was opened on the leading files from both sides of the river. The main body moved rapidly forward to support the advance guard and the whole force was immediately engaged. Captains Carr and Davis Canning, two gentlemen who had accompanied Colonel Whitmore from Napier as volunteers, were shot dead. Te Kooti was in force, and Colonel Whitmore soon found that he was not strong enough to dislodge the Natives from their position. The fight was, however, kept up until night, which falls quickly in those deep ravines, threw its kindly mantle over the scene of bloodshed and put an end to the unequal conflict. Colonel Whitmore immediately fell back, but with great difficulty, owing to the darkness and broken nature of the country. The same causes prevented the enemy from following in pursuit, or the wounded, amongst whom was Capt. Tuke, could not have been saved. As it was, the killed, six in number, were left in the gorge where they fell, and where they remained unburied for some time afterwards. In this engagement Te Kooti was wounded in the foot, and partly on that account did not perhaps follow the next day in pursuit of Colonel Whitmore, whose force he could easily have overtaken and decimated—hampered as it was with the wounded, short of provisions and with no supports, the expedition could have offered but a feeble resistance to any attacking party. Te Kooti must have suffered pretty severely in the fight, for the next day he struck camp and fell further back into the ranges. Colonel Whitmore's expedition arrived back at Turanganui thoroughly dispirited, and the Colonel's well-known ardour for the time considerably cooled.

CHAPTER IV.

TE KOOTI MASSACRES THE SETTLERS AT POVERTY BAY.

Lieut. Sanders, who had been out on a scouting expedition from the Wairoa to ascertain the whereabouts of the enemy, returned on the 2nd of September and reported that he found Te Kooti strongly entrenched at Puketapu, not far from the scene of the fight which took place a few weeks before with Col. Whitmore. Lieut. Sanders got within 8 miles of the pa, and could plainly see the palisades. A few days after news was brought that a friendly young chief named Karaitiana and three of his tribe, who were watching the movements of Te Kooti, were killed. Directly after this event Te Kooti made a demonstration in force against the Wairoa settlement, then occupied by military settlers, who, upon the approach of the enemy, retired to the redoubts on the Clyde. Between the 27th of September and 4th of October, 200 Ngatiporou under Ropata and Hotene, about 300 Hawke's Bay natives under Renata and Tomoana, about 120 Wairoa natives, and about 40 of the A.C. Force, making altogether an expedition of nearly 700 men, under the command of Capt. Tuke, was hastily despatched from Napier to assist in defending the Wairoa district. When the party arrived, however, Te Kooti had retired. The relieving force followed in pursuit, but failed in their efforts to find the whereabouts of the enemy. At a Native village named Whatoroa they discovered the bodies of the young chief Karaitiana and his three men dreadfully mutilated. Karaitiana had been tomahawked and his heart and liver taken out and roasted in a sacred fire as an offering to Whiro, the God of Evil, a very ancient Maori custom. He was split open as a butcher dresses a sheep. The settlement had been burnt, and an old Maori found in the plantation was shot, and an old woman taken prisoner. The expedition then returned to Napier. The settlers on the East Coast for a hundred miles were now in a most excited state, not knowing when or where Te Kooti might not fall upon and destroy them. At Matawhero, Poverty Bay, a numerously attended meeting was held, when the following resolutions were unanimously carried:—

1. That scouts be at once sent out on the three main outlets from the interior to obtain, if possible, some insight into the movements of the enemy.

2. That a redoubt be erected in some central position to serve as a refuge for Natives and Europeans.

3. That a memorial be addressed to the Government begging that an efficient force may forthwith be stationed there.

4. That this meeting seeks to express in the strongest terms its disapproval of Colonel Whitmore's management while in command here, it being notorious that he took every opportunity of insulting the people of this place, both Native and European, and that his conduct generally was calculated to excite ill-feeling beween the Natives and the Government.

The fact of the above resolutions being carried shows that a very lamentable state of affairs existed at that time in the district, and that the settlers, having no confidence in the officers in charge of the district, had determined to take the reins into their own hands and look after their own safety themselves. A Vigilance Committee was formed. Scouts were sent out, and two strong redoubts were commenced—one at Turanganui, and the other at Matawhero, near the home of Major Biggs, now senior officer, having received promotion, Col. Whitmore, after his defeat, having returned to Napier. On the 5th of November the Vigilance Committee informed Major Biggs that Te Kooti was on the move, descending the Patutahi Valley. The Major informed the committee that they need not be alarmed, as he had scouts out under Lieut. Gascoigne, who would keep him posted as to the movements of the enemy. The committee, satisfied that all was well, returned to their homes and the settlers relaxed their vigilance. Before dawn on Tuesday morning, November 10th, 1868, a never-to-be-forgotten day in the annals of the Poverty Bay district, the settlement at Matawhero lay wrapped in slumber, no sound broke the stillness of early morn except the occasional bark of some watchful sheep dog, the distant cry of the swamp hen, or morepoke (night owl); and although Te Kooti and his triumphant fanatics were known to be hovering in the vicinity on vengeance bent, no sentinels guarded the peaceful homes of the sleeping settlers. During the night a large band of Te Kooti's men crossed the Patutahi ford, moving in the direction of Matawhero. Major Biggs, confident in the alertness of his scouts, had, with the rest of the settlers, retired the night before lulled into a false sense of security, for he had received no news concerning the movements of the enemy. Suddenly he was aroused from his slumbers by the sounds of Maoris talking. Thinking that it was some of his Native scouts arrived with important news, he hastily jumped out of bed and questioned the new arrivals, who instantly fired at him, wounding him severely. Running back into the house, the Major called out to his wife to fly for her life, and asked a lad named C. James, who was in the house and worked for the Major, where his gun was. The boy replied that it was not loaded, but handed it to him. The Major, whilst in the act of loading, was fired at again, and fell. The Natives then rushed into the house, lit a fire and commenced devouring all the eatables handy. Mrs. Biggs all this time was standing by her wounded husband, with her child in her arms. The Major implored her to fly for her life, but she heroically expressed her determination to remain with him to the last, and begged her servant, Mrs. Farrell, to make her escape whilst there was yet time; but Mrs. Farrell obstinately refused to leave her master and mistress. The boy James attempted to escape out of the back door, but finding a number of Maoris there he returned, and, squeezing himself through the Natives crowding the front of the house, under cover of the gloom crawled into a flax bush, and from thence into the surrounding scrub. The boy escaped not a minute too soon, for the Maoris immediately commenced to beat out the brains of the Major, and murdered Mrs. Biggs, her infant, and Mrs. Farrell, who were afterwards found mutilated in a most horrible and shocking manner.

At the same time as Major Biggs and his family were killed, another party of Natives attacked the home of Capt. Wilson, a short distance away. After firing several volleys at the inmates, they set fire to the house, the flames casting a lurid glare over the surrounding country. Capt. Wilson was killed and his wife and three children were bayonetted. The eldest boy, about 9 years of age, escaped in the confusion, and was found several days afterwards. Mrs. Wilson was also alive when found, but afterwards died of her wounds at Napier. The body of John Moran, servant to Capt. Wilson, was found cut into three pieces. The boy, Charles James, after escaping from the house of Major Biggs, ran to Mrs. Bloomfield's, which was not far distant, and gave the alarm. He knocked loudly at the door, calling out that the Maoris were murdering everybody. Mrs. Bloomfield and her sister, who resided in the house, could hardly realise their dreadful situation, but when they were thoroughly awakened they got up, and, snatching up Mrs. Bloomfield's three children, fled towards Turanganui, about six miles distant. They were accompanied in their flight by a boy named Tom Finukin, who worked about the house. By his advice they kept in the scrub skirting the coast to avoid being seen. They could see, as they travelled, Lieut. Wilson's house in flames, and could plainly hear the loud shouting and firing of the Maoris. In an exhausted state they at length reached Turanganui. Mr. Walsh, his wife, a child, and infant were surprised and murdered; also, Messrs. Padbury and Cadell, single men, living in a house by themselves. Mr. and Mrs. McCulloch and baby, with Mary McDonald, a niece of Mr. McCulloch, were surprised in their house and killed; also Mr. and Mrs. Mann and a little boy one year old. Mr. Goldsmith, stockman to Captain Reid, of Turanganui, being in the vicinity and hearing shouting and firing of guns, rode over to the spot and was horrified to see the body of Mrs. Mann lying on the ground terribly scorched. The savages had killed her, and then set fire to her clothes. Two natives were standing near at the time of Goldsmith's arrival, and they attempted to seize the horse's bridle, but Goldsmith, putting spurs to his horse, threw them off and galloped away. Fortunately at the time the guns of the natives were not loaded. Passing along, he saw the body of Mrs. Walsh, and her child, shot through the head, moaning piteously by her side; and outside of Mr. Cadell's house were lying the bodies of Messrs. Cadell and Padbury. Hastening on at full speed through Makaraka, he reached Turanganui with the dreadful news. Messrs. Dodd and Pepperd, who resided on their run beyond Matawhero, were probably the first of the settlers who were killed, for the natives on their way to Matawhero passed their place, and a man named Butters going there early in the morning to shear, found them lying dead from gunshot wounds. The house of Mr. Goldsmith was situated in a height of the river Waipaoa, and was attacked with the others. Goldsmith was not at home at the time, but the natives killed his half-caste daughter Maria and her baby. Mrs. James, who was living in an outhouse belonging to Goldsmith, was alarmed by a boy named Tarr, and managed to escape with her six children. Mr. Munn, who lived between Waerengahika and Matawhero, was on horseback near his house on Tuesday morning, and seeing some natives moving about whom he knew in Napier, he called out to them. One of the Maoris by way of answer, drew a revolver and fired, the ball striking Mr. Munn on the shoulder. He, however, galloped off and escaped. A man named James Garland had a miraculous escape. He lived in a little hut near Mrs. Bloomfield's, but, strange to say, was not awakened by the noise going on around, and in the morning at about 5 o'clock he got up to milk the cows as usual, and was horrified to behold what had occurred during the night. Not a native was to be seen at the time, although they were still in the neighbourhood, and remained the greater part of the day ransacking and burning the settlers' homesteads. A number of friendly natives living at Matawhero also fell victims to the rebels. At the time the news of the massacre reached Turanganui, between four and five in the morning, the schooner Tawera was standing out of the bay, bound for Auckland. Captain Reid at once got a boat and crew and pulled after the schooner, which he succeeded in overhauling after rowing hard for several hours. The vessel was put about, and returned to her anchorage in the bay.

The following particulars of the operations which preceded the Poverty Bay massacre have been gathered from a journal kept by Captain George A. Preece, N.Z.C. It appears from Captain Preece's journal that Te Kooti had refused to surrender. Captain (afterwards Major) Biggs marched men up, but Te Kooti got through his lines at night and directly inland. Captain Biggs sent a messenger through to Wairoa to Captain Deighton, R.M., asking him to obtain Ihaka Whanga's tribe at Te Mahia to come to his assistance. Captain Deighton was holding Court at Te Mahia at the time, and after interviewing the loyal chief Ihaka Whanga, he desired to return to Wairoa and forward arms and ammunition for Ihaka's men, who were at once to move to Te Mahanga, the place where the Poverty Bay leaves the sea beach. He rode to Wairoa and sent Mr. (now Captain) George A. Preece, N.Z.C., with ammunition and food on pack horses, instructing him to accompany Ihaka's men and join Cáptain Biggs, he having previously informed the latter of his action, sending his own messenger.

Mr. Preece reached the appointed place at 5 a.m., having travelled all night. The force was just starting when a messenger from Captain Biggs galloped in stating that Te Kooti was making for the Arai Valley and asking that a force be sent up from Wairoa to intercept him at Whenuakura. After consultation with Ihaka, Mr. Preece decided to return at once to Wairoa, starting from there the same day with a few Europeans and Maoris—40 in all.

In the meantime Captain Biggs returned to Turanga (Gisborne) collected a force of old Military Settlers and Forest Rangers under Captain Westrup, and moved up the Arai Valley, where a severe engagement took place between Captain Westrup's party and the whole of Te Kooti's forces, in which we lost three men and a number wounded, including Mr. Evans, of the Volunteers. Te Kooti outflanked Westrup's force, capturing their camp and baggage.

The small Wairoa party moved to Whenuakura, about five miles above Te Reinga Falls, where some ex-rebels of 1866, under their fighting chief Te Rakiroa, were living. He professed ignorance of the escape of the Chatham Island prisoners, and volunteered to give assistance.

Captain Biggs sent Lieut. (now Major) Gascoigne through to Wairoa by the inland road in front of the enemy with a despatch to Captain Deighton, R.M. He passed the camp occupied by Mr. Preece and the

TE KOOTI EXPEDITIONS. 181

European volunteers at midnight, got a fresh horse and rode on, after reporting that he had heard heavy firing on his left in the distance.

The next day the small force at Whenuakura moved on towards Poverty Bay. Under instructions from Captain Biggs. Lieut. Gascoigne returned from Wairoa and went right on to Poverty Bay, rendering splendid service on these two occasions. Mr. Preece's force camped on a high point, keeping a sharp look-out all night.

The following morning (July 25th) an early start was made, and the force had just got past the second crossing of the Hangaroa river when they met Lieut. (afterwards Captain) Wilson and a single native scout named Netana, with a letter from Captain Biggs stating that Westrup had been defeated at Paparatu, at the head of the Arai Valley, losing all the baggage and three killed and several wounded; that Te Kooti was moving with his whole force to Waihau Lakes, and instructing the small force to return at once and take up a position in the vicinity of Waihau Lakes, or at Whenuakura. Lieut. Wilson and Netana returned to Poverty Bay.

The small force with Preece, on nearing Waihau Lakes just at dusk, saw a large force of mounted foot coming over the Akimana range from the direction of Paparatu, comprising Te Kooti's army in large numbers. Torrential rains set in, and when the force reached Whenuakura drenched to the skin, they found Captain Richardson, A.C. Force, who had been at Napier on leave, with a few more old Military Settlers and others; also the Chief Paora Apatu and a hundred of his men.

The following morning was spent cleaning and drying their arms from the complete saturation of the previous night, also awaiting arrival of pack horses with supplies. A strong picket under Mr. Preece was sent up the hill toward Waihau Lake, and at 2 p.m. he captured one of the enemy's scouts named Hotama, who was sent to the rear under guard.

A general engagement then ensued. Captain Richardson moved up with the main body, and the enemy was kept in check. We lost one man killed, the enemy at least two.

An unfortunate occurrence then took place. The chief Paora Apatu, never remarkable for his courage, withdrew with his whole force, retiring towards Wairoa, thus leaving Richardson with only about 66 men, including the Packers, to contend with the overwhelming force of the enemy.

Captain Richardson then determined to retire to the next ridge, overlooking and just beyond the native settlement at Whenuakura. Here the fight was continued till late in the evening, when Richardson decided to retire toward Wairoa, as his ammunition was nearly exhausted, leaving Mr. Preece and about 16 men as a rear guard, and supplementing their ammunition. He directed them to keep up a constant fire on the enemy, who by this time had occupied the Whenuakura Valley, he retired towards Wairoa. After keeping up a constant fire till dark our rear guard also retired, Te Rakiroa and three of his men deserting to the enemy during the action. The whole force reached Opoiti that night after a most arduous march about 11 p.m.

TE KOOTI EXPEDITIONS.

Captain Richardson decided to go right on to Wairoa to procure picked Maoris and to act in conjunction with Capt. Biggs and the Poverty Bay men. He took the prisoner Hotama to be sent to Napier. Heavy rain set in lasting for several days. After which Capt. Richardson, having obtained some more reliable natives and the Mohaka Volunteers under Ensign Lavin (subsequently killed during Te Kooti's raid on Mohaka in March, 1869), he moved forward up to Te Reinga to find that the Ngatikohatu, Te Rakiroa's people had joined Te Kooti. Whenuakura was found to be deserted, and Te Kooti's trail had gone inland towards Ruakituri.

The party returned to Captain Richardson's camp at Opoiti. The latter returned to Wairoa to await fresh orders from Captain Biggs. An orderly arrived with a letter from Colonel Whitmore, stating that he had reached Whenuakura with No. 1 Division Armed Constabulary, under Major Fraser; that the Poverty Bay Volunteers had refused to go further, and he was pushing on with the A.C., some Ngatiporou and some Hawke's Bay natives, and instructing Captain Richardson to follow on his trail, bringing up food and ammunition.

Mr. Preece, having been engaged through the campaign of 1865, and knowing the district thoroughly, strongly urged Captain Richardson not to go via Whenuakura, but to take the Marumaru and Te Tuhi track, thus cutting off two sides of a triangle and saving a day and a-half marching. Richardson, however, determined to adhere to the other plan, the result being that as he was descending into the Ruakituri River about 2 p.m. on August 9th he met the Ngatiporou, under Hotene Porourangi, who reported that an engagement had taken place the previous day in the river bed near Puketapu, resulting in the death of Captain Carr, late Royal Artillery, Lieut. Davis Canning, and four men of Major Fraser's A.C. Division, and Captain Arthur Tuke and several natives wounded. Also that Major Fraser was marching with the A.C. Force and Hawke's Bay natives, via Te Tuhi track, for Wairoa. Had Captain Richardson acted on Preece's urgent advice, instead of following Colonel Whitmore's trail, the result would have been different, as the latter would have had fresh men with a good supply of ammunition and food. Colonel Whitmore only had rations up to the 8th, and was short of ammunition as well. Te Kooti was himself wounded and suffered loss in this engagement. The enemy was in fact beaten and made no attempt to follow Colonel Whitmore when he retired. His (the Colonel's) force had been reduced to about 150 men by the Poverty Bay Volunteers returning from Whenuakura. Captain Richardson then went via the latter place to Wairoa, arriving the following day. Major Fraser, with the A.C., Hawke's Bay natives, and the wounded had arrived the previous day.

* * * * * *

Lieut. Sanders was well acquainted with the district and with Te Waru, having lived in his village and appeared to place very great dependence upon him. Shortly after his return a second scouting party was sent out —four picked men who had been with Preece in his advanced position prior to Captain Richardson's engagement. These were Karaitiana Rotoatara, a young chief, Ahitana, Te Reweti and another. They went to Nama's settlement at Opoiti. The latter had been among the rebels in 1865-66, but now professed to be friendly, and one of his men Hone Pereha, joined the party, and all proceeded toward Whataroa, Te Waru's settlement. On their way they met one Paraki, another of Nama's men, who told them that Te Waru's people had been scouting and had seen fires at Te Kooti's stronghold Puketapu, but they knew nothing more. After kai, Hone Pereha had some private conversation with Paraki, and said he would return with him as he felt ill; the rest went on.

This was on October 4th and some days elapsed, but nothing had been heard of Karaitiana and his companions, while Nama professed entire ignorance. But Mr. George Barton, who had been surveying on the Waiau branch of the Wairoa River, reported that a woman had joined Te Kooti, that the four scouts had arrived at Te Waru's settlement during his absence, and received a welcome by Reihana, Te Waru's brother, feasted and put in the best wharepuni (sleeping house) for the night, Reihana Horotiu alone staying with the guests. Towards midnight, all were asleep except Karaitiana and Reihana, when the latter asked the former to lean over and give him a coal wherewith to light his pipe. The former hesitated, as he thought the request a strange one, and immediately Reihana struck him dead with a blow from his tomahawk, and with the agility of a tiger tomahawked two of his sleeping companions. Te Reweti, aroused from slumber, made for the door where he was met by Reihana's men, who were waiting expectantly, and was quickly slain. Colonel Lambert was now in command at Wairoa. Nama and his people had deserted their villages directly they knew that their treachery had been discovered.

When this news came Mr. (afterwards Sir Donald) Maclean immediately sent for Ropata Wahawaha, Hotene Porourangi and 200 Ngatiporou from the East Cape, 300 Ngatikahungunu or Hawke's Bay natives under Tareha and Henare Tomoana, 100 Wairoa natives. About 30 A.C. men and 4 European officers under Captain Tuke, left Wairoa with instructions that they were to attack Whataroa if it were fortified, then proceed to Puketapu and attack Te Kooti there. This expedition took a considerable time to organise, men having to be brought from the East Cape and Napier. It was therefore about the 28th of October before they left Wairoa. Travelling up the Waiau a considerable distance, moving by night these were approaching Te Waru's settlement at Whataroa, when they were overtaken by Colonel Lambert, who assumed command. They reached Whataroa at noon next day, finding it deserted, but a prisoner was taken in a neighbouring village, who stated that Te Waru and all his people had joined Te Kooti, to assist him in a raid on Poverty Bay. Strangely and unfortunately, this information was disbelieved by the Commanding officer, for the extraordinary reason that were Te Kooti to march on Poverty Bay he would leave his rear unprotected, which would be contrary to all military rules. At Whataroa the bodies of Karaitiana, Ahitana, Maaka and Reweti were exhumed. They had all been fearfully

MAJOR ROPATA.

mutilated, and the former's chest had been cut open and his heart removed. Colonel Lambert, being a Justice of the Peace, held an inquest and a verdict of wilful murder returned against persons unknown.

The next day parties were sent out to scout the surrounding country toward Puketapu, and on the following night a consultation was held with the chiefs. Ropata Wahawaha and Hotene Porourangi urged that the expedition should go straight on to Puketapu the next day. Colonel Lambert said, however, that owing to the rough country and extent of bush to be gone through it would be in constant danger of falling into ambuscades and incur heavy casualties, to which Ropata replied, "We don't go to fight and come back with the same number of men." Tareha and the Hawke's Bay men were in favour of retiring to Wairoa and collecting a larger force. The Wairoa natives also agreed, much to the indignation of Ropata and Hotene, who were urgent for an attack on Te Kooti at Puketapu. But Colonel Lambert, though an excellent officer who had done good service in India, had no experience of bush fighting, and the result was the whole force moved to Orewha, about 18 miles from Puketapu, and then went back to Wairoa, the Hawke's Bay natives having previously shot the unfortunate old prisoner who had given the most valuable information (which was disbelieved by the Commanding Officer). They danced a war dance on the occasion and thought they had done a very meritorious act. Had the force gone on, as was at first intended, they would have found the pa at Puketapu empty and could have followed Te Kooti's trail and attacked him in the rear before he could have reached Poverty Bay.

The expedition went back to Wairoa on the 4th November. The mail left for Poverty Bay the following morning, yet no notice was sent to Major Biggs conveying the information given by the poor old prisoner. Had the command of the expedition remained under Captain Tuke, who had proved himself an experienced bush fighter during the East Cape campaign of 1865, and in fighting against the Urewera, from the Opotiki side under Major St. John, there is no moral doubt that the first intention against Te Kooti at Puketapu would have been carried out, and consequently the Poverty Bay massacre averted. As it was, he was permitted to march undeterred on the unfortunate, ill-protected and unwarned settlement. Major Mair, by paying £15 to a friendly native on Friday, two days before Te Kooti's attack, had sent Major Biggs a letter warning him that he would be attacked in a day or two, and it is a fact that Biggs received the letter, but probably too late to take decisive action.

CHAPTER V.

TURANGA AFTER THE MASSACRE.

When the settlers at Turanga were apprised of the massacre that had taken place at Matawhero, only a few miles outside the township, the whole settlement was thrown into the greatest state of excitement and disorder. Any moment Te Kooti's bloodthirsty followers might put in an appearance, and pillage the town, if such it could then be called. There were no officers present to direct any defensive measures, and the only thing to be done was for everyone to rush for the Redoubt, which, however, was not finished, but would afford some sort of shelter in case of attack. The number that made for the redoubt was greatly swelled by the constant arrival of families from the district round about, who, leaving everything in their houses, made for the township. It seems almost incredible that a district that had been for some time in daily dread of an attack from a powerful and bloodthirsty enemy, should have been allowed to remain in such a defenceless and unprepared state. Inside the redoubt were huddled together nearly 100 Europeans, including women and children, and 150 friendly natives of the Ngatiporou tribe, who resided near the township. Turanga, now called Gisborne, was at that time but a mere setttlement consisting of one or two hotels and two or three stores, but being the port for the surrounding district, which had a large native population, carried on, with Auckland chiefly, a thriving and lucrative trade. Captain Read's store was the principal house of business. The captain was also the local banker, for when, as very often happened, cash was short, he used to issue his I O U for various amounts, which passed current the same as a banknote. As soon as possible a number of women and children, principally those who had escaped from the massacre at Matawhero, were embarked on board the schooner Tawera, which immediately sailed for Napier. In Hawke's Bay the schooner spoke the s.s. Lord Ashley, bound north for Auckland, and transhipped some of her passengers who wished to go to that port. The Lord Ashley carried the news of the massacre to Auckland. Besides the Tawera, the schooner Success and ketch Eagle (Captain Loverock) were at anchor in the bay, off Turanga, and were kept in readiness to receive the women and children from the redoubt in case of an attack, which, however, for some reason, did not take place. Te Kooti's men contented themselves with the plunder they got from the homes at Matawhero. At night the sky was red with the glare from the burning houses. Mrs. Bloomfield's house was a substantial structure, erected at a cost of £1500, and was well finished. The roof was of slate, with leaden gutters, and this was stripped off by the natives before they set fire to the building. Before the next morning Te Kooti's men had retreated back to their mountain fastness, carrying with them a large amount of loot, and well pleased with their murderous work. Their victims lay dead and mutilated amidst and by the side of the blackened and charred remains of their former happy homes. Lieut. Gascoigne, who at the time of the attack was out with his scouts, hearing that the enemy had slipped by him, immediately made the best of his way to Turanga, where he arrived after a perilous jouney, and assumed command of the district, Major Biggs being killed and Capt. Westrup having escaped along the coast from Matawhero with a number of settlers. Capt. Loverock sailed slowly along the coast in the Eagle looking out for stragglers, burning during the night flares to attract the attention of any fugitives who might be on the beach. Early the following morning he was fortunate enough to rescue about forty settlers—men, women and children—who were on the beach, having escaped overland from Matawhero. Their delight at being taken on board was unbounded, and they will ever feel grateful to Capt. Loverock for going to their rescue. As soon as it was ascertained that the enemy had retired from Matawhero, a burial party started from Turanga for the scene of the massacre. The victims were found to have been nearly all mutilated. The remains of Major Biggs and his wife and servant, mangled and partly devoured by pigs, were brought in and interred, with the bodies of the other victims, in the Makaraka Cemetery, where now may be seen a handsome memorial stone, on which is set forth the names of the victims and the date of the massacre. Having performed their mournful duty, the burial party returned to Turanga. In all thirty-eight Europeans and thirty-two friendly natives were killed in the massacre at Matawhero. Some years after, when Te Kooti was at Paeroa, Ohinemuri, Mr. Mitchell, of the "Hauraki Tribune," interviewed him, and referred to the massacre. Te Kooti denied having been present or that he ordered the attack, but said that Biggs had been warned by the natives that he would be attacked. Te Kooti at the time was suffering from the wound in his foot which he received on the banks of the Ruakiture River in the skirmish with Col. Whitmore, so that it is very probable that he was not personally present. Mrs. Wilson, who was found alive, although dreadfully wounded, was conveyed to Turanga, where she was tenderly nursed, and it was hoped at the time that she would have recovered, but after her arrival at Napier she succumbed to the dreadful wounds that had been inflicted upon her. Before her death she left the following detailed statement of the native attack upon their house:—Capt. Wilson had just gone to bed. He had been writing letters for the overland mail, when a Maori knocked at the door, and wanted Capt. Wilson to open it, saying that he had a letter from Hirini. Capt. Wilson's suspicions were aroused, and he told the man to put it under the door. Soon afterwards he looked out, saw the outline of a number of heads, and suspected that mischief was intended. The natives finding it of no use to try and get the door opened by artifice, proceeded to batter it in with a piece of timber, but when they had done so they seemed afraid to enter the house. Edward Moran was sleeping in an outhouse, and Capt. Wilson called him to come into the house, which he did, although the natives tried to catch him as he ran across. After a time the natives began to fire into the house. Mrs. Wilson lay on the floor with one of her children; the others were upstairs. Capt. Wilson and Moran returned the fire of the natives, who then proceeded to fire the house at both ends. The flames and smoke soon drove the inmates out, the heat being so great that Mrs. Wilson's hair and the feet of the little ones were scorched as they escaped. Capt. Wilson had his revolver, and was prepared to use it, but the natives stopped him, saying that they would not kill him. They then started to walk towards Goldsmith's place. One of the natives took up Edward, Mrs. Wilson carried Jessie, Moran Alice, and Jimmy was on his father's back. They had very little clothing on, having to leave the house so quickly. Mrs. Wilson had a shawl over her night dress, and little Jimmy had his father's coat on over his night dress. After walking two or three hundred yards along the bank of the old river bed, one of the natives suddenly rushed upon Moran, another then stabbed Capt. Wilson through the body with a bayonet. Mrs. Wilson upon hearing her husband call out, turned round, and as she uttered a cry of horror she received a thrust with a bayonet, her arm being pierced trying to shield Jessie. She then fell down unconscious. When she regained consciousness it was daylight, and she saw her husband, Moran, and the children, with the exception of Jimmy, lying dead around her. She wondered what they had done with Jimmy, and never expected to see him again. Mrs. Wilson lay in the same place the whole of Tuesday, on which day an old native came and took her shawl, and it was not until the next day that she was able to crawl back again to what had been her home. There she found a small tea-kettle, which she filled with water from the tank, and got a broken bottle to drink out of. She then hid herself in a small shed that was left standing. Jimmy, when his father fell, had a difficulty in getting away, as his arm was under his father's body. Extricating himself at last he ran towards Mrs. Bloomfield's. It was then quite dark. Arriving at the house he lay on the verandah, and whilst there he heard the boy James rousing the inmates, but he did not see anyone leave the house. In the morning he wandered about from one place to another, and then returned to Bloomfield's, where he slept all night. The next day he returned to his own place, and saw his father, brother and sisters and Moran lying dead, and thought, not seeing his mother, that the natives had taken her away to eat her. At last, going into the shed, he found his mother. The little fellow then went to a nest, and found some eggs, and getting a firestick from the still-smouldering ruins, made a fire, put the kettle on and boiled some eggs. He also got some potatoes from the old Maori who had taken the shawl from Mrs. Wilson, and who lived not far away. Knowing that the Captain had his pocket-book in his coat-pocket and a pencil, Mrs. Wilson sent Jimmy for them, but she was so exhausted that it was only after many attempts that she was able to scrawl a few lines on a card requesting help. Jimmy was then sent off with the card, to carry it, if possible, to Turanga, but he could not manage to find his way farther than Makaraka, about halfway. Twice he tried. At last he saw a dog trotting along. He followed in the track it took, and after a while he reached the main road. Two miles outside of Turanga Jimmy was met by a party going to reconnoitre, who, upon learning Jimmy's errand, pushed forward and brought Mrs. Wilson back into the township.

CHAPTER VI.

FIGHGTING ON THE EAST COAST.—TE KOOTI CAPTURES 16,000 ROUNDS OF AMMUNITION.

A few days after the massacre large reinforcements, consisting principally of friendly natives, arrived at Poverty Bay from Napier and the coast under the command of Major Westrup and Capt. Tuke. The excitement at Turanga gradually abated; settlers returned to their homesteads, and Major Westrup made preparations for an advance against Te Kooti. The news of the massacre fell like a thunderbolt upon the citizens of Auckland when the Lord Ashley arrived with particulars and some of the fugitives. The deed was so horrible that it could scarcely be realised, and a deep gloom settled upon the people, who congregated in knots discussing the dire catastrophe. The 18th Regiment was at the time in garrison at Auckland, but under strict orders from the Home Government not to take the field. The man-o'-war Rosario (Capt. Palmer) was also in the harbour, and directly the news arrived, Capt. Palmer got up steam and left for Turanga, where the warship remained for some time as a guard ship for the protection of the town in case of an attack. The s.s. Tauranga was chartered by Dr. Pollen, Government Agent, and Mr. James Mackay proceeded in her down the East Coast to raise, if necessary, a corps of Arawas. There was no European force at the time available for service, the Armed Constabulary having more than they could do on the West Coast. On November 23 a strong force of friendly natives, who had started from Turanganui after Te Kooti, whilst following up the trail in the direction of Patutahi, came suddenly, at about 4 p.m., upon a horse saddled, standing in the track. The rider, no doubt alarmed by the sudden appearance of the friendlies, had escaped into the surrounding scrub. Following the track, the expedition emerged into a well-made road, the streams, where necessary, being roughly bridged. This work was done to enable the enemy to carry off the large amount of loot which they had secured from the settlers in the bay. After proceeding along the road for some distance, a hill was mounted at a place called Te Karetu, about thirty miles from Turanganui, and beneath them they beheld the object of their search—Te Kooti's camp. The position chosen was in a hollow on the edge of a densely-wooded creek, with high banks. It was a regular tent encampment, and numbers of horses and sheep were seen. There were no signs of the enemy, who were evidently asleep in their tents. It seems strange that they should have had no sentries on the watch. After extending well round the encampment, the friendlies suddenly poured volley after volley into the tents below. The fusillade had the effect of causing the surprised inmates to rush out of their canvas in all directions, and make for the nearest cover. Not being rushed, the enemy soon recovered themselves, and returned the fire of the friendlies, and a straggling fight commenced, which lasted all night, when Te Kooti's men, for some reason, ceased firing, and the friendlies had to reduce their fire on account of their ammunition running short. During the night two friendly natives were killed and six wounded. Lieut. Gascoigne, who was in charge of a party of scouts, had a narrow escape, a ball passing through his cap. In this affair Te Kooti is said to have lost about thirty men. The friendlies, throwing up some rough entrenchments, waited for a fresh supply of ammunition from Patutahi, where a depot had been formed, before resuming the offensive. The expected supply of ammunition, however, never arrived, for the party escorting the ammunition, in charge of Sergt.-Major Butters, formerly of Von Tempsky's Forest Rangers, were intercepted by about fifty of Te Kooti's men, and forced to retire, leaving in the hands of the enemy over 16,000 rounds of ammunition, besides stores. The men under Sergt.-Major. Butters, being mostly natives, bolted, and, although a stand was made behind an old fence, Sergt.-Major Butters was compelled to retreat back to the redoubt at Turanga. Shortly afterwards the friendlies, investing Te Kooti's camp, finding no ammunition forthcoming, also made their way back to Patutahi, whilst Te Kooti struck camp, and retreated still further back into the mountains to Ngatapa. The force of friendly natives—part Hawke's Bay, under the chief Karauria Pupu, part Mahia men under Ihaka Whanga and others, with a few Poverty Bay natives and Europeans, under Lieut. Gascoigne, held the position for three days' continual fighting. It was while this fighting was going on that Te Kooti sent a party to intercept the convoy under Sergt. Butters with the supply of ammunition. In the meanwhile a party of 370 men left Wairoa, viz., 200 Ngatiporou, under Ropata, Wahawaha and Hotene Porourangi, and 170 Wairoa natives under Lieut. Preece, to co-operate with the force engaged with Te Kooti. They left Wairoa on November 25th, making good marching and reaching the last crossing on the third day, when Mr. Ormond and Mr. George Burton, from Wairoa, overtook them with despatches from Colonel Lambert, stating that news had come via the coast to the effect that Te Kooti had intercepted the ammunition convoy between Patutahi and the front. The force moved on the following morning at daybreak, reaching Patutahi at dark and reported themselves to Sub-Inspector Arthur Tuke, Armed Constabulary. Having been supplied with ammunition and rations, they moved off early next morning, reached Te Wharekopae river and camped for the night. The following morning Ropata and Preece went on to the firing line and consulted with Lieut. Gascoigne and the friendly native chiefs who had been holding up the enemy at Makaretu for four days. It was then decided that the Wairoa force was to move under cover of the hills to the right and attack the enemy's left flank. This force had to make its way through heavy fern and broken manuka country without the least track. They attacked the enemy's left flank position at 3 p.m. The Hawke's Bay natives, under their own chiefs and Lieut. Gascoigne, at the same time making a frontal attack on the enemy's main position, with the result it was captured, sixty-five dead being found in the rifle pits, including the chief Nama and other prominent men. On the following morning Ropata and Preece moved forward and ascertained that the enemy was entrenching on the summit of Ngatapa, a position of great natural strength. A few stragglers were captured, but it was considered to be more advisable to retire and move out with a larger force the following day, when the Hawke's Bay natives would have rested somewhat after their five previous days' arduous fighting in the trenches.

Accordingly, on the morning of December 3rd it was arranged for the force to move out to a general attack. The Wairoa force, under Ropata and Lieut. Preece, and some Poverty Bay natives took the lead, capturing Te Kooti's uncle, Rihari Rikirangi, who was immediately shot. On reaching a high point of the range it was seen that the enemy was strongly entrenched on Ngatapa, and had cut down all trees and scrub in front of the position for a considerable distance. On reaching the clearing, Preece who was leading the advanced guard, halted his men in the track and sent a scouting party to the left with instructions to ascertain strength of that side of the position and return and report, but on no account were they to fire. Presently shots were fired by the scouts on the enemy's eastern left front, followed by a heavy fire from the rebels' works, which caused a panic, but Ropata came up at this juncture, and with Preece's help rallied the men, and with a small party went forward and attacked the right of the pa, getting up to within a few yards of the defences, preparatory to delivering an assault. Lieut. Preece then went back to bring up the main body, but after going twice, he only succeeded in getting about 90 men to join in the attack. Late in the afternoon, a portion of the enemy's works was taken and fighting continued at close quarters. Had the main body only joined, the whole position would have been captured. Ropata remained at his post all night with about 100 men, but had to retire at daylight, having lost six killed and six wounded, besides being without food or ammunition. They reached Makaraka just as Lieut. Gascoigne and the Hawke's Bay natives under their chiefs were moving out to Ropata's assistance, but he was so disgusted at their behaviour and by some of his own men deserting him at a critical time, that he decided to return home and bring his own tribe from the East Coast, upon whom he knew he could depend. The whole force then retired to Patutahi, where Colonel Whitmore met them, he having arrived from the West Coast with No. 1 Division A.C., under Colonel James Fraser. Ropata Wahawaha received the rank of Major in the N.Z. Militia for these services, and both he and his subaltern, Lieut. Preece, were awarded the New Zealand Cross for bravery.

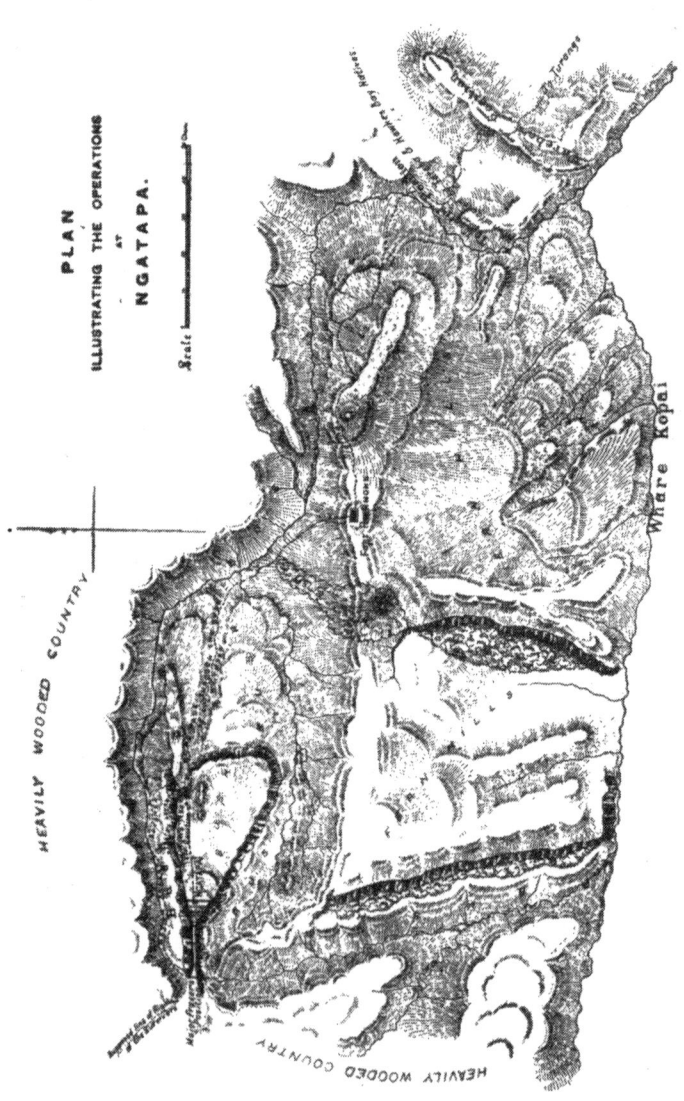

CHAPTER VII.

THE SIEGE OF NGATAPA.

Colonel Whitmore arrived at Turanga from the West Coast in the s.s. Ladybird with 300 men of the Armed Constabulary. Before proceeding to attack Te Kooti, Colonel Whitmore sent forward a party of scouts to ascertain if the enemy still occupied the same position. The scouts, upon their return, reported that they saw large fires at Ngatapa, as if Te Kooti was burning his whares before retreating. Acting on this report, Col. Whitmore ordered his men to re-embark for the West Coast. The Government steamer Sturt, having the force on board, in steaming out, ran on to a rock and knocked a hole in her bottom. At this juncture news came into Turanga that the enemy, instead of retreating, had again made their appearance on the plains, and murdered several settlers. A dog belonging to a young man named Fergusson, who was known to be at Mr. Harris' sheep station, came by itself to the redoubt at Turanga, and as the dog was known never to leave its master, it was considered that something wrong had happened, and a strong party, upon proceeding to the station of Mr. Harris, discovered the bodies of young Wylie, Fergusson, and a Maori all terribly mutilated. Col. Whitmore at once landed his Constabulary, and on December 24 marched against Ngatapa, where the column, about 400 strong, arrived on the 27th, and found Te Kooti strongly entrenched. Ropata shortly afterwards joined the attacking force with 350 natives.

After the native force had retired from the first attack on Ngatapa, Lieut. Preece, who had injured his foot on the return, was sent to Wairoa about middle of December, and about 400 Hawke's Bay natives, under their chiefs, Te Hapuku, Henare Tomoana Tareha and others arrived, having been sent to co-operate with Colonel Whitmore's force in a second attack on Ngatapa. These, together with 170 Wairoa natives and a few Europeans, with Mr. Deighton. R.M., and Lieut. Preece, left Wairoa intending to go to Puketapu, Te Kooti's original stronghold, from whence he had made his fatal raid on Poverty Bay. From here the force was to follow his trail and get in at his rear behind Ngatapa through the forest. This was a well designed plan, but, unfortunately, failed in execution. On reaching Omaruhakeke, on the Mangaruhe River, December 25th (the exact spot where three years before we had an engagement, losing Captain Hussey. Here the Maori prophets began to dream dreams. Captain Deighton remained at Erepeti, on the Ruakituri, with a few Europeans. On reaching Puketapu the place was found to be deserted, and on descending into the Papunui Valley a native, with his rifle capped and hammer down, fell, his gun going off, shooting his front rank man through the knee. The Hawke's Bay prophet at once declared this to be an "Aitua" (evil portent), and decided to return in spite of Preece's entreaties. He urged in vain for them to follow Te Kooti's broad trail from Te Papunui and get into Te Kooti's rear, behind Ngatapa, where by that time Colonel Whitmore's column would be attacking and the force went back to Wairoa, having accomplished nothing beyond discovering that Puketapu was unoccupied and burying the remains of Captains Carr and Davis Canning, and the others who fell at the Ruakituri fight, on the 8th August. Had this force gone on, as originally intended, it is more than probable that Te Kooti would have been captured, he having no knowledge that a force was moving in that direction. But it was not to be.

Having gathered his forces in front of the enemy's stronghold, Colonel Whitmore immediately invested the pa by throwing up lines of entrenchments, which, when finished, commanded Ngatapa, which was a natural fortress, being situated on the top of a pinnacle on one of the highest peaks of the mountain range some 2,000 feet above sea-level. The ground in the rear of the pa narrowed into a razor-back ridge, down which a track led, and which was available for retreat with the help of rope ladders to descend the rock terraces into the gorge below. The front slope of the position was defended by three lines of earth and fern-built parapets, with ditches in front. These parapets abutted at either end on the steep scarfed slopes. The outer or first line was about 250 yards long and seven feet high, the second line was shorter as the peak contracted, and the third or last line was a most formidable work, nearly fourteen feet high, with sandbag loopholes to enable the defenders to fire in safety. Each line was connected with the next by covered ways. A conical hill on the same ridge as the pa, but separated from it by a deep ravine, Colonel Whitmore made the base of his operations. This was called the Crow's Nest, and the two positions were about 700 yards apart. A mortar, after much labour, having been got into position, opened a vertical fire of shell with great effect. Colonel Fraser, with 100 of the Armed Constabulary and 100 Ngatiporous, was ordered round the right flank to cut off the enemy's retreat in the rear, and a long line of friendly natives, with No. 6 Company Armed Constabulary, under Major Roberts, connected the two parties, forming a line 700 yards long. The whole of the enemy's position was surrounded, with the exception of a small part of the cliff, which was considered too steep to admit of the enemy's escape, and was, moreover, exposed to a flanking fire from either party. Rain now set in, and continued for several days, increasing the hardships of the siege as the men were obliged to lie in the rifle pits, which were soon filled with water. In the meantime a heavy fire was kept up on both sides, but caused only trifling casualties. On the 2nd January Captain Brown, No. 7 Company A.C., was shot dead, and on the following day Captain Capel, of the same corps, was wounded. A few men under Captain Swindley climbed the precipitous razor-back ridge in the rear of the pa, and formed rifle pits under the rock terrace that formed the summit of Ngatapa. From here the party commanded the position of the enemy, who made desperate attempts to dislodge Captain Swindley. He, although losing several of his men, succeeded in holding the vantage-ground, and Privates Biddle and Black received the New Zealand Cross of Valour for their intrepid conduct on this occasion. Ropata, the friendly chief, after consulting with Col. Whitmore, determined to storm the outer line of the enemy's parapets. For this purpose he told off fifty picked men, and sent them down the ravine with orders to scale the cliff immediately under the end of the first parapet. The enemy, noticing the advance of Ropata's men, crowded to the end of the trench, and fired down on the storming party, wounding five men, but at the same time, being in an exposed position, suffered severely from the fire that was poured into them. The storming party, under cover of the fire from the rifle pits, climbed the outer face of the parapets, which they cut through with spades, and pouring a raking fire up the trench drove the occupants out, and took possession of the first line. In this affair about eight men were killed on each side and several wounded. A sap was then commenced from this base to the second line of trenches, the work being carried on all night, with the intention of blowing up the parapet and storming the main work the next morning. The enemy in the meantime kept up a heavy and well-directed fire on the working party, who had to keep well under cover to avoid being shot. Two men, who were incautious, were killed. In the meanwhile the storming party, numbering 200 men, sat in the trenches, and waited for the dawn. At about 2 a.m. the fire from the pa ceased, and a woman in the enemy's position called out that Te Kooti and his men had escaped. At the break of dawn the storming party cautiously advanced, and found that what the woman had said was true, for the only occupants were several wounded men, who were immediately tomahawked. The retreating foe were followed through the bush by a party of Ropata's men, who succeeded in capturing about 120 of the fugitives, who were dragged to the edge of the cliff, made to stand in a row, stripped, then shot, and thrown into the ravine below, where their bleached bones may still be found. Te Kooti himself, with a number of his followers, however, got away. The stronghold of Ngatapa having been destroyed, Colonel Whitmore marched his Armed Constabulary back to Poverty Bay, but Ropata returned to the coast across country, capturing on his way about eighty men, women and children belonging to Te Kooti's band. These he did not kill, as he had done the others, saying that if he did the Europeans would call him the butcher.

CHAPTER VIII.

TE KOOTI ATTACKS WHAKATANE AND THREATENS TAURANGA.

Te Kooti having been driven out of the Poverty Bay district, and his force dispersed, it was not considered necessary to retain any longer Colonel Whitmore and his Armed Constabulary, who embarked again for Wanganui, where a large number of West Coast natives were still in open rebellion. Ropata and his friendly natives returned to their different settlements along the coast, and peace once more reigned in the district. But Te Kooti was still at large, and roaming, none knew where, in the Urewera Mountains, and any day might make his appearance again at some settlement along the coast. But week after week passed away, and there was no sign of the guerilla chief, who might possibly have had enough of fighting and intended to rest satisfied with the mischief he had already done. Occasionally smoke was noticed rising from some of the ranges in the mountains, but it might have been caused by the fires of other natives, who had their settlements in the ranges, and so little notice was taken of the circumstance. About one hundred miles to the northward of Turanga, Poverty Bay, is situated the native settlement of Whakatane, in the Bay of Plenty, and two or three months after the capture of Ngatapa, Te Kooti, with a band of followers, estimated about 400 in number, descended from the mountains, and suddenly attacked the Whakatane natives. A Frenchman named Jean Gerraud, who had a store at the settlement, was tomahawked after making a desperate resistance and killing several of his adversaries. In the attempt to take the pa, or fortified place, where the natives of the settlement had rushed into upon the approach of the enemy, Te Kooti was unsuccessful, and forced to retire. He then commenced to sap up to the palisading of the pa, which he reached after two days' work, when the inmates surrendered. Te Kooti then sacked and burned the settlement, including the stores of Messrs. Simpkins and Milburne. Te Kooti's scouts having reported the advance of a strong party of Europeans and natives, under Major Mair, sent to the relief of the settlement, he hurriedly retired back again to the mountains, followed by Major Mair's party, who, however, did not succeed in capturing their wily foe. He again managed to get away. The fact that Te Kooti was again on the warpath caused no little uneasiness at all the settlements along the coast, and especially at Tauranga, distant about sixty miles north of Whakatane, and where there was settled a large number of European women and children, totally unprotected, excepting by the small force of settlers located in the township and its environs. An urgent request was despatched to Auckland for reinforcements. The 18th Regiment in garrison there were at the time of the Poverty Bay massacre not available for service in the field, and the Government, at Wellington, under the circumstances, requested the Auckland Naval Artillery Volunteers, under Lieut. E. H. Featon with 26 pounder Armstrong guns, to

TE KOOTI EXPEDITIONS.

proceed to Tauranga for the relief of the settlers. The request of the Government was cheerfully complied with, and as soon as possible the Artillery embarked on board the s.s. Tauranga, and steamed away for their destination, receiving on their departure an ovation from the large crowd assembled on the wharf to see them off.

After Te Kooti was pursued by Major Mair from Whakatane to Tauaroa, he made for Ahikereru, and from thence almost at once to Waikaremoana. Avoiding the Wairoa Waikaremoana road, he crossed the Waiau River and went by Te Putere. At this time, an expedition of Wairoa, Mahia and Mohaka natives accompanied by a few Europeans, was on its way to Waikaremoana, as the rebels were supposed to be in force there. Two friendly native scouts having been killed at the Waiau River, Mohaka was therefore denuded of its fighting natives of the Ngatipahauwera, a small but splendid fighting tribe. Te Kooti ascertained this from a native at Te Putere. His whole force struck for Upper Mohaka, killing the European settlers—men, women and children and some natives employed by them—as he went down the valley. There were two fortified pas at Lower Mohaka, but these were only held by a few men each, with women and children, the main body of natives being away on the expedition to Waikaremoana. Te Kooti at once attacked both pas, one being out on the flat, the other with a steep cliff in front of it. The occupants, men and women, fought bravely. The Europeans on the other side of the river had in the meanwhile escaped towards Napier. The stores, hotel, and houses having been looted and burned, needless to say that numbers of natives were drunk, and this probably prevented them pursuing those who had escaped. The rebels continued their attack on both pas. On the second day a force of Wairoa natives, under Hamana Tiakiwai, a poor fighter, accompanied by that splendid old chief Ihaka Ihanga, reached within a mile of the pas when they were attacked by the rebels and fled, leaving Ihaka Ihanga wounded. Notwithstanding this, the old man climbed up a tree and remained there while the rebels were passing under him.

Trooper Rowley Hill was with this party, and he, with a few natives, worked their way round to the back of the pa in the open. They got in, and through his splendid fighting example, they held out against the enemy. At the other pa, the rebels sapped up to it. Te Kooti demanded their surrender. A son of Paora Rerepu, who himself was away on the Waikaremoana expedition, fired at him, but Te Kooti threw himself down and was not touched. A general massacre then took place, some ten or twelve men and a number of women and children were killed. Young Ropita Rerepu, though wounded, escaped over the cliff. After this the rebels, finding that reinforcements were coming from both Wairoa and Napier, withdrew and made off for the Urewera country again, sending a party towards Wairoa to make it appear they were going to attack that settlement, but really to cover their own retreat. Constable Rowley Hill was promoted to be Sergeant for this service, and was afterwards awarded the New Zealand Cross.

LIEUT.-COLONEL ST. JOHN.

CHAPTER IX.

TE KOOTI ATTACKED IN THE UREWERA COUNTRY—DEATH OF CAPT. TRAVERS.—A MILITARY POST SURPRISED.

Col. Whitmore was again ordered from Wanganui with his Armed Constabulary to the East Coast, via Auckland, and this time the Government were determined to put an end to Te Kooti and his murderous escapades, and a number of additional men were enrolled for service with Col. Whitmore's column. Arriving in Auckland a number of Col. Whitmore's men, who had been for some months constantly fighting in the field, broke away, and the embarkation of the force was delayed owing to the time lost in hunting up the lost sheep. In the meantime Te Kooti had not been idle, for he had again collected a considerable number of restless spirits to join his standard, and considered himself in the rugged passes and mountains of the Urewera Country able to defy any force that might be sent against him.

When Colonel Whitmore passed through Auckland the force shipped for Tauranga, and from thence moved overland to Matata. Part of the force under Colonel St. John had gone round the North Cape and landed at Whakatane. Some considerable time was spent in organising and arranging for native allies to accompany the two separate columns which were to move against Te Kooti and the Urewera tribe. It was arranged that Colonel Whitmore's force, consisting of No. 1, 2, and 6 Divisions of A.C., Ngatipikiao and Ngatiwhakaue friendly Arawas, under their chiefs Te Pokiha Taranui, Henare Te Pukuatua, and others, should proceed up the Rangitaike and establish posts as they went along, making Matata the base, while St. John with another force of A.C. and friendly natives, from Whakatane and beyond Opotiki, moved up Whakatane River, the objective being Ruatahuna, the stronghold of the Urewera, where both columns should meet.

At about the same time that Colonel Whitmore arrived at Whakatane a force under Colonel Herrick started from Napier province for the rebels' strong position, situated on the edge of the Waikaremoana Lake, and it was arranged that Col. Whitmore's forces, after sweeping the enemy out of the Urewera mountains at the back of the Bay of Plenty, should join Col. Herrick at Waikaremoana. This event, however, did not come to pass, owing to the difficulties encountered by Col. Herrick, in his failure to build boats to cross Waikaremoana lake.

Captain Travers, late of 70th Regiment, marched up the Whakatane River with Colonel St. John's column, and during the attack on the enemy's position, Tatahoata was sent by that officer to hold the edge of a point of bush above the pa in order to cut off the retreat of its defenders, should they abandon it. His company of A.C. lay down along a rotten old fence twenty yards outside the bush, and were heavily fired on immediately from the natives hidden inside. The decayed fence offered no protection, and several were killed or wounded by the first volley. The gallant Travers stood on a stump, directing his men to take good aim. Seeing his danger his batman ran up and tried to make him take cover, but he replied, "A British officer never takes cover, my lad!" Next moment he was mortally wounded, only uttering the words, "I have tried to do my duty as a soldier and a Briton." Captain David White, leader of the guides, was killed while going up the Whakatane River two days previously. He was about the finest bush fighter in our forces.

While Colonel St. John's column marched up the Whakatane River, Colonel Whitmore's went via Te Teko to Galatea. Colonel Whitmore established a post at the end of the navigable part of Rangitaike River, which was named Fort Alfred—another, twelve miles further, named Fort Clarke (after Mr. Commissioner Clarke, who accompanied the forces); another called Fort Galatea. This was made the starting point. A garrison was left at each post, and a transport service was arranged from Matata by canoes to Fort Alfred and thence by pack horses to Fort Galatea. This force moved towards Ahihereru, and it was arranged that Ngatipikiao, under the Chief Pokiha Taranui and Lieut. Gilbert Mair, should take the lead through the bush to a certain point near the open country and there await the arrival of the main body. This was carried out, and Pokiha Taranui with his men, and Lieut. G. Mair, were given three hours to move through the bush to the right and get to the back of the pa, which had been located. This was well carried out, and a simultaneous attack was made from front and rear, with the result that the Pa was taken and five natives killed and a number of women taken prisoners. The force moved on the following day, and in the afternoon fell into an ambuscade, which resulted in one of the Corps of Guides being mortally wounded and two others wounded. On the following day the force saw from the top of Tatahoata range that Colonel St. John's force was in possession of the Tatahaoata Pa. They camped at Oputao, the foot of the hill, that night. Colonel Whitmore, accompanied by Captain Swindley, Lieut. Preece and Sergt. Maling, with his Corps of Guides, 16 in number, and a Maori guide, pushed on through the bush and joined Colonel St. John's force at 11 p.m. that night.

The column, under Major Roberts, A.C., joined Colonels Whitmore and St. John at Tatahoata. The whole force concentrating, resumed their march, the Corps of Scouts, under Captain Swindley, leading the way. For several days there were small skirmishes with parties of the enemy. They were then seen to be in force on the track leading from Waikare-moana. A portion of the force moved out and took possession of a hill. The Ngatipikiao, under their chiefs Te Pokiha Taranui and Matene, and Lieut. Gilbert Mair, engaged with the enemy in the bush in a creek, killing four, one of whom was at once recognised by Lieut. Preece to be a Wairoa native named Hamiora, who had joined Te Kooti just before the Poverty Bay massacre. After this, the native allies made up their minds that they would not go to Waikaremoana. Colonel Whitmore appealed to them to help him to carry out his plans, but without effect. In this decision they were justified by the state of the weather, the lack of provisions and ammunition, and the fact that Te Kooti, with a strong force, occupied a narrow gorge through which they would have been obliged to pass. The force then moved out, Major Mair, with the sick and wounded, accompanied by the Whakatane and Opotiki natives and some Constabulary, moved via Horomanga Gorge. These were followed, and had to fight a rear guard action. The main body, under Colonels Whitmore and St. John, moved out via Ahikereru to Fort Galatea.

Winter being now fairly set in, Colonel Whitmore decided to hold his posts and await a more favourable opportunity for dealing with the enemy. Accordingly he left Colonel St. John in charge at Fort Galatea, and left with his staff and the Corps of Guides intending to go by sea to Wairoa to consult with Colonel Herrick, also taking with him No. 2 Division A.C. to strengthen that officer's force at Waikaremoana. The A.C. and Corps of Guides were left at Wairoa, and Colonel Whitmore, after conferring with Colonel Herrick, left with his staff for Wellington to recruit his health.

In the meanwhile, Colonel St. John, who had been instructed to occupy Taupo in the near future, started out with the intention of consulting the friendly natives there, taking a party of about twenty of the Bay of Plenty Cavalry with him. He camped at Opepe, nine miles from Taupo. Leaving most of his men there under Cornet Angus Smith, he pushed on with Captain Morrison and a few others to consult with Captain St. George about establishing a military post at Tapuaeharuru on Lake Taupo.

Opepe was a most dangerous position, at the forest edge, with a number of deep dry gullies converging on the small plateau, where the whares our men were occupying stood. Te Kooti, having intercepted and shot Trooper Donald McDonald the previous day at Heruiri, who, with Trooper Black, was carrying despatches from Galatea for Colonel St. John, became aware of the latter being ahead of him, followed quickly. It had been raining heavily, and the men left behind in camp were drying their clothes when a native came up who knew one of the troopers. He said that there were friendly natives coming; they would be there soon. Suddenly the party were attacked by a large force from the bush, which was close by, and most of them were killed. Cornet Smith and Troopers Dette, Croswell and Lockhart escaped. Cornet Smith was nine days out before he reached Fort Galatea. Two young surveyors, named Hallett, who were engaged surveying a few miles away came up in the morning and found the bodies of the men who were killed. They at once rode on to Tapuaeharuru and informed Colonel St. John.

Te Kooti had, in the meanwhile, moved on to Waitahanui, on the Lake, on his way to Tokaanu. Colonel St. John and the remainder of his party and some Taupo natives arrived in the course of the day and buried the bodies of the dead troopers. He returned with his men to Fort Galatea, where he found three of the troopers who escaped and made their way there on foot.

CHAPTER X.

EXPEDITIONS IN TAUPO AND BAY OF PLENTY DISTRICTS.

While Colonel Whitmore was in Wellington recruiting his health a change of Government took place, the Stafford Government being defeated and Mr. Fox formed a Ministry, with Mr. Donald McLean as Defence Minister. Colonel Harington was placed in command of the Field Force in the Bay of Plenty, This officer recommended the withdrawal of Colonel St. John's forces from all stations from Matata to Galatea, and only holding Whakatane and Opotiki. This was acted on and the force was put through a course of drill at Tauranga. Te Kooti was still in the Waikato country with his whole force. Captain St. George was in charge of friendly natives at Tapuaeharuru, and he kept the Government posted with information of many movements of the rebels. Late in August it was ascertained that Te Kooti was leaving Waikato and was moving towards the southern end of Taupo Lake. Captain St. George's force was strengthened by Arawa natives, under Henare Pukuatua and Lieut. Preece, who had been ordered up from Tauranga. At the same time, Colonel Herrick's A.C. force was withdrawn from Waikaremoana, which was abandoned, and a line of posts was established from Napier to Runanga on the Taupo Road. The chief Henare Tomoana, with about 150 Hawke's Bay natives, were sent up to act with Colonel Herrick. When these arrived, instructions were sent to Captain St. George to move with his Taupo and Arawa contingents by canoe to the southern end of the Lake and act in conjunction with Colonel Herrick and Henare Tomoana. These movements took time, and it was towards the middle of September before the force arrived at Runanga. Henare Tomoana, however, pushed on, without awaiting the arrival of Colonel Herrick. He met Te Kooti in full force at Tauranga, on the shores of Lake Taupo, where Te Kooti at once attacked him. He, however, fortified the Maori pa, and after a day and night's fighting repelled the enemy with loss, who retired towards Tokaanu and Rotoaira Lake. Captain St. George's contingent, having been detained by heavy sea on the Lake, arrived in a fleet of canoes just too late to take part in the fight. Both columns then moved on towards Tokaanu, St. George's party by canoe and Henare Tomoana's by land. They found that place deserted, the enemy having retired towards Lake Rotoaira. The Government force camped at Tokaanu, and word came in that Colonel Herrick's force of A.C. had arrived at Tauranga, Taupo, and would join up the following day.

It should be here mentioned, that while this force was moving up from Napier another force was sent up from Napier via inland Patea, under the chief Renata Kawepo. This force was to junction at Rotoaira Lake with another party of natives sent up the Wanganui River to Pipiriki by canoes, thence to march to via Karioi. The Wanganui force was under Colonel McDonnell and Major Kemp (a native chief). The plan was well carried out, and word came through the same day that the two forces had arrived at Rotoaira, and that the enemy was in great strength on the opposite side of the Lake. Captain St. George at once left for Rotoaira to consult with Colonel McDonnell. On the following morning (the 27th of September) a party of Taupo and Arawa contingent, under Lieut. Preece, were scouting on the trail of the rebels over the hill, leading towards the western side of Rotoaira, when they were heavily attacked by rebels. They were soon supported by Henare Tomoana's Hawke's Bay men, and a general engagement took place in which the enemy was driven back up the hill, where he was entrenched in rifle pits. At this moment, Captain St. George, who was riding from Rotoaira with Colonel McDonnell, and had heard the firing, arrived and took command. The rifle pits were taken at a charge and a number of natives killed, amongst whom was Wi Piro, a Chatham Island ex-prisoner, who was one of the leading spirits in the Poverty Bay massacre. The enemy were completely routed with loss, while on our side a Hawke's Bay native and a young Taupo chief, Maniapoto, were killed.

Colonel Herrick's force joined up the same day, and Colonel McDonnell assumed command. A few days were spent in scouting the country from the scene of the late engagement towards the western side of the Rotoaira Lake. Parties were sent out under Captain Northcroft, A.C., Lieut. Preece, and Sergt. C. Maling, of the Corps of Guides, to locate the enemy's position. It was ascertained that he was in force at the southern end of the Lake, and the Wanganui natives from Rotoaira reported that he was building a pa on a hill beyond Papakai settlement. A general move was now ordered, the A.C. force under Colonel Herrick; the Taupo and Arawa contingent under Captain St. George, and the Hawke's Bay natives under Henare Tomoana, to Poutu, on the Rotoaira Lake, where the Hawke's Bay and Wanganui native contingents were located, under Colonel McDonnell. Tokaanu was occupied as a base of operations, and a sufficient force left there to hold it.

On the 3rd of October, the whole force moved out and occupied Papakai settlement, the enemy retiring to three forts on the hills. It was then arranged that Major Kemp, with his Wanganui native contingent should work, under cover of a ridge, to the left at a given time. They were to attack the small redoubt on the left. The Armed Constabulary, under Colonel McDonnell, and Hawke's Bay natives to attack the main redoubt; Te Porere and the Taupo and Arawa contingent to attack the small redoubt on the right, and then converge to the left of the main redoubt.

Major Kemp and his men carried out their duties well. After crossing the Wanganui River, which is a deep creek at this point. Captain St. George sent Lieut. Preece, with part of the Taupo contingent, to attack the extreme right of the position, and with the rest of the contingent joining in the frontal attack. The operations were entirely successful. The position was taken by assault, and over thirty left dead on the field. Our loss consisted of Captain St. George, a brave officer, Komene, an Arawa chief; Winiata, a splendid fighter of the Wanganui contingent; and Pape (Pompey), also of the Wanganui contingent, killed. The chief Renata

LIEUT-COLONEL. McDONNELL.

Kawepo, of the Hawke's Bay contingent, bayoneted a rebel and was attacked by the man's wife, who gouged his eye out and inflicted other injuries.

The rebels were followed into the bush, but it was too late in the day to continue the pursuit. It was afterwards ascertained that Te Kooti was himself wounded, losing a finger and receiving a flesh wound on his side. The force occupied Papakai that night and returned to Poutu the next day, where the dead were buried.

After this, Te Heuheu, chief of the southern end of Taupo Lake, surrendered with all his people, and reported that Te Kooti and his people had made for Manganui-a-Te Ao, on the Wanganui River. The Hawke's Bay natives and the Wanganui natives then returned to their respective settlements. Colonel Herrick, who was a Hawke's Bay settler, left the force and retired to his farm at Ongaonga, having been continuously in the field since August, 1868. Colonel McDonnell abandoned Poutu and moved the force to Tokaanu on Lake Taupo.

The force remained in Tapuo, with Tokaanu as headquarters and base of operations, from that time until the middle of January, 1870. Expeditions were made through the bush towards the Wanganui River, and some small skirmishes took place with local natives at some of their old settlements. Expeditions were also made to the country to the west of Taupo Lake, and the natives of that part surrendered and were handed over to the custody of the friendly Taupo natives. Reports came in from time to time that Te Kooti had overstayed his welcome amongst the natives of Manganui-a-Te Ao, on the Wanganui River, and that his position there had been made awkward by the fact that Topia Turoa, a leading chief of Upper Wanganui, had surrendered to Mr. Fox, the Premier, at Jerusalem, on the Wanganui River, and had expressed his willingness to place the services of himself and his tribe at the disposal of the Government to act in conjunction with Major Kemp, against Te Kooti in the field, and that his services had been accepted.

It is worth while here to mention two cases of great bravery displayed by friendly natives about this time. Colonel McDonnell wished to send a despatch to Mr. Fox. The district through which the orderly would have to travel was principally through enemy country, consisting for some 60 miles of fairly open country, then 30 miles of bush track. Lieut. Preece was asked by Colonel McDonnell to detail one of the Taupo contingent, who knew the country, for the service, but one and all professed ignorance of the country or they only had a partial knowledge of it. Then, thinking of a man named Te Puia, who had been in a division of A.C. on the West Coast, and was partly Arawa and partly Wanganui native, Lieut. Preece asked him if he knew the road. He replied "Yes," and when told that the Colonel wanted him to carry a despatch, he said, "If the Colonel will give me a troop horse and authorise me to take any other horse I find on the road I will go." When informed that this would be done he went to his whare, got his saddle and bridle, and went up to headquarters for the despatch. He caught three horses on his sixty mile ride, then camped in the bush beyond Karioi, reaching Pipiriki on foot next day, and from thence went by canoe to Jerusalem, where he delivered the despatch to Mr. Fox. He was kept there for two days, until Mr. Fox was in a position to state when the force under Major Kemp and Topia Turoa would start, and on his return walked 30 miles and rode 60 in one day, picking up each horse where he had left it. He arrived at Tokaanu at 4 a.m., doing the distance of 90 miles, partly on foot, partly on horseback, in 24 hours. This service was never properly recognised. His only reward was £5.

The second act of bravery was as follows:—Two natives of the Arawa contingent—Te Honiana and another—volunteered to go on a scouting party by themselves, from Tokaanu to Taumarunui, where Te Kooti and his war party were supposed to have then reached. The distance was 40 to 45 miles, partly through bush, partly through open country. They went armed, and travelled at night where the country was open, and by day in the bush. They reached the hill overlooking Taumarunui, where the station now stands, and from their position in the bush saw the large assemblage of natives in the settlement below and heard all their speeches, giving full information that they were making for Tapapa, at the back of Tauranga (near what is now known as the Putaruru railway station). Having heard this, they made their way back to Tokaanu and reported to Colonel McDonnell, after an absence of six days, when fears were entertained that they might have fallen into the hands of the enemy. For this service these two men were given £10 each, and were presented with the Terry carbines they carried. This was certainly a very inadequate reward.

Colonel McDonnell having been advised by the despatch from Mr. Fox that Major Kemp and Topia Turoa were on their way to join him, determined to push on at once with all speed and send word to Kemp to follow as quickly as possible. Accordingly, the whole force moved to Tapnaeharuru, at the extreme northern end of the Lake, and from thence to Waimahana, on the Waikato River, where they arrived on the 19th of January. Here Colonel McDonnell decided to halt and await the arrival of Major Kemp and Topia. Lieut. Preece was sent across the Waikato River and through the bush with an advance party to locate the enemy, and managed to surprise and capture a party of Ngatiraukawa at Tewe. They were local Hauhaus. They said that Te Kooti was at Tapapa in great force, but that they did not want to join him, although some of the tribe had done so. They themselves wished to be left alone. Lieut. Preece sent word back to Colonel McDonnell to say that he thought it advisable to stay where he was, in order to keep the natives under control. He camped there and maintained a good guard. Late in the night a call some distance off their front, was heard. They challenged, and after a while heard an English voice, to which they replied, and found it was Sergt. Maling, of the Corps of Guides, who, with a native orderly named Raimona, had been sent from Tauranga by Colonel Fraser with despatches to Colonel McDonnell. They had crossed Te Kooti's trail on the Tokoroa plains, and got between the Colonial forces and the enemy. This was only one of Sergt. Maling's many plucky acts. He was afterwards awarded the New Zealand Cross.

TE KOOTI EXPEDITIONS.

Two days afterwards, lying low by day and marching by night, Tapapa pa was attacked and captured. On the following day, Te Kooti reversed the order and attacked the Government troops just as they were about to move out against him. This was fortunate, because if his attack had been delayed he would have found only a small force there. The attack proceeded from the bush side. One of the Whanganui contingent, was with others gathering potatoes when he was killed by a blow from a "mere pounamu" by a man who approached from the bush. The alarm was given by the man's companions, and the fighting became general. To Kooti's people were flying the Union Jack, and were at first mistaken for the Whanganui natives, and had got between the Whanganui natives and a point of bush where our troops were engaged with the enemy. Lieut. Preece was instructed to clear this point when a Maori passed just in front of him at the edge of the bush. Thinking he was a Whanganui native, Lieut. Preece asked which way the rebels had retired; the native who was at the edge of the bush, pointed in front of him, got behind a tree and fired missing Lieut. Preece but mortally wounding Private Etherington of the Corps of Guides, who was a few paces behind him. The enemy was driven off with the loss of a few men and two on our side.

A number of small engagements took place in the Tapapa bush during the month the force was there. Expeditions were made in different directions through the bush, resulting in skirmishes with detached parties of the enemy and killing a few of them without loss to our forces, but as it was dense bush the work was very difficult. After getting through and joining Colonel Fraser's force at Akeake, a small engagement took place in which one European and two natives were killed.

Te Kooti then made for Ohinemutu, and would probably have taken the place, if it had not been for the determination of Lieut. Gilbert Mair, who forced an action while Petera Pukuatua and other natives were parleying with him, under his flag of truce. The result was a running fight extending for over fourteen miles. Te Kooti's loss was severe, including Peka Te Makarini, a half-caste, shot by Mair, Timoti Te Kaka of Opotiki, and others. The rebels escaped into the Urewera Country.

The force then moved to Tauranga, and thence to Maketu and Matata, with the intention of working against Te Kooti in conjunction with the Ngatiporou under Major Ropata and Captain Porter from the Poverty Bay side, and from the Bay of Plenty by way of Waimana or Ahikereru and Ruatahuna.

The Wanganui natives, under Major Kemp and Topia Turoa, had moved to Ohiwa, and Colonel McDonnell proceeded from there to Opotiki, to interview the Defence Minister, Mr. (afterwards Sir Donald McLean). Captain Preece was instructed to go to Tarawera and then on to Fort Galatea, with a body of Arawas, and, as soon as a column arrived, to make a movement on the Urewera through Ahikereru. Soon afterwards, they were ordered back to Tarawera, and later to Te Teko, on the Rangitaiki River.

CHAPTER XI.

ARDUOUS BUSH FIGHTING.
EXPEDITIONS UNDER CAPTAINS MAIR AND PREECE.

It had then been decided by Mr. McLean to relieve Colonel McDonnell of his command. The field force of the Armed Constabulary was sent to occupy a line of posts at Taupo and several points on the Bay of Plenty. Meanwhile the field work was to be carried on by natives under their own chiefs and a few European officers. About the 26th of March, Captain Preece received instructions to disband the Arawa and Taupo native contingents, and to enroll a special corps of not more than one hundred picked Maoris, who should be drilled in the same way as the European force. Captain Preece was to be stationed at Te Teko and work from there as a base. Captain Mair had been instructed to raise a similar number, and would be stationed at Kaiteriria. Both officers were under the officer commanding the Tauranga district. They were ordered to scout together and meet at Fort Galatea, patrolling the country, and at the same time to keep in touch with Major Roberts, commanding the Taupo district; but a good deal of discretion was allowed to both officers. Captain Preece picked his men from all tribes, and avoided choosing any chiefs in order to have them under his own control, as he had had a sickening of native chiefs. He had considerable opposition from the chiefs, but selected good men in spite of them, and was fortunate in getting some excellent European and Maori non-commissioned officers, and never regretted the composition of the force. The men worked well together. The Europeans were experienced Armed Constabulary men, and one of the sergeants, a native, had been many years in the Auckland Police Force, and was well drilled.

In the meanwhile the Whanganui natives, under Major Kemp and Topia Turoa, Ngatiporou under Major Ropata and Captain Porter; the loyal Ngaitai tribe, under the chief Wiremu Kingi; and the Ngatiawa and Ngatipukeko under Hohaia and Hori Kawakura, attacked Te Kooti at Maraetai, in the Waioeka Gorge, after he had raided Opape, a settlement near Opotiki, where he had captured a number of the Whakatohea tribe and taken them inland with him. These operations were very successful. Ropata drove the natives out of their stronghold, and as they escaped from him they fell into the hands of Major Kemp and his men. The local natives, who had been taken prisoners, or who had joined Te Kooti recently, were spared, but the ex-Chatham Island prisoners, belonging to Te Kooti's band, got no mercy; a great many were killed. Hakaraia, a noted old ruffian, was among them. Of Te Kooti's Whakatahea captives, 270 men, women and children were taken by us. A letter was discovered from one of their chiefs to Te Kooti asking him to make the raid, which explained why he had spared their lives when he took them.

CAPTAIN MAIR.

From the 6th April, 1870, onwards, Captains Mair and Preece made expeditions on the borders of the Urewera Country, and had a few unimportant skirmishes with the enemy in different places. On the 17th of April a Ngatiwhare, named Paraone Te Tuhi, and four others, who had been in one of the skirmishes, came in under a flag of truce and surrendered. Paraone said to us: "I am the rope; pull me and the horse will follow," intimating that he was the first to give himself up, and that if we sent him back to his tribes they would also surrender. Shortly after this, the whole of the Ngatiwhare tribe from Ahikereru, under their chiefs Hapurona Kohi, before mentioned, and Hamiora Potakurua, came in and laid down their arms at Fort Galatea. They were conveyed to the coast, near Matata. Subsequently, the Warahoe and Patuheuhu tribe surrendered under their chiefs Wi Patene and Manuera, and were settled near the redoubt at Te Teko, the Government providing them with food until they could gather their crops from seed supplied to them. In all cases they gave up their arms.

It must be mentioned that when Major Kemp and his Whanganui natives advanced from Ohiwa up the Waimana River, Tamaikoha, the Urewera chief of Waimana, who had been the leading spirit in the rebellion in the Opotiki country in 1867 and 1868, met Kemp and made peace. He declared that he had never joined Te Kooti, and promised that our troops could go through his country in pursuit of the rebel chief without being molested by his men. Tamaikoha did not want two Richmonds in the field. Some time after the junction of Major Kemp's party with Ropata's, and their successful fight at Maraetai, and after they had left the neighbourhood, Colonel St. John, who then commanded the district, heard that rebels were afoot, and made a raid up the Waimana. He fired on some men he saw, killing one, who, unfortunately, turned out to be Tamaikoha's uncle, named Tipene. This naturally caused trouble, because Tamaikoha said that we had made a treacherous peace and then attacked him. Colonel St. John was removed from the district, and Major Mair was sent to try and patch matters up. His efforts were successful, and Tamaikoha was ever afterwards our firm friend. This is mentioned for a reason that will appear later.

The Urewera tribe were growing weary of allowing themselves to be used by the rebel leader. Early in May Captain Preece had heard that the Urewera chiefs, Paerau Te Rangikaitipuake and Te Whenuanui, of Ruatahuna, were inclined to break away from Te Kooti, who, after his defeat at Maraetai, had taken up a position with the remnant of his followers at Te Houpapa, in the bush at the head waters of the Waioeka and Hangaroa Rivers, about midway between Opotiki and Wairoa, on the Hawke's Bay side. He accordingly sent letters by a surrendered Ngatiwhare chief, telling them that if they would come in and give up their arms, we would merely go through their country in pursuit of Te Kooti, and would not harm them. They replied that the peace made with Tamaikoha had resulted in blood being spilt, and that they would not surrender. However, shortly after this, Te Whenuanui met Major Mair at Ruatoki, and peace was made with his party. A little while later, Paerau Te Rangikaitipuake met Capt. Preece at Ahikereru, and his people made peace and opened their country to us. After these important surrenders, the only chief of the Urewera on the Ruatahuna side of the country who supported Te Kooti was Kereru Te Pukenui, who occupied the lower end of the valley and Maungapowhatu. One chief of the latter place, Timoti Takangahau, had previously surrendered with Ngatiwhare.

About this time a body of Wairoa natives, under Mr. F. E. Hamlin and Lieut. Witty, took up a position at Onepoto, Waikaremoana, the position abandoned by Colonel Herrick in 1869. The Urewera wrote to Captain Preece saying that we were fighting them on one side of their country and making peace on the other. After a few skirmishes, Hona Te Makarini and his people surrendered to Mr. Hamlin, and with a few other chiefs went to Napier to confer with Mr. Ormond, the General Government agent at that town.

This ended the war against the Urewera, although a small section of them from Maungapoohatu, under Te Whiu, were still out with Te Kooti at Te Wera or Te Houpapa. Among them was Kepa Te Ahuru, N.Z.C., a Trooper of No. 1 Division A.C., who had been captured by Te Kooti at Rotorua just before Lieut. Mair's engagement with him at that place, on the 7th of February. This man afterwards, during a skirmish with Major Pitt, when Te Kooti raided Tologa Bay, made his way through the bush to Maungapowhata and surrendered to Captain Preece at Horomanga, near Fort Galatea. He was sent to Tauranga to report himself to Colonel Moull, who having satisfied himself that he was forcibly detained and had taken the first opportunity of escaping, sent him to duty and gave him his back pay. Kepa was at once attached to Captain Preece's force. He served in it for several years, and was on all the subsequent expeditions through the Urewera Country.

Te Waru and his tribe of Wairoa natives, who dared not show themselves at Wairoa on account of the treacherous murder of Karaitiana Rotoatara and his three fellow scouts at his (Te Waru's) pa at Whataroa, in October, 1868, just before the Poverty Bay massacre, surrendered unconditionally to Capt. Preece at Horomanga and laid down their arms. They were informed that any murderers would be tried for their offences according to law. They were being sent to Tauranga under strong escort when Mr. Clarke, the Civil Commissioner, intervened and the Government decided to place them on the coast at Maketu, under charge of the loyal Maoris. They were afterwards settled at Waiotahi, near Opotiki, on land allotted to them by the Government, but were never allowed to return to the Wairoa district. It may be interesting to know that the grandson of Karaitiana Rotoatara above mentioned, was a sergeant in the Great War and was awarded the military medal for service in France, thus proving himself a worthy descendant of his grandfather.

On one of the many expeditions made by Captains Mair and Preece, during the latter part of 1870, scouring the borderlands of the Urewera, they intercepted a party of Te Kooti's men trying to get through to Waikato, and drive them back into the bush near Heruiwi. One of these men, Paora Wakahoehoe, was afterwards killed at Waipaoa in August, 1871. Another named Maka was captured by Captain Ferris in the early part of 1872. He was one of the ringleaders of Te Kooti's butchers who committed the atrocities in Poerty Bay in November, 1868. He was tried in Napier and condemned to death. The sentence, however, was commuted to penal servitude for life, and after serving ten years he was released.

From April, 1870, to April, 1871, Captains Mair and Preece, with their respective contingents, patrolled the country from Te Teko as far as Heruiwi, in the Taupo district, and through the bush from Waiohau to Horomanga and Ahikereru, keeping in constant touch with the Armed Constabulary under Major Roberts at Taupo and Major Mair at Opotiki. Then orders came that they were to hold themselves in readiness to take the field against Te Kooti, as it was reported that he was making for Waikaremoana to avoid Major Ropata and Captain Porter, who were moving up towards Te Houpapa from Poverty Bay.

On the 27th of May, 1871, Captains Mair and Preece started from Fort Galatea, on their first expedition after Te Kooti through the Urewera Country. They had about 50 men of each contingent, and had brought up three weeks' rations from Te Teko. They arrived at Ahikereru on the following day, and then got deep into the Urewera mountains, where the knowledge of the country that they had obtained on Colonel Whitmore's Ruatahuna expedition was of great service to them. On arrival at Ruatahuna they were welcomed by the natives under Te Whenuanui and Paerau Te Rangikaitipuake, this being the first visit of troops to their country since peace had been made with them in 1870. They camped there one day and buried the remains of Captain Travers, A.C., and five men, whose bodies had been exhumed by Te Kooti's orders in May, 1869. With them was old Hapurona Kohi, previously mentioned as having killed one of our men with a mere pounamu at Tapapa in January, 1870, the chief of the first Urewaras who surrendered to us in April, 1870, and could be trusted to give reliable information. He was a man of great influence, and his "mana" extended from Ahikereru to Ruatahuna and Waikaremoana.

The passage of these forces through the country was not without risk of opposition from the more irreconcilable of this wild hill tribe. Indeed before they left Ruatahuna they received a defiant message from Kereru Te Pukenui, a chief who occupied the lower end of the Ruatahuna Valley, warning them to return or they might get into trouble. This man's influence extended as far as Maungapowhatu.

The first march was over the Huiarau range, and thence through rugged country, and down the river ved to Hereheretaunga, on the Waikaremoana Lake. They had previously sent on a Urewera native with a message to Hona Te Makarini, the chief who had surrendered to Mr. F. E. Hamlin in the latter part of the previous year, bidding him to have canoes to take the force over to his settlement and to be ready to meet them. They found the canoes duly provided, and having crossed to Waitohi, sent them back for Captain Mair and his men. On the following day they went over to Tikitiki, Te Makarini's settlement. Captain Mair remained there, while

TE KOOTI EXPEDITIONS.

CAPTAIN MAIR'S ARAWA FLYING COLUMN.
Returning to camp, after defeating Te Kooti, February 7, 1870.

Captain Preece advanced with Sergeant Bluett and 12 men, and a prisoner named Hone Pereha, one of Te Kooti's men who had recently turned up at Tikitiki. Other Wairoa natives were there who had left Te Kooti, and they promised to surrender to Major Cumming at Wairoa, Te Makarini undertaking to take them out. Captain Preece and party proceeded to Wairoa to get further provisions and boats for the men. Though they had exceptionally bad weather they got back ten days later with a good supply.

Taking Hapurona Kohi, who proved a very useful guide, the expedition crossed the Lake to the eastern arm towards Maungapowhatu, travelling for one day up the Houpuruwahine Stream, and then ascended a range by a very old track. On the third day they arrived at Maungapowhatu, surrounded the settlement of Kakari, and then sent Hapurona Kohi to tell the natives that the Government had no quarrel with anyone but Te Kooti's people, who must surrender. When they found that the troops were in possession of the place they made no trouble. Captain Preece afterwards learned that Kereopa, the murderer of the Rev. Volkner, had escaped out of the other side of the fort. The force then pushed through the bush to Tauaki, the next settlement, by a well used track. Their intention was to go as far as Te Wera, at the head of the Waioeke and Hangaroa rivers, where Te Kooti was believed to be, but bad weather set in again, and they halted until Tamaikoha arrived on the 21st of June. He advised the force not to go on to Te Wera as supplies were running low, but to make for Opotiki, by way of Waimana. It was now late in the season, and the weather being unfavourable, it was decided to follow his advice. The force went on to Opokere and from there to Whakamau, where the track to Te Wera branches off. Thence to Tawhana, the junction of the Tauranga and Tawhana streams, which form the Waimana valley. The objective was Tauwharemanuka, where Tamaikoha had built a large meeting house. It had been named Runanga to commemorate the making of peace, but he, with grim humour, renamed it Tipene, after the man who was shot by Colonel St. John's party after peace had been made.

A long march down the stream, which we crossed no less than forty-two times, took the force into the Waimana Valley proper, and here an extract from one of the officer's notes may be interesting: "The Waimana is a very fine valley for small farms; the land is of the best quality." On the 28th the force arrived at Opotiki, and after some more bad weather, reached Te Teko on the 2nd of July. It had been over a month going through some of the roughest country in New Zealand, and although the expedition had not achieved much in the way of fighting, it had shown the Urewera that troops could go through their country in the depth of winter. Later events proved that it was fortunate that the force did not go to Te Wera country, for Te Kooti was close to Waikaremoana at the time, and had a distant view of Captain Preece's small party as they returned from Wairoa.

On the 17th of July, a telegram was received stating that Te Kooti was at Waikaremoana, and that Major Ropata and Captain Porter were seeking for him in that direction. Major Cumming and 50 men were also going to Waikaremoana, and Captain Preece was instructed to keep a sharp look-out. On the 19th instructions came that the force was to proceed to Ruatahuna. Captain Preece got ready and started the same day for Fort Galatea, where Captain Mair joined with his force from Kaiteriria. Here Captains Mair and Preece encountered fearful weather. Flooded rivers forced them to make a detour of over twenty miles before they could cross the Rangitaiki River by the natural bridge at Te Arawhata, and then they were compelled to fell trees to make a crossing over a branch of the river, and had to send to Major Roberts at Opeke for a further supply of rations.

In spite of the weather, which still continued to be very bad, they were kept constantly busy. Captain Mair started with twelve men towards Runanga, where Captain Gudgeon was stationed. Captain Preece sent out a sergeant and party to scout towards Ahikereru. Mr. Ormond telegraphed that Te Kooti was supposed to be at Ruatahuna. Captain Scannell arrived, with a body of Armed Constabulary, to take up a position at Okoromatuakiwi, between the forces under Captains Preece and Mair and the force under Captain Gudgeon, to prevent Te Kooti breaking through. On the 29th rations arrived by pack-horses from Opepe. In the meanwhile, in reply to a message which Captain Preece had sent to the Urewera to enquire if Te Kooti had been heard of near Ruatahuna, word came that he had not been in that locality, but that it was reported that he had disappeared from Waikaremoana on the 31st. Captain Mair returned from Runanga, but found no traces of him in that direction. On the same day a telegram arrived instructing the force to march for Waikaremoana with the least possible delay by whatever route was thought advisable. They started at once, making for Pareranui through the bush. The Whirinaki River was flooded, and great difficulty was experienced in crossing. but in the open valley of Te Whaiti there was good marching for about five miles. Then the expedition took to the bush again and camped at Manawahiwi. The next day they marched over the ranges to Oputao, in the Ruatahuna valley, and thence to Whatakoko, where a camp was established, and a message sent to Paerau Te Rangikaitupuake telling him to keep his people together for fear Te Kooti should get hold of them.

Starting at daylight next morning, the troops marched through the bush, crossed the Huiarau range at 11 a.m., and soon reached Hehereretaunga on the Lake. There were no canoes, although a wire had been sent to Wairoa that canoes were to await the arrival of the force there. consequently they had to cut a way through the bush, skirting the Lake over very rough country to Mahungarerewai, where guns were fired to attract the attention of Te Makarini's people at Tikitiki. It was impossible to get further round the Lake, owing to the nature of the country. The force had, therefore, to take the risk that Te Kooti might hear the guns and make off, or the force would be cut off without food. Two men came over in canoes. They reported that Major Cumming was at Onepoto, on the other side of the Lake, and though his men had followed Te Kooti's trail on the Whanganui-a-Parua arm of the Lake, they could see no fires. All

CAPTAIN PREECE.

that night and all the next day it snowed heavily, and there was a very heavy sea on the Lake. Fortunately, the camp was on a point which had been an old cultivation, and the troops were able to get a few potatoes by digging through the snow.

On the 4th of August, two men arrived in a small boat with a letter from Captain McDonnell. Captain Mair remained in camp and Captain Preece went in the boat to arrange with Major Cumming for rations. We were unable to get to Onepoto owing to the heavy sea, and remained at Te Makarini's pa, at Tikitiki, for the night. Early next morning he got over to Major Cumming's post at Onepoto, secured three days' rations and arrived at Captain Mair's camp to find his people nearly starving. Next day the troops moved over in canoes to Whanganui-a-Parua, and leaving ten men to guard the canoes, started through the bush to the top of the range, from where Lake Waikareiti could be seen. Sergeant Bluett, who climbed a tree, was the first white man who ever saw it.

It was thought likely that Te Kooti might be making in that direction, Captain Mair therefore returned with ten men to search the shores of the main Lake and ascertain if there were any traces leading towards that locality, and also towards Onepoto, while Captain Preece went over the range, and followed the trail of one man until it joined others, and at last brought the expedition to a camp which appeared to have been left about four days. From there he sent word back that they were on the trail. That night a dog was caught, indicating that the enemy was not far away. Early next morning the troops started to follow the trail. They had not gone far when a volley was fired as the men were going up a ridge. There were no casualties, and our men returned the fire, but the enemy got away into the bush, and scattered. As the expedition only had food for one day it was deemed advisable to let the enemy know that the force had retired. It was evident that they were making along the Matakuhia range. Knowing the country, Captain Preece thought that if their troops returned to Onepoto and got fresh supplies they could make for the same direction as the enemy by keeping on the Waikareiti side of the range, while avoiding ambuscades.

At Onepoto, Captain Mair was found with Sergeant Bluett and the whole force, and then decided to go back over the same ground with all the men. After a forced march they came upon a camp of Te Kooti's at the base of the Matakuhia range, and found there a letter from him, written in hinau dye, which ran as follows:—

"Ki nga Wawanatanga katoa. E hoa ma, he kupu tenei kia koutou, me mutu te whaiwhai i au notemea kei taku nohonga ano au e nohoana, kei te puihi, engari ka puta au ki te moana whaia, ko tenei mahi kohuru a koutou me te kiore te ketu ana i te hamuti me whakarere, he whai na koutou i au tonoa mai he tangata kia haere atu au ki waho na tatou riri ai kapai.

"He kupu ke tenei ko taku mahara ko te maungarongo te oranga ko te mahi kai hoki, kati kei te whakarite whau i enei mahara kia oti. E ahau ma, ko tena mahara a tatou ko te riri kaore ano i tae mai ki au engari ka tata whou te whakarite ia koutou mahara, engari kia tupato kei ki koutou kaore.

HEOI ANO.

"E hoa ma, i tonoa atu e au aku tamariki ki te kawe i taku pukapuka whakahoki mo koutou, tahuri ana koutou ki te whawhai. Kati kauaka hei haku ki to koutou matenga, ko ana tamariki hoki ko Hata Tipoki, ko Epiha Puairangi ko Patoromu ko Ruru he tamariki ena i tohia ki te tohi a Tu i whangaia ki te whatunui a rua. He tamariki hoki e whakaaro nui ana ki te whenua.

"Heoi ano, ki te kino koutou ki ena korero me aha mo koutou na ano ia.

"Na to koutou hoa riri,
"NA TE TURUKI."

(Translation of Te Kooti's letter.)
TO ALL GOVERNMENT MEN.

Sirs,—

"This is a word of mine to you. You must give up chasing me about, because I am dwelling in my own abiding place, the bush. But if I come out to the coast then pursue me. This murderous purpose of yours in pursuing me is like a rat rooting in excrement. You must give it up. Send a man to tell me to come out to you in the open, where we can fight. That would be fair.

THIS IS ANOTHER WORD.

"My thought is that in the maintenance of peace and in the cultivation of food is safety. I am trying to carry out these thoughts and to accomplish them. Sirs, that idea of yours that we should fight has not come to me yet; but I am about to adopt your idea. So, beware. Do not say it will not be.

THAT IS ALL.

Sirs,—

"I sent to you some of my young men to carry my letter warning you and you attacked them. Cease then to complain about your misfortune. Those young men, Te Hata Tipoki, Epiha Puairangi, Patoromu and Ruru, were young men consecrated by the rites of Tu (the God of War) and fed with the bread of rua (hinau berries). They were young men who loved their country. That is all. If you dislike these words, what does it matter? All the worse for you.

"From your enemy,
"TE TURUKI."

The troops camped for the night, but not wishing to attract the attention of the enemy, did not light fires until 9 p.m., and then only with dry supplejacks to boil tea. On the following morning, Captains Mair and Preece went forward with forty men without swags, and came to an old kainga, a few miles from Eripeti, on the Ruakituri River. They struck back into the bush, where they heard a dog bark, but, not finding it, kept along the bush pararellel with the track. Traces of people who had been pig-hunting were found. Te Kooti's party appeared to have broken up into small parties in their usual way, and our men were at a great disadvantage in not being able to get supplies without going back for them.

On the following day, Captain Preece went out with Sergeant Blue<ins>tt</ins> and thirty men. They climbed the Matakuhia range, and after crossing several gullies, at length struck the enemy's trail, which they followed until they found his camp, which seemed to have been abandoned three days earlier. The trail appeared to go down towards Papuni, but scattered again.

It may be interesting here to state that on a very high point on the Matakuhia range they came on a very old Maori pa, with large carved posts, and old earthworks round it. It must have been very old, as large birch trees were growing in it and around it. The troops then returned to camp.

On the following day, Captains Mair and Preece decided to go back to Onepoto for a fresh supply of rations, and to follow the course that they at first thought of as the only means of overtaking the enemy, namely, to start from Whanganui-a-Parua across country at the back of Matakuhia range towards the Waipaoa River.

On the 13th of August the expedition drew ten days' rations from Major Cumming, intending to get across the Lake next day; but the sea was too high, and the men were obliged to make their way round the Lake through very rough country. They then struck through the trackless bush, guided by compass and cutting their way, until they reached high tableland, where there was no undergrowth and travelling was easier. Heavy snow fell, and the men had to camp early and prepare wood for fires at night, as it was unsafe to light them in daytime. It is very difficult to get a fire in black birch country. On the following day, the expedition marched through more difficult country. The men complained of cold, but were still cheerful, believing that they were making for Maungapowhata. Next day it was still snowing when the expedition reached the top of the dividing range. A man was sent up a tree to observe the country in the Waiparoa valley. He beckoned to Captains Mair and Preece to climb up, saying he saw smoke. They soon saw he was right, and at once began to descend the range into the Waipaoa valley. It was necessary to go very carefully and with as little noise as possible, and it took them four hours to reach the valley across an intervening ridge. At the river they found a camp a day or two old. Leaving a guard of thirty men there, they hurried on, and after two hours came on the trail. Kepa Te Ahuru, N.Z.C., captured a woman named Mere Maihi, who was at once recognised by Captain Mair as an Opotiki woman. From her he ascertained that Te Kooti's camp was not far off, though many of the men were out in different directions pig-hunting, and might come in from any side. Te Kooti and some of his followers, however, were in camp, and as it was already late in the day and there was no time to be lost it was decided to attack at once. The enemy was completely taken by surprise and made no stand. Four men, Paora Te Wakahoehoe, of

Wairoa (a Chatham Island prisoner, who Captain Preece at once recognised), Mehaka Hare, a Bay of Islands native, Patara Te Whata (a Chatham Island prisoner, concerned in the Poverty Bay massacre). One prisoner, Wi Heretaunga, a Chatham Island prisoner, who was also one of the leaders in the Poverty Bay massacre, was captured. This man met with summary execution when it was found out who he was. As the troops entered the camp, getting over a bank, Captain Mair shot the sentry at the gate (Patara Te Whata). The main body charged towards the huts. Captain Preece, with a few men, turned to the left, where there was a large hut and some men ran out of it. This was close to the Waipaoa River, which was then a deep stream. Before they had reached the bank two men were seen climbing the cliff on the other side; one was shot and fell back dead into the river. The other man, who had just reached the top of the cliff, was fired at but not hit. He fired one return shot. This man, it was afterwards ascertained, was Te Kooti. The man who fell into the river was recognised by Captain Preece as Paora Te Wakahoehoe, an ex-Chatham Island prisoner. He had been mailman from Wairoa to Napier. He joined the Hau Haus at Omarunui, the day before the fight at that place on the 12th of October, 1866. He was taken with the other prisoners and afterwards sent to the Chatham Islands, from which place he escaped with Te Kooti. In Te Kooti's hut was found a celebrated greenstone mere, named Tawatahi, which was presented to the Hon. Mr. J. D. Ormond, also his Defence Force shoulder belt full of Spencer rifle ammunition, all he had except the one shot he fired. Four women and two children were taken prisoners. The capture included nine Enfield rifles, two breech-loading carbines, four revolvers and four fowling pieces. Te Kooti's escape was a mere fluke. Had our men not been delayed a little in scrambling up the bank of a small creek they must have got him, either in the river or before he reached the top of the cliff. However it was not to be.

It may be interesting to know that Mehaka Hare was a son of Captain James Tautari, who owned two schooners trading to the Bay of Islands in the early fifties and sixties, and also traded to Rarotonga in the "Sea Breeze." He understood navigation and was a highly respectable native, being thoroughly trusted by all settlers and traders. His son had married an Opotiki woman and took up his abode there. Te Kooti's shoulder belt, which was probably that of Captain James Wilson, who was killed in the Poverty Bay massacre, is now to be seen, with the cartridges therein, in the Museum at Palmerston North, where it was deposited by Captain Preece some years ago.

If most of the men had not been away our success would have been greater. We followed the few men who escaped through the dense bush, but as night was falling the force had to abandon the chase. They camped there the next day, as it was snowing, and raining, and after two days' hard marching got out of the bush into the open country. where they camped on an old potato cultivation, a welcome find, as food was becoming short. Arrangements had been made with Major Cumming, at Waikaremoana, to send a party with pack-horses with supplies along the open country towards Whataroa, and a corporal with nine men was sent to meet them. In the meanwhile, as the expedition had had a very hard time, it was determined to try and communicate with the Ngatiporou under Captain Porter, who were believed to be in the vicinity of Te Papuni.

It was decided that Captain Preece and forty men should make a forced march up the Ruakituri River for the purpose of overtaking Captain Porter's force. He knew the country well, having been through it both during the fighting in 1865, 66 and also 1868. Heavy rain, however, prevented him getting away until the 22nd, and he was again delayed on the 24th at Eripeti by flood. The force crossed the Ruakituri by felling a tree and bridging it at a narrow place, and had a hard march over the hills by Colonel Whitmore's track, then cutting a track to escape the river. Seven sick men belonging to Ngatiporou were met who said that Captain Porter and the Ngatiporou were ahead; Major Ropata, having divided his force, was at Waiau River. On the morning of the 25th of August Captain Preece's party reached Papanui. Leaving Sergeant Bluett in charge of the men there, Captain Preece, with twenty men, pushed on and caught up to the Ngatiporous on top of the range, nine miles from Topuni, where they had just found the trail of one man, which led into a larger one. They were following it up slowly. After reporting the engagement with Te Kooti to Captain Porter and Mr. Large, who were in charge of the Ngatiporou, and telling them that Te Kooti was probably making for Maungapowhata, Captain Preece's force returned to Papuni that night, covering six Ngatiporou camps in one day. Next morning they got away early and got to Captain Mair's camp that night. On the 27th of August Captains Mair and Preece marched towards Wairoa, taking the arms they had captured from the enemy, also the prisoner women and children. They reached Omaruhakeke (the place where Captain Hussey was killed on Christmas Day, 1865), at 5 p.m., and finally, on the 28th, reached Wairoa, having been constantly on the move from the 17th of July through the roughest country in New Zealand, carrying supplies on their backs. The force remained at Wairoa waiting for a steamer, and ultimately shipped from Whangawehi for Whakatane, getting back to Te Teko on 8th of September. Captain Mair returned to his post at Kaiteriria.

On September 14 news was received that the Ngatiporou, under Captain Porter, followed Te Kooti's trail to Opokere at Maungapowhata, where they surprised him one morning, killing four men and taking seven prisoners, including one of Te Kooti's wives. On the 17th of September Captain Preece started from Te Teko with some fresh men and all who were in good condition from the former expedition, arrived at Fort Galatea next day, where Captain Mair had already reached with his men from Kaiteriria. On the 22nd September Captains Mair and Preece started from Fort Galatea on another expedition up the Horomanga Gorge. Their way lay over rough country to Omaruteani, on the Whakatane River, one of Kereru Te Pukenui's settlements, where they met Paerau Te Rangikaitupuake, Te Whenuanui and other Urewera chiefs, but not by Kereru Te Pukenui. On the 26th they got a letter from Te Purewa, a chief of

MAJOR (LATER COLONEL) PORTER.

TE KOOTI EXPEDITIONS.

Maungapowhata, saying that he had found Te Kooti's trail and was following it. They reached their old camping ground at Kakari next day, and were well received by the Maoris, who reported that Te Kooti's men who had left him had got guns and rejoined him. The expedition then started for Ngaturi, for the purpose of hunting up Kereopa, who they heard was there, and to endeavour to pick up Te Kooti's trail. Sergeant Huta and ten men went in another direction, but Te Kooti had four weeks' start, and the heavy rain had obliterated his tracks. For several days the expedition divided into small parties under Captains Mair and Preece, Sergeant Bluett, and Sergeant Huta, each going in a different direction through the bush, one main camp being at Te Kakari. On the 30th of September Captain Mair sent word that he had found a small trail leading towards Ruatahuna or Waikaremoana, and Sergeant Bluett came in with his party and reported that Hemi Kakitu and twenty of Tamaikoha's men had joined in the pursuit on their own account. They then spread their men out in three parties to follow up the trail, Captain Mair moving by Tatahoata with the main body. One day two camps were passed. Te Kooti had about twenty followers, and was avoiding the settlements of the Urewera, keeping well away from the tracks. When the expedition reached Tatahoata they found that a trail had been found at Paterangi, inland of Ahikerere, and that Captain Mair had started by the ordinary track with thirty men and intended to sleep at Tarapounamu. Within an hour Captain Preece's force was off once more, and reached Tahuaroa that night. On the following morning they made a splendid march over the ranges to the foot of Pukiore, where they found that though Capt. Mair had not passed Paerau, Te Rangikaitupuake with ten men had gone by. The river being low it was decided to go by Okehu stream. Captain Mair caught Preece's party about a mile and a-half from Ahikereru. Paerau Te Rangikaitupuake and his men there reported that the trail had been seen on the 30th on the Okehu stream, beyond Paterangi, evidently several days old, so sending the sick men to Fort Galatea, under Sergeant Matutaera, a start was made for Whataroa. It was evident that Te Kooti was making for Waikato. A start was made next morning in heavy rain, and trouble was experienced in crossing the Whirinaki River. Captain Mair went with his column by way of Te Tapiri, and Captain Preece struck through the bush by a very old track. At Ohihape a trail was found, but it was apparently old. Here Captain Mair joined but went off again with thirty-five men and Sergeant Bluett with ten men; Captain Preece started with the column for Te Arawhata to communicate with Captain Morrison, at Opepe, and get fresh supplies therefrom. He went on to Ngahuinga. Next day Captain Mair had a brush with Te Kooti in the bush. There were no casualties on either side, but the encounter showed that Te Kooti had not escaped to Waikato.

The weather continued very bad for several days, and we had so little food that we could not move. Starting again on the 10th of October for the bush in very cold weather with snow and hail, we found a trail of Te Kooti's people in small parties of twos and threes, which we followed until we lost it in the open ground. Tamaikoha's men reported that they had seen signs of the enemy in a creek in the bush, and we followed them until night. Tamaikoha, with twenty Urewera men, now joined us, and Rakuraku, another of the Urewera chiefs, went to Ruatahuna to cut in ahead of Te Kuiti in case he should double back that way. A long and arduous chase followed through rough country. One woman captured stated that Te Kooti was trying to get to Waikato, but that sme of his men were not willing to venture it. Scouting parties were sent out right and left, scouring the bush at the back of Ahikerera and towards the head of Okehu stream, but without finding any more signs of the rebels. The heavy rains, flooded streams, and shortness of food combined to make it dangerous to remain in the bush, so a return march was made to Ahikereru, and on the 4th of November Te Teko was reached, leaving men at Fort Galatea. On the 22nd of November it was reported that Major Ropata and Captain Porter, with the Ngatiporou, had been to Ruatahuna and had captured Kereopa, who was being sent to Wairoa, Hawke's Bay.

On the 17th of December, Major Ropata and Captain Porter, with their party of Ngatiporou, reached Whakatane from Ruatahuna. A month passed quietly, and on the 18th of January, 1872, Captains Mair and Preece made an expedition up the Horomanga Gorge, on a rumour that Te Kooti was in the vicinity of Tutaepukepuke. They captured two Urewera men, who denied that he had been in the locality. However, the men were detained and the settlement surrounded, but the natives denied all knowledge of Te Kooti's whereabouts. The country was scoured for four days without result.

On the 31st of January, 1872, Captain Preece, with Sergeant Bluett and party of men, left for Ahikereru, travelling by their old October trail, then through rough rocky country, following the bed of the upper branch of the Waiau. Here a hot spring was discovered just above the junction of the main stream. In recent years this spring was claimed by the Tourist Department as a most important discovery, which quite unknown even to the Maoris of the district. As a matter of fact Captain Preece's expedition came across several hot springs, one hot creek and one place where hot water bursts up in the middle of the river. The Waiau proper comes in on the left, rising at the head waters of the Whakatane behind Ruatahuna.

Old Hapurona stated that the hot springs were well known to the old natives, and that the range between the branches of the Waiau had in the old times been a favourite hunting ground for kakapo and the indigenous rats, which were considered a most delicious food amongst the natives. The pursuit was continued to the Marau end of Lake Waikaremoana. Captains Ferris and Preece joined hands, but neither of them had any success to report. Capt. Preece then worked towards Te Purtere and on the morning of the 13th of February, Captain Preece sent out parties scouting right and left. Sergeant Bluett marched up the Mangaone Stream, and Sergeant Huta up a small creek where a camp was found with the fires still quite warm. The occupants had recently left. The trail was followed for seven miles, to the mouth of the Mangaone. The fugitives

TE KOOTI EXPEDITIONS.

were sighted as they were climbing a cliff on the opposite of the stream. Captain Preece called on them to surrender, but, receiving no reply, fired on them. Unfortunately, the ammunition had been damaged by the heavy rain and was very defective. The Terry carbine was not a good weapon, the ammunition being easily damaged. The enemy got safely up the cliff, returned the fire, and made good their escape.

This was the last engagement in the New Zealand War, the last shot being fired by Private Nikora Te Tuhi. Both Captain Preece and Captain Ferris continued to follow Te Kooti, but they never actually came across him again, although Capt. Ferris captured Anaru Matete, a Poverty Bay chief, who had been in rebellion continuously since 1865, Paora Tu, Hohepa and Maka (Te Kooti's chief executioner), near Te Reinga some weeks after. The latter was tried at the Supreme Court at Napier and sentenced to death, but this was commuted to penal servitude for life. He was liberated after serving ten years. On the following day Captain Preece followed the trail to Whataroa, where Captain Ferris took it up. Captain Preece's force remained at the Lake for a few days to rest, after its long and trying marches. When the men arrived at Fort Galatea they had been a month constantly travelling through trackless country.

On the 19th of April Captain Preece started on his last expedition after Te Kooti, by way of Ahikereru and Maungapowhata, Puketapu. The expedition reached Waikaremoana through Whataroa, and found that Captain Ferris had started from the Marau end of the Lake with ten Armed Constabulary and ten natives. Te Kooti was now again making for Waikato. Steps were taken by Captains Preece, Mair and Ferris, operating in different directions, to intercept the fugitive, but though the country was traversed in every direction that was thought likely to reveal Te Kooti's trail, no trace of him was discovered. On the 17th of May a telegram arrived from Mr. McLean, the Defence Minister, stating that Te Kooti had got through to Arowhenua, near the Waikato River, above Cambridge, on the 15th, and left there for Te Kuiti on the 16th. So ended all the expeditions organised in pursuit of this crafty rebel. Captain Ferris had followed the trail through dense bush as far as Heruwi, but he got there too late. Lieut. Way, who met Captain Preece at Tarawera, had seen nothing of the trail. Captain Ferris deserved great credit for the persistent way in which he had followed the trail from the time it was handed over to him at Whataroa (15th February) through to Te Reinga, thence to the bush at the back of Mahaka, then doubling on his own tracks and striking his old hiding place at the head of the Waiau River behind the western end of Lake Waikaremoana, through dense bush, rough country, and up the beds of rivers, and ultimately reaching the open country, unfortunately just too late to capture the fugitive.

Captains Mair and Preece worked well together. There was never any question of seniority between them. They consulted one another on every detail, and worked loyally together, for the good of the public service, during a very trying time, giving every possible assistance and information to other officers who were operating against Te Kooti from different points.

P

CHAPTER XII.

THE WAIKAREMOANA EXPEDITION, UNDER MESSRS. HAMLIN AND WITTY.

The Waikaremoana is one of the largest and most beautiful lakes in New Zealand, stretching star-shaped its picturesque arms and fiords into the encircling forest-clad mountains. Dr. Scott, who accompanied the native force under Messrs. Hamlin and Witty, gives the following graphic account of the expedition in his reminiscences. He says:—"From Capt. Newland, the officer commanding the Wairoa district, I learned that the expedition which I had been ordered to join as medical attendant had been organised mainly with a view of crossing Lake Waikaremoana, and reducing Te Kooti's stronghold within the Urewera fastnesses of the western side, to which, when he sustained a reverse in the field, or retired inland after a successful raid on the coast settlements, he invariably resorted, and securely ensconced within his (said to be unassailable) citadel of the hills, therefrom bade defiance to the efforts of the Government. Waikaremoana, or Sea of Rippling Waters, in addition to its possessing a fortress of supposed impregnability, which had long been the headquarters of Te Kooti's truculent band, formed also a nucleus of disaffection to which resorted all original bad characters and ne'er-do-wells from all parts of the island, who, being welcomed by him or his Urewera allies, constituted a constant supply of recruits wherewith to replace his losses by desertion, capture, or loss in the field. Likewise, the geographical position and features of Waikaremoana, situated as it is in the "bosom of the mountains," rendered its western shore, on which Te Kooti had founded several villages with extensive cultivations and stores of provisions, all but inaccessible by land otherwise than by a long and tedious route through the Urewera country, via Ruatahuna, which has never yet been achieved by any expeditionary force that I am aware of, without crossing the lake itself in the face of the enemy; and as the western seaboard is forest clad almost to the water's edge and the only accessible landing places are comparatively narrow margins of boulder strewn, rocky plateaux, the difficulty and risk of effecting a landing and assailing such positions, if hostilely occupied, may be easily estimated. At the time of my arrival at Wairoa the field force, numbering about 350 Ngatikahungunu, had been in military occupation of the eastern side of the lake for some weeks and were occupied in hewing out canoes from timber growing on the spot, as a means of transit. They had not as yet come into serious collision with the enemy, armed with at least one piece of artillery on the western side; but were in full view of the fortifications, and also of another facing it called Tiki Tiki, from which every evening the big gun was discharged with a tremendous boom among the mountains, a continued blowing of horns and war dancing being kept up during the day. Leaving the opposing belligerents thus in the presence of each other on opposite sides of the lake, the Government natives making diligent preparations for an advance, and the insurgents apparently fully prepared to give them a warm reception on their landing, if not before, as they possessed quite a mosquito fleet of canoes, I will return to a description of the lake. The "sea of Waikare" is of extraordinary configuration, and its geographical position over 2,000ft. above the sea level, together with other remarkable attributes, probably renders it unique among the lakes of New Zealand. Situated about thirty miles inland from Te Wairoa, Hawke's Bay, whence it is approached by a gradual ascent by a line of the Waikare Taheke river (of which it is the source). While of lesser magnitude than Lake Taupo and altogether lacking the wondrous volcanic phenomena which distinguish the shores and vicinage of that magnificent expanse of water, with the exception of the grand prospect of Tongariro from Tapuaeharuru and other points of view, Waikaremoana completely surpasses the former in the majestic scenery of its mountain environment, rocky precipitous shores, and cyclopean boundaries. Far away to the westward as one stands on the elevated plateau of Onepoto overlooking the lake and the landing place—towers darkly green the gigantic outline of the inhospitable Huiarau, partly forest clad range of mountains, which at its greater altitudes during the winter months presents all the repellent features and perils of our New Zealand Southern Alps or snowy ranges of the Mackenzie country. These slips, slides, and overwhelms, the treacherous avalanche, and blinding snowstorms, obliterate the devious and little used track, to the utter bewilderment, discomfiture, and probable death of the unfortunate wayfarer or fugitive from exposure, cold or famine. There many of the miserable Urewera denizens of the lake, accustomed to the journey and climate, met their end while striving to escape to Ruatahuna on our advance and occupation of their pa, and as tradition has it, many hundreds of the primeval Maoris, old time invaders of the Urewera, lie entombed amid the mountain fastnesses.

Mr. Hamlin, Lieut. Witty, Sub-Lieut. Large, Saunders, and James Carroll, with the narrator in medical charge, and three armed constabulary for dispatch work with Wairoa, constituted all the Europeans attached to the force, and must have possessed patience, firmness, and long suffering in no ordinary degree in order to reconcile and bring to unanimity of action the heterogeneous crowd of which they really at times seemed to have only nominal command. Difficulties of tribal jealousies, old feuds not quite extinct, and possible sympathy with the enemy were not the only factors of discord. I ought also here to observe that another great difficulty in exerting authority among the natives was the absence of any energetic and plucky chief of note or high standing. True, three rangatiras of sufficiently high rank accompanied their several contingents to the field, but of these Ihaka Whanga, a noble old warrier, was feeble and almost in his dotage from wounds, infirmity and age; while Paora te Apatu, also of blue blood, was no warrior; and Rahurahu, though an excellent fellow and devoted to the Government, was—well, say constitutionally unfit for campaigning. Thus the onus of every undertaking fell upon the European leaders, but triumphing over all obstacles, they at length succeeded in getting two canoes formed from the trees felled and shaped in the vicinity of the camp, whence they launched them with great labour upon the lake and, having secured a small boat, found themselves possessed of a miniature fleet of three small craft, which they were not long in using to the best advantage. The enemy responded by the firing of musketry, braying of horns and derisive yells from the Hauhau pas and villages. On the 22nd there came off from Matuahu in a canoe a delegation under a flag of truce, which, lying off the camp at Onepoto, opened negotiations with Hamana and Te Hapimana, two chiefs on the Government side. A long korero ensued, when in response to a demand for surrender they replied that they would hold a consultation at their pa and report the result the next day. The whole proceeding was, however, only a ruse to gain time or to reconnoitre our position, for shortly afterwards the outlying scouts reported the passage of eight canoes, four of them very large ones, and the whaleboat fully manned from Tikitiki and thence to Ohiringa, thus menacing the rear of our position and our communication with Wairoa. As Lieut. Witty counted 25 men in one canoe, there is little doubt that the detachment numbered fully 160 strong; and this force in our rear was by no means a pleasant prospect for our armed constabulary, mounted men, Troopers McMillan, Campbell and Jones, who, however, continued to carry their dispatches as required with praiseworthy zeal and no little pluck, passing on every journey the thicket where their comrade was ambuscaded and shot some months before. On the 8th of June the expedition commenced its first movement on the offensive by land and water. One portion of the force marched or scrambled from Onepoto to Te Tikitiki, while a second detachment accompanied them along the coast in the canoes and dinghy, under Lieut. Large. These proceedings did not escape the watchful Hauhaus, and two armed canoes at once came out from Motuohu to reconnoitre. This apparently just suited the adventurous Ngaietus, who at once started in chase. On the canoes nearing each other in mid-lake considerable firing took place, and as Sub-Lieut. Large described it, a mimic naval engagement ensued, without, however, any casualties on either side. The Hauhaus retired round the sheltering promontory of Matuahu, our canoes pursuing until they got within range of the hostile shore, when they also retired to Matakitaki. On arrival at the new camping ground it was found impossible by the European leaders to induce the majority of the Maoris to make any further aggressive movement, and as it was thought that the Ureweras were only awaiting reinforcements in order to attack both in front and rear, the European officers resolved upon vigorous action at once. In consequence of this resolution, on receipt of instructions from Mr. Hamlin, Lieut. Witty, accompanied by Messrs. Large and Saunders, selected about eighty of the best men, including Witty's contingent of Mohaka natives, and Large's Ngaietus, and pushed off for Whanganui-o-parua, ostensibly to procure potatoes from the cultivations at the whares, but really, if possible, to effect a landing on the opposite shore. The perilous landing having been effected without opposition, the force proceeded on to Taumataua, a large clearing immediately opposite Matakitaki. The party in the boat and one of the canoes reached the cultivation or clearing without opposition, and under the impression that the place was abandoned, were searching about in whares, of which there were about a dozen, when a volley was fired at them from the bush skirting the clearing. Although the enemy could not have been more than one hundred yards distant, fortunately not one shot took effect. At the same time heavy firing commenced from the south side of a bush clad ridge, which commanded the landing place, at another party who were in the act of landing from the canoes. Here again the Hauhaus fired high and most of the bullets went whizzing over their heads. A few, however, ploughed in among them wounding one of the Ngatipahauwera. The natives behaved well, taking cover behind logs, boulders, etc., and returned the fire briskly, holding the enemy in check until the return of the canoes with the rest of the party, when charging on the front and right flank of the Hauhaus, animated by the example of their officers, and greatly stimulated by the frantic ejaculations of their minister, a veritable member of the church militant named Pita Tauhou, they charged into the bush, driving the enemy before them in the direction of Matuahu, the large pa before alluded to. Darkness coming on they returned to Taumataua, the clearing where they were first ambushed, sent the boat and canoes across to Matakitaki and, carefully posting sentries and out-pickets, made themselves comfortable for the night, not a little elated at having achieved with such limited means their present success and with no loss of life. It was anticipated that a sharp attack would be made at daybreak, the usual hour for Maori surprises. Consequently at daybreak all were on the qui vive, but nothing occurred to disturb them until about 1 p.m., when the Hauhaus attacked an out picket of Witty's men under Sergeant Keef, a Mohaka half-caste. The picket held its own bravely until reinforced from the main body, killing Enoka (Te Waru's fighting lieutenant) and wounding several others without loss to themselves. Another charge was made into the bush, fully demonstrating that the coast natives, if properly led, are more than a match for the Urewera mountain tribes. At the same time that the picket was attacked, the whaleboat and five canoes fully manned put out from Matuahu, evidently intending to assail Witty's detachment from the rear, and capturing their canoe, cut it off from the main body, but being signalled from the high hill at the back of the pa of the repulse of the land attack, withdrew again to its shelter and protection. At this time the Hauhaus, no doubt thoroughly cowed by the adverse omens, fruitless volleys at short range, which were really remarkable, and loss of one of their principal leaders, Enoka, formed the intention which they afterwards carried out of evacuating. Next day, Monday, the entire force, some 250 strong (excepting 60 or 70 left to garrison Matakitaki and keep open communication with Wairoa), crossed to Taumataua, and on Tuesday started, carefully feeling their way through the dense bush which intervenes between Taumataua and Matuahu. The line of march led through dense bush, deep ravines and was nearly trackless, offering every facility for the favourite ambuscading tactics of the enemy. But the march was accomplished without incident in three hours, the force arriving about noon at the rear and base of the high hill which dominates the redoubtable pa (Matuahu). Very steep forest clad and menacing looked the mountainous acclivity, within the woodland recesses of which it was thought a last stand would be made by the Ureweras in defence of their long vaunted stronghold. Careful dispositions were made accordingly for the attack. These completed, the force divided into three storming parties. Wairoa natives under Hamlin constituted the main advance, while two flanking divisions of Ngatipahauwera and Ngaietu were under Lieut. Witty and Sub-Lieut. Large respectively. These started simultaneously, advancing from tree to tree and clearing to clearing with speed, caution and determination, until the summit was successfully and bloodlessly gained, much to everybody's astonishment and gratification. The expedition looked down upon the famous citadel of the hills, scarcely believing their senses that the pa was evacuated—"Kua horo a Matuahu." A rush down the hill followed, and in ten minutes the village was full of shouting friendlies, ransacking the whares, probing the ground with their bayonets for hidden loot and holding high jinks generally with the favoured haunt of their hereditary enemies. Having gained this redoubtable Hauhau stronghold on the western side of the lake, the expedition made it their base of operations, and from this centre detachments were dispatched in various directions to harass and injure the enemy. In one of these forays Sub-Lieut. Large captured the whaleboat, a number of large canoes and four prisoners. Although Sub-Lieut. Large got into disgrace for starting without orders, the capture of the whaleboat and canoes gave the expedition complete means of transit, but the act received neither thanks nor mention inasmuch it was done without the knowledge and sanction of the commanding officer. The Ureweras appeared to be quite dispirited and disorganised with the continued success of the Government, and the principal men soon made overtures for peace and surrendered; while the Wairoa chiefs hearing such doleful accounts from them of the number of their people who had perished in the snows of the Huiarau range in flying to Ruatahuna, would not agree to any forward movement in that direction. So the expedition, after destroying all the stores of food and canoes of the enemy, recrossed the lake and returned to Wairoa, where Te Makarini and several other Urewera chiefs of note and their people, soon after surrendered themselves to the Government.

CHAPTER XIII.

TE KOOTI PARDONED BY THE GOVERNMENT—HE STARTS TO REVISIT THE SCENE OF HIS FORMER EXPLOITS, BUT IS STOPPED AND PUT INTO GAOL, AFTERWARDS RELEASED AND SENT BACK TO HIS SETTLEMENT.

Te Kooti now settled down in the so-called King Country surrounded by the tribes that had fled from the Imperial troops after their last stand at Orakau. No attempt was made by the New Zealand Government to follow him, not considering it advisable to start a fresh campaign in the heart of the country. The forces raised for service were gradually disbanded and Te Kooti was severely left alone, although if he had at any time ventured near any of the European settlements, no doubt an attempt would have been made to capture him. Ten years passed away and the Government, finding Te Kooti was a great stumbling block to all attempts made to approach the King Country natives with a view to the opening of their part of the country, determined to pardon the guerilla chief. Accordingly on Monday, 12th February, 1883, Mr. Bryce, then Native Minister, informed Te Kooti that he would be included with other criminals who had been pardoned and that he would be covered by the Amnesty Act. The meeting took place at a native settlement called Manga-o-Rongo, about 17 miles from Kihikihi. The Government party consisted of Mr. Bryce, Mr. T. W. Lewis (Native Department) Mr. George T. Wilkinson, Government Native agent, who acted as interpreter throughout the proceedings, Messrs. Butler, C. W. Hursthouse, R. N. Campbell, and the chief Rewi. There also were present three or four mounted orderlies. When Te Kooti came forward and took Mr. Bryce's hand, he exclaimed, "Righteousness and Peace have met together; mercy and truth have kissed one another." Te Kooti was now at liberty to move about without fear of molestation. The free pardon accorded to Te Kooti was not acceptable to the people of New Zealand, who raised a great outcry against the Government, and Mr Bryce in particular, for shaking hands with such a notorious murderer. After a time Te Kooti evinced a strong desire to visit the scenes of his former exploits and announced his intention of returning to Gisborne. Although the Government had pardoned Te Kooti, the Poverty Bay people had not, and openly avowed their determination to kill him on sight. Mr. Geo. Wilkinson succeeded in stopping Te Kooti from carrying out his project, but in a few months more Te Kooti again seemed to have an irresistible desire to start on his journey, and again the persuasive powers of Mr. Geo. Wilkinson were successful, but in 1889, Mr Wilkinson being absent from the district, Te Kooti suddenly made a start, not heeding the request of the Government that he should stay where he was. When it became known that the instigator of the Poverty Bay massacre was actually on his way with a band of followers, there was the greatest excitement all along the East Coast and especially at Gisborne, the people at which place announced their determination at all hazards to prevent their old enemy from entering the district. If the Government would not assist them they would take the law into their own hands, they declared. In the meantime Te Kooti was on his way to the Coast, the number of his followers increasing as he went along. The Hon. E. Mitchelson (Native Minister) finding all attempts to dissuade Te Kooti from carrying out his expressed intention to revisit the scenes of the Poverty Bay massacre failed, it was at last determined by the Government to prevent him by force, and a mixed corps of Police, Permanent Artillery and Volunteers was hurriedly dispatched from Auckland to the Opotiki district, where Te Kooti had arrived, It was expected that he would have resisted any attempt at his capture, but upon the arrival of a squad of police who were sent in advance, he quietly gave himself up, and was taken before Mr. Bush, R.M. Te Kooti was informed that the fact of his travelling through the country with a large number of followers was likely to lead to a breach of the peace, and that the Government had decided to escort him back to the King Country. This was accordingly done, Te Kooti making no objection, and his followers returned to their different kaingas or villages. After some few years Te Kooti, then getting old and feeble, was again seized with a strong desire to revisit the scenes where he had been the chief actor in those terrible tragedies. He accordingly quietly went back to the East Coast; there were no followers this time, and the Government did not interfere, and this was the end of it all. After another few years of seclusion he died at a settlement he had formed at Ohiwa, Bay of Plenty, on April 17th, 1893, aged 79 years. According to the idea of a large number of natives, mostly Ureweras, his was an honoured old age and death. This is verified by the fact of the natives raising a substantial sum of money for the erection of a monument over his grave, on which is engraved the legend that he was a god and priest (a sort of Moses), a great general and minister. In concluding this brief account of a very remarkable man it may not be out of place to append the following translation of the inscription: —

IN MEMORY OF TE KOOTI RIKIRANGI, PROPHET AND GENERAL.

Who died on the 17th day of April, in the year 1893; aged 79 years.

He was a chief and a hero. He displayed great gallantry in great battles fought in Ao-tea-roa (the North Island of New Zealand). The Government made peace with him and gave him and his people some land and also confirmed his religion (known as "Ringatu"). These matters were settled and fully confirmed in the presence of the Native Minister in the year 1883.

[THE END.]

www.ingramcontent.com/pod-product-compliance
Lightning Source LLC
Chambersburg PA
CBHW031141160426
43193CB00008B/210